THE NONVIOLENT ATONEMENT

J. Denny Weaver

WILLIAM B. EERDMANS PUBLISHING COMPANY
GRAND RAPIDS, MICHIGAN / CAMBRIDGE, U.K.

Wm. B. Eerdmans Publishing Co.
2140 Oak Industrial Drive N.E., Grand Rapids, Michigan 49505 /
P.O. Box 163, Cambridge CB3 9PU U.K.

Printed in the United States of America

12 11 10 09 08 07   9 8 7 6 5 4

Library of Congress Cataloging-in-Publication Data

Weaver, J. Denny, 1941-
    The nonviolent atonement / J. Denny Weaver.
        p.   cm.
    Includes bibliographical references.
    ISBN 978-0-8028-4908-3 (pbk.: alk. paper)
        1. Atonement.   2. Black theology.   3. Feminist theology.
    4. Nonviolence — Religious aspects — Christianity.   I. Title.

BT265.2 W43   2001
232′.3 — dc21

                                                2001040375

www.eerdmans.com

THE NONVIOLENT ATONEMENT

For Samuel and Katherine, Simon and Seth

May they keep the faith

Contents

Preface

Although I did not recognize it at the time, I started writing this book more than twenty-five years ago, when I taught my first college theology course. That course had been a struggle both for myself as a very inexperienced professor and for the students who endured it. Toward the end of the term, a student whose name now escapes me asked just what exactly was going on with the atonement formulas that I had sketched for them. A comparison that I had not previously recognized flashed through my mind, and on an impulse I threw out that new insight as a suggestion about what was going on. Although the question and my answer were both spontaneous, they stuck with me, and I spent the next several years testing whether that spur-of-the-moment answer was indeed true. This book is my attestation to that student that the answer he received in embryonic form those many years ago was indeed correct. I hope that he remembers the question and recognizes this book as the real answer.

While the manuscript builds on much research, it does not develop a thesis that comes from research in the traditional sense. Rather, the book is the result of what has recently been dubbed "thinking out of the box," being willing to view an ancient and classic question from a new and different standpoint.

I could list a number of "aha" experiences dotted over a quarter century when pieces of the puzzle that is this book fell into place — an article or book read, a conversation with a critic of my developing view, a comment from a supporter suggesting additional evidence, a student's query that forced me into new territory for an answer, a literary challenge that prompted a new layer of questioning and analysis. While the specifics might interest only the individuals involved, scrolling through the list in my mind's eye shows that this book is a matter of looking for pieces outside of the usual box. And the existence of the book indicates that the process of reflection has reached a culmination. It is an effort finally to bring all the pieces together in one place. While the result is a relatively small book, it carries the weight of twenty-five plus years of conversation and reflection.

The long process means that many more people have contributed something to this book than I can possibly name. The list includes the student who asked about the meaning of the atonement formulas in my first theology course. It includes a professor to whom I posed what I considered a subversive question in a seminary theology course. Somehow I retained that question as well, and I now view it very differently than when it was first posed — thus the list of contributors includes J. C. Wenger, who absorbed that question. I learned much from John H. Yoder, who first pointed out to me the significance of identifying the particular perspective of classic creedal statements. On the list I would include the name of Charles de Gaulle, president of France, whose war memoirs I read in French while I was in Algeria with the Mennonite Central Committee in 1966-68. In those three volumes, written some two decades earlier, I observed how de Gaulle's policies of 1968, which much of the world found incoherent, actually reflected an integrated worldview that had been shaped by de Gaulle's experiences with the allies during the second world war. That insight led me to shift the primary focus of my remaining seminary and then graduate work from biblical to historical studies as the way to gain insight into contemporary issues. Eventually it produced the historically located, narrative theology of this book. In the recent past, persons who read chapters or made other contributions at some stage of development of the manuscript include Duane Beachy, Gerald Biesecker-Mast, J. R. Burkholder, Will Coleman, James H. Cone, John Day, Duane Friesen, Dwight Hopkins, Loren Johns, John Kampen, Robert Kreider, Daniel Liechty, Weldon Nisly, Ray Person, John Powell, Lisa Robeson, Lee Snyder, John Stahl-Wert, Susan Brooks Thistlethwaite, Alain Epp Weaver, and Sonia Weaver. Those who read the entire manuscript include Don Blosser, Ted Grimsrud, Rachel Reesor, Stanley Hauerwas, Leanne Van Dyk, Delores Williams, and Walter Wink. Even when I did not incorporate every piece of their advice and chose instead to follow my own inclination, I appreciate the thought and stimulation of the critiques. I am very grateful to Bethel College, Newton, Kansas, whose invitation to present their biennial Bible Lectures provided opportunity for four lectures and a workshop for pastors in which I could do a major, public testing of the theses of this manuscript. I owe much to the two institutions that made possible a year's research and writing. This book would not have happened without the six-month sabbatical leave granted by Bluffton College, and an additional six-month leave from teaching funded by a grant from The Louisville Institute. It has been a pleasure to work with Eerdmans editor John Simpson, who always believed in this project. Anna Diller did very fine work on the index. Last and most importantly, I am grateful for the unwavering support of this project by my wife Mary, who was also the critic I most wanted to satisfy.

This book is written for the present — the issues debated are both contemporary and real. In that present task, it offers new interpretations of some elements of the history of doctrine. Since the past is, in part, what contemporary persons understand that it is, the book is also written for the past. But since both past and present open vistas to come, ultimately the book charts a direction for the future. It is my fervent hope that this essay about the past for the present will make *Christian* faith more Christ-like in future years. As a symbol of that hope, I dedicate the book to my grandchildren, Samuel and Katherine, Simon and Seth.

J. Denny Weaver
Bluffton College

1 *Introduction*

Sharp debates about the death of Jesus sparked by feminist and womanist theologians are the current cutting edge of discussions about Christology and atonement — what classic language calls the person and work of Christ — that have churned throughout the twentieth century. The century ended as it began — with searches for the historical Jesus. Along the way, this century featured frequently pointed debates on atonement, carried on under a variety of nomenclatures, between adherents and theological descendants of medieval theologians Anselm of Canterbury (c. 1033-1109) and Abelard (1079-1142). In fact, except perhaps for the sixteenth-century debates about the characteristics of Christ with respect to his presence within and outside of the sacrament, the twentieth century may well have experienced the most important, sustained conversation about the person and work of Christ since early church debates eventuated in the fourth- and fifth-century formulas from Nicea and Chalcedon, which became the benchmark of christological thought since that time. Thus in spite of the new feeling to the discussion brought by women's voices and perspectives, this book on atonement is not about a new debate. On the contrary, it joins a very long-running conversation. At the same time, it makes a bold claim as it joins the conversation, namely that it brings some new arguments to the long discussion and charts a new route through much explored territory. Specifically, it charts a path of nonviolent atonement through territory strewn with images and assumptions of violence.

Although the roots of modern atonement arguments always pass through Anselm on their way back to the early church, it has preoccupied Protestants more than Catholics. Since Catholic belief accords believers immediate access to the saving grace of Christ in the sacraments, Catholicism has not sensed the same need as Protestants to guarantee access to God's grace via a correct doctrine of atonement.[1] But whatever their persuasion, for those who thought about atonement and staked out a position for much of the past millennium, the prevailing choice was for Anselm or another version of satisfaction atonement, with Abelard's moral theory as the minority alternative. In the last half of the twentieth century, the so-called classic theory, given renewed visibility in the modern era by Gustaf Aulén's *Christus Victor*,[2] has achieved renewed visibility as an alternative to both Anselm and Abelard.

Atonement theology starts with violence, namely the killing of Jesus. The commonplace assumption is that something good happened, namely the salvation of sinners, when or because Jesus was killed. It follows that the doctrine of atonement then explains how and why Christians believe that the death of Jesus — the killing of Jesus — resulted in the salvation of sinful humankind.

In the western world generally and in the United States in particular, the prevailing assumption behind the criminal justice system is that to "do justice" means to punish criminal perpetrators appropriately. "Appropriately" means that the more serious the offense, the greater the penalty (punishment) to be imposed, with death as the ultimate penalty for most serious crimes. There is thus a very pervasive use of violence in the criminal justice system when it operates on the belief that justice is accomplished by inflicting punishment. Called retributive justice, this system assumes that doing justice consists of administering quid pro quo violence — an evil deed involving some level of violence on one side, balanced by an equivalent violence of punishment on the other. The level of violence in the punishment corresponds to the level of violence in the criminal act.[3]

---

1. Timothy Gorringe, *God's Just Vengeance: Crime, Violence and the Rhetoric of Salvation*, Cambridge Studies in Ideology and Religion, no. 9 (Cambridge: Cambridge University Press, 1996), pp. 107-8.

2. Gustaf Aulén, *Christus Victor: An Historical Study of the Three Main Types of the Idea of Atonement*, trans. A. G. Herbert (New York: Macmillan, 1969).

3. Gorringe, *God's Just Vengeance*, pp. 1-29.

Retributive justice fails both victims and offenders, although obviously in very different ways. Stated briefly, the system of determining guilt and inflicting punishment on an of-

Satisfaction atonement assumes that the sin of humankind against God has earned the penalty of death, but that Jesus satisfied the offended honor of God on their behalf or took the place of sinful humankind and bore their punishment or satisfied the required penalty on their behalf. Sin was atoned for because it was punished — punished vicariously through the death of Jesus, which saved sinful humankind from the punishment of death that they deserved. That is, sinful humankind can enjoy salvation because Jesus was killed in their place, satisfying the requirement of divine justice on their behalf. While the discussion of satisfaction atonement involves much more than this exceedingly brief account, this description is sufficient to portray how satisfaction atonement, which assumes that God's justice requires compensatory punishment for evil deeds committed, can seem self-evident in the context of contemporary understandings of retributive justice in the North American (and western) system of criminal justice.

The link between satisfaction atonement and systems of retributive justice cannot be denied. Timothy Gorringe's *God's Just Vengeance* provides a thorough analysis of satisfaction atonement's foundation in assumptions of retributive violence, as well as an extended discussion of the mutual interrelations between theories of satisfaction atonement and understandings of punishment and criminal justice in the western world since the time of Anselm.

In recent years, all theories of atonement, and above all Anselm's satisfaction atonement motif, have come under critique from a number of quarters. One cluster of challenges comes from writers influenced by Mennonite and peace church impulses. Following the direction of Gustaf Aulén, already more than thirty years ago Mennonite Gordon Kaufman developed a demythologized revisioning of the classic image that avoided the compensatory violence of satisfaction atonement.[4] Using different

---

fender does nothing for the victim, who is a passive observer of the process. On the offender's side, punishment or exacting vengeance in the name of the state does not teach the perpetrator a better way to live. For analysis of the criminal justice system as retributive justice as well as for the alternative of restorative justice, see Howard Zehr, *Changing Lenses: A New Focus for Crime and Justice*, A Christian Peace Shelf Selection (Scottdale, Pa.: Herald Press, 1990).

4. Gordon D. Kaufman, *Systematic Theology: A Historicist Perspective*, reprint, 1968 (New York: Scribner's, 1978), pp. 389-410. In his continuing theological program, Kaufman later abandoned the Christus Victor language entirely and constructed a new set of theologi-

methodology and a much different approach to the history of doctrine, Mennonite John Howard Yoder's *Preface to Theology* opened the door to an alternative, free church perspective on the classic issues of Christology and atonement.[5] Neither Kaufman nor Yoder was as specific about the assumption of violence in satisfaction atonement as has been my ongoing work in that area,[6] which has followed Yoder's lead. That work culminates with the book in hand.

A different kind of challenge to satisfaction atonement comes from a Catholic writer who works out of the theory of mimetic violence and the scapegoat mechanism developed by René Girard. As an alternative to the assumption that God orchestrates evil that punishes Jesus for the sins of humankind, Edmund Schwager developed a dramatistic understanding of the New Testament's depiction of Jesus, which shows that punishment is what sinful humanity does to itself through rejection of the reign of God.[7]

Other recent challenges to satisfaction atonement have come from theologians who articulate what are sometimes called contextual theologies. Among such theologies, this book deals with the interrelated triumvirate of black, feminist, and womanist theologies. In *God of the Oppressed*,[8] James H. Cone, the founder of the black theology movement, pointed out that the dominant Anselmian doctrine posed atonement in terms of an abstract theory that lacked ethical dimensions in the historical arena. Consequently, it allowed white people to claim salvation while accommodating and advocating the violence of racism and slavery.

Some of the most well-known and explicit feminist challenges are Joanne Carlson Brown and Rebecca Parker's essay in *Christianity, Patriarchy, and Abuse*,[9] and Rita Nakashima Brock's analysis of atonement in

---

cal images. See Gordon D. Kaufman, *In Face of Mystery: A Constructive Theology* (Cambridge, Mass.: Harvard University Press, 1993), esp. ch. 25 on "A Wider Christology."

5. John H. Yoder, *Preface to Theology: Christology and Theological Method* (Elkhart, Ind.: Goshen Biblical Seminary; distributed by Co-op Bookstore, 1981), pp. 120-58, 206-43.

6. For example, see J. Denny Weaver, "Atonement for the NonConstantinian Church," *Modern Theology* 6, no. 4 (July 1990): 307-23.

7. Raymund Schwager, *Jesus in the Drama of Salvation* (New York: Crossroad, 1999), pp. 160-69.

8. James H. Cone, *God of the Oppressed*, rev. ed. (Maryknoll, N.Y.: Orbis Books, 1997).

9. Joanne Carlson Brown and Rebecca Parker, "For God So Loved the World?" in *Christianity, Patriarchy, and Abuse: A Feminist Critique*, ed. Joanne Carlson Brown and Carole R. Bohn (New York: Pilgrim Press, 1989), pp. 1-30.

Journeys by Heart.[10] Delores Williams's argument in *Sisters in the Wilderness*[11] presented a womanist critique of satisfaction atonement. Each of these writers depicts classic atonement doctrine as images of divine child abuse or divine surrogacy, and as models of Jesus' work that encourage women to submit passively to abuse.

Black, feminist, and womanist theologies have brought new questions to the atonement discussions in recent years. Each of these theologies is sensitive to earlier theological efforts to justify violence or oppression of women and people of color by appeal to the suffering of Jesus or the submission of Jesus to suffering required by a divine mandate. Consequently, black and feminist and womanist voices have challenged any understanding of atonement that presumes salvation or reconciliation to God that would understand the killing of Jesus as an act required in order to satisfy divine justice. The sharpest challenges would eliminate the ideas of atonement and redemptive suffering entirely from Christian theology.

Putting the discussions about atonement from the contextual theologies in the same conversation with my nonviolent theology is the culmination of a number of years of encounters and reflection. As I discovered these several contextual critiques over a period of years, their notes played familiar melodies. For some years, I had been thinking about issues of violence and atonement from the pacifist perspective of the Mennonite tradition to which I choose to belong. I had concluded that Anselmian atonement was an abstract legal transaction that enabled the Christian believers of Christendom to claim salvation via the death of Christ while actively accommodating the violence of the sword. With that insight already in mind, encountering the critique of Anselm in Cone's *God of the Oppressed* was startling. Where I had been arguing that the abstract legal formula allowed accommodation of the sword, Cone was arguing that it had accommodated chattel slavery and racism. Rapidly I saw that critique of Anselm was an agenda item that extended well beyond the pacifist perspective from which I had been working. Going on to discover similar and parallel

---

10. Rita Nakashima Brock, *Journeys by Heart: A Christology of Erotic Power* (New York: Crossroad, 1988), pp. 53-57. See also Rita Nakashima Brock, "And a Little Child Will Lead Us: Christology and Child Abuse," in *Christianity, Patriarchy, and Abuse: A Feminist Critique,* ed. Joanne Carlson Brown and Carole R. Bohn (New York: Pilgrim Press, 1989), pp. 50-54.

11. Delores S. Williams, *Sisters in the Wilderness: The Challenge of Womanist God-Talk* (Maryknoll, N.Y.: Orbis Books, 1993), pp. 161-67.

as well as additional arguments in feminist and womanist theology widened the theological picture even more.

These discoveries were both exciting and challenging. For one thing, they provided additional reasons why Anselm's atonement motif was inadequate and problematic. More significantly, by extending the discussion of atonement and violence beyond the pacifist context, they brought to the fore a new perspective on traditional theology, in particular the classic formulas of Christology and atonement.

By being aware of and articulating their own contexts, black and feminist and womanist theologies shone a bright light on the fact that the received theology of Christendom in general and satisfaction atonement in particular *also have a context.* In the case of atonement theology, it became evident that the dominant tradition of Anselmian atonement was not general theology, not a universally recognizable, uncontestable foundation of common truth that all right-thinking Christians were bound to accept. Rather, Anselm's atonement doctrine was just as much a particular formulation that reflected a particular context as are any of the theological expressions from the so-called contextual theologies.

"Postmodernity" is the current terminology of choice for describing the recognition that each theology reflects a particular context and the abandonment of the idea of a universally recognizable and independently verifiable foundation of truth.[12] While postmodernity does not necessarily mean abandonment of the idea of universal truth or universally true religion, it does mean abandoning the idea that such truth will be readily apparent and thus accepted by anyone of right mind. Thus in postmodern perspective, Anselm's satisfaction atonement theology emerges as a theology that reflected a particular context just as surely as does James Cone's black theology or Delores Williams's womanist theology. It becomes clear that the atonement debate is then not about truth (such as Anselm) on the one side and deviants from the truth (the critics of Anselm) on the other. Rather the discussion concerns how the several theologies, whether Anselmian or womanist, reflect Christian sources such as the Bible and the story of Jesus, and whether some of these contextual theologies reflect and

12. For a more extensive discussion of my view on postmodernity, see the Introduction of my *Anabaptist Theology in Face of Postmodernity: A Proposal for the Third Millennium*, with a foreword by Glen Stassen, The C. Henry Smith Series, vol. 2 (Telford, Pa.: Pandora Press U.S.; co-publisher Herald Press, 2000).

restate more of the meaning of those sources better than others. The results articulated in the pages that follow present an understanding of atonement that is firmly anchored in biblical material but that does not pass through the previously presumed-to-be-general atonement theology of Anselm of Canterbury. Black, feminist, and womanist writers make similar claims.

Encountering the array of critiques from contexts different from my own also presented an important challenge to my work, namely whether the understanding of narrative Christus Victor that I was formulating could respond to the sets of problems raised by the writings of black and feminist and womanist theologians. The challenge was twofold. On the one hand, since Christian faith confesses that God's reign encompasses every person, an understanding of the work of Christ had to make sense to black and feminist and womanist theologians. Stated in terms reflecting postmodernity, did each context have its own atonement theology, or was there a way to talk about the work of Jesus Christ so that Christians in different particular contexts could understand the death of Jesus as an event with universal significance? At the same time, any reconstruction of atonement had to respect the particularity of these contextual theologies, and not merely claim to incorporate and co-opt pieces of them into someone else's supposedly wider and more general understanding. This book presents the results of the efforts to develop an understanding of atonement that made sense in its own right as a statement about the universal significance of Jesus Christ but that also answered questions raised by the contextual theologies.

I have called the resulting model of the life and work of Christ narrative Christus Victor. While narrative Christus Victor displays continuity with classic Christus Victor, it differs from the classic view in many important ways, and it deals with a number of issues not usually included in the discussion of atonement. The working assumption in development of this model is that the rejection of violence, whether the direct violence of the sword or the systemic violence of racism or sexism, should be visible in expressions of Christology and atonement. Developing an understanding shaped by nonviolence then lays bare the extent to which satisfaction atonement is founded on violent assumptions. Thus proposing narrative Christus Victor as a nonviolent atonement motif also poses a fundamental challenge to and ultimately a rejection of satisfaction atonement.

Since violence covers a multitude of sins and issues, examining biblical and historical material from a "nonviolent perspective" requires definitions for both violence and nonviolence. I am using "violence" to mean harm or damage. This definition obviously includes killing — in war, in murder, and in capital punishment. Violence as harm or damage includes physical harm or injury to bodily integrity. And it incorporates a range of acts and conditions that include damage to a person's dignity or self-esteem. Abuse comes in psychological and sociological as well as physical forms: parents who belittle a child and thus nurture a person without self-worth; teachers who brand a child a failure and destroy confidence to learn; a husband who continually puts down his wife; and more. Killing is not the sole instance of violence, but one of its more extreme forms. The system of chattel slavery that existed in colonial America and in the United States for two and a half centuries was most certainly violence. But the continuation of racist practices today under other names is also violence. Social practices that proscribe set roles for women and limit their opportunities are examples of violence. Social structures that impose poverty are violent. Such forms as racism, sexism, and poverty are frequently referred to as systemic violence. It is necessary to keep all of these forms of violence in mind, from direct violence of bodily injury and killing through psychological abuse and the multiple forms of systemic violence. Each of these forms of violence appears at some point in the discussion of atonement images to follow.

One important dimension of violence is the way it is assumed and used in the criminal justice system. As was already noted, the prevailing assumption behind the criminal justice system is that to do justice means to inflict punishment, with the intensity of punishment dependent on the seriousness of the misdeed. In theory then, the death penalty differs quantitatively but not qualitatively from lesser punishments. But recognizing the assumption that justice means punishment shows that a very pervasive use of violence surrounds us in the criminal justice system, a use of violence whose commonness renders it virtually invisible. The assumed violence of justice as punishment will appear at several stages in the discussion of atonement, particularly in the context of feminist and womanist arguments and in the arguments of the defenders of Anselm in Chapter 7.

If violence covers a variety of issues, "nonviolence" also covers a spectrum of stances and actions ranging from passive nonresistance at one end to active nonviolent resistance at the other. In this regard, it is very important to distinguish violence defined as harm or damage from nonviolence as force or social coercion that respects bodily integrity. Since we have no term that carries the specific meaning of coercion used positively, I will here describe it as identifying a spectrum of acts stretching from persuasion to physical coercion. Persuasion attempts to affect and guide the action of others without denying their freedom or harming their person. At a low level of intensity, it includes the gentle coercion of parents who restrain children from disruptive behavior and teachers who require pupils to raise their hands and wait for permission to speak in class. At a high level of intensity at the other end of the spectrum, positive coercion that constrains or compels the acts of others through pressure would include such actions as social ostracism, public marches and protests, and eventually strikes and economic boycotts. Examples of physical force used positively or in a way to prevent an act that an individual wants to perform might include some forms of punishment for children, physically restraining children from running into the street, knocking a person out of the path of a vehicle, and physically restraining a person attempting suicide.[13]

One specific point to make clear about nonviolence is that it does resist violence in any of its forms. The question is not whether nonviolent Christians should resist. It is rather *how* Christians should resist. And the answer is to resist nonviolently. As the treatment of the story of Jesus in the following chapter demonstrates, Jesus engaged in nonviolent resistance. He broke the conventions of the prevailing order and posed alternatives to them by healing on the sabbath, by traveling through Samaria, by his dealings with women, and much more. As I use the term in this book, these actions of Jesus constitute nonviolent resistance.

This brief survey of the meanings of violence and nonviolence means that the study of violence and atonement needs to address two related sets of questions. One focus of this discussion is to come to terms with the assumed violence in the traditional images of atonement, and most particularly of satisfaction atonement. Each of the forms of violence noted above appears in traditional atonement imagery: accommodation of the violence of sword and of various forms of systemic violence by the abstract formulas of satisfaction atonement; modeling of submission to abusive author-

---

13. Two examples of developing these understandings of violence and force or coercion in some detail are Duane K. Friesen, *Christian Peacemaking and International Conflict: A Realist Pacifist Perspective* (Scottdale, Pa.: Herald Press, 1986), pp. 143-57, and Walter Wink, *Engaging the Powers: Discernment and Resistance in a World of Domination*, The powers, vol. 3 (Minneapolis: Fortress, 1992), pp. 175-257.

ity; modeling the assumption that doing justice or making right depends on punishment or sanctioned violence. The second focus of the argument is to show how narrative Christus Victor provides a reading of Jesus' life and work that avoids all the dimensions of violence in traditional atonement imagery.

Discussion of atonement and violence is a complex argument with many components. One could open the discussion at any number of places. This book begins at the end. That is, I first pose my complete suggestion for atonement from a nonviolent perspective, and then explain the problems which this answer solves. This method provides a tangible, biblical model to hold on to through the twists and turns of the discussion. It also make it easier to understand the particular arguments of other theologies encountered along the way.

Against a backdrop of sketches of the traditional images of atonement, Chapter 2 lays out my proposal for a nonviolent understanding of atonement that I have called narrative Christus Victor. While it stands in continuity with the classic view described by Gustaf Aulén, narrative Christus Victor differs significantly from the classic image, and it bears little resemblance to the Christus Victor rejected by feminist writers such as Brown and Parker. The argument considers narrative Christus Victor in three biblical settings: in the book of Revelation at the end of the New Testament, in the Gospels at its beginning, and in terms of its compatibility with Paul, the New Testament's most important theologian. Additional discussion of biblical material rounds out this chapter.

Not all the dimensions of narrative Christus Victor as a thoroughgoing nonviolent approach to atonement are clear at first glance. The biblical materials in Chapter 2 constitute only one part of the argument. Chapter 3 develops additional nonviolent dimensions by exploring answers to some systematic questions and by correlating the demise of narrative Christus Victor and the eventual rise of satisfaction atonement imagery with changes in ecclesiology that followed the church's eventual identification with the social order. Chapter 3 deals primarily with violence of the sword and killing, with awareness of systemic forms of violence.

Putting narrative Christus Victor in conversation with black, feminist, and womanist theologies in Chapters 4, 5, and 6 shifts focus to issues related to the systemic violence of racism and sexism. Chapter 4 engages examples of black theology, which has raised questions about abstract formulas and the accommodation of slavery and racism, and about theology divorced from the reality of history. Chapter 5 enters conversation with representative feminist theologians who have raised concerns about the model of innocent and passive submission to abuse in satisfaction atonement. Chapter 6 engages womanist theology, which supports elements of the feminist critique of atonement but also raises additional issues of surrogacy, racism, and the efficacy of innocent suffering. Finally, Chapter 7 brings the critique from all these theologies into conversation with the modern defenders and advocates of Anselm and provides a new analysis of Anselm's *Cur Deus Homo.* The final conclusion is that, even at its best, Anselm's satisfaction theory of atonement cannot escape its foundation in the idea of retributive violence. It can be kept and defended, I conclude, only if one is willing to defend the compatibility of violence and retribution with the gospel of Jesus Christ.

2 Narrative Christus Victor: The Revisioning of Atonement

The Nonviolence of Jesus

That Jesus lived and taught nonviolence seems generally, if not universally, accepted.[1] What has been almost universally doubted, it seems, is that Jesus' example and teaching apply to the contemporary church, to the church through the ages that now stands on the doorstep of the third millennium. The time-honored idea of a justifiable war, which has been articulated in some form since Augustine's version of it in the fourth century, actually assumes that Jesus' rejection of the sword is the norm for Christians — but then sets out the circumstances in which that norm need not or cannot be applied. In the first chapter of his seminal *Politics of Jesus,* John H. Yoder listed six ways, taken "from every age in the history of Christian thought about society," that Jesus' irrelevance for social ethics has been proclaimed.[2] In response, Yoder wrote *Politics of Jesus* to show

---

1. Walter Wink's reinterpretation of Jesus' words, "Do not resist an evildoer" (Matt. 5:39) in the Sermon on the Mount shows that Jesus suggested an active response to evil that does not violate the nonviolent character of Jesus' teaching. While Jesus was providing strategies of resistance, Wink argued, they were nonviolent strategies that disarmed the oppressor. See Walter Wink, *Engaging the Powers: Discernment and Resistance in a World of Domination,* The Powers, vol. 3 (Minneapolis: Fortress, 1992), pp. 175-89.

2. John Howard Yoder, *The Politics of Jesus: Vicit Agnus Noster,* 2nd ed. (Grand Rapids: Eerdmans, 1993), pp. 5-8, also pp. 13-20.

that Jesus' rejection of the sword had clear social implications for contemporary Christians, if they truly took Jesus seriously.

The book in hand is a theological parallel to *Politics of Jesus*. Where Yoder articulated ethics that assumed the nonviolence of the narrative of Jesus, this book constructs theology from that perspective. It demonstrates that nonviolence is far from being a category restricted to ethics. Beyond ethics, Jesus' rejection of the sword has the potential to shape our understandings of all other dimensions of theology, and in particular what theology has said about Jesus and how the contemporary church should understand the work of Christ.

My discussion has several components. It surveys biblical material from the Gospels through Paul and Hebrews to the book of Revelation. The biblical discussion makes two points. One is that narrative Christus Victor clearly fits and gives meaning to the story of Jesus, and that it accords with recent scholarship on the apostle Paul and the letter to the Hebrews. Further, it makes clear that this atonement motif presumes nonviolence and is in fact meaningless apart from that presumption. Beyond the biblical material, a second component of the argument appears in Chapter 3, which offers a new reading of the development of Christology and atonement in the history of doctrine. This discussion shows that the standard account of the development of doctrine has presumed the accommodation of violence as the self-evident norm. The book provides an alternative reading of the history of doctrine that is an extension of the biblical interpretation that presumed nonviolence. These biblical and historical insights will make quite visible the fact that atonement has ecclesiological implications and that narrative Christus Victor is an ecclesiological motif as well as a model of atonement. Together these biblical and historical insights bring a critique shaped by nonviolence to the internal logic of atonement motifs themselves. The result is a statement of narrative Christus Victor as a comprehensive theology that responds to a variety of violence issues raised by contemporary theologies.

This multifaceted discussion comprises a theological alternative to the sixth way described by Yoder to make Jesus irrelevant for ethics. Jesus is deemed irrelevant for "dogmatic" reasons, Yoder wrote, in that it is claimed that he gave "his life for the sins of humankind. The work of atonement . . . is a forensic act, a gracious gift . . . but never should it be correlated with ethics."[3] The book in hand demonstrates that interpreta-

3. Yoder, *The Politics of Jesus*, pp. 7-8.

tions of biblical material related to atonement, the history of dogma, and contemporary reconstructions of atonement are in fact impacted when issues of atonement are examined through a lens focused by the nonviolence of Jesus.

Images of Atonement

This book proposes narrative Christus Victor as an image of atonement. As a backdrop, it is important to begin with sketches of the prevailing models of atonement in mind. Gustaf Aulén's *Christus Victor* lent credibility to a threefold taxonomy of atonement models or atonement images: the classic model or Christus Victor, the satisfaction theory, and the moral influence theory. Each of these is actually a family of views with several variants.[4]

Christus Victor Motif

What Aulén called the classic view stressed the theme of victory. This atonement image used the image of cosmic battle between good and evil, between the forces of God and those of Satan. In that fray God's son Jesus

---

4. For three families of atonement images, see Gustaf Aulén, *Christus Victor: An Historical Study of the Three Main Types of the Idea of Atonement,* trans. A. G. Herbert (New York: Macmillan, 1969), which first appeared in 1930; and Robert S. Paul, *The Atonement and the Sacraments: The Relation of the Atonement to the Sacraments of Baptism and the Lord's Supper* (New York: Abingdon, 1960). Some more recent surveys include John H. Yoder, *Preface to Theology: Christology and Theological Method* (Elkhart, Ind.: Goshen Biblical Seminary; distributed by Co-op Bookstore, 1981), pp. 206-43; H. D. McDonald, *The Atonement of the Death of Christ in Faith, Revelation, and History* (Grand Rapids: Baker, 1985), pp. 125-46; Thomas N. Finger, *Christian Theology: An Eschatological Approach, Volume 1* (Scottdale, Pa.: Herald Press [reprint, Thomas Nelson], 1985), pp. 317-24; John Driver, *Understanding the Atonement for the Mission of the Church,* foreword by C. René Padilla (Scottdale, Pa.: Herald Press, 1986); C. Norman Kraus, *Jesus Christ Our Lord: Christology from a Disciple's Perspective,* rev. ed., reprint, 1987 (Scottdale, Pa.: Herald Press, 1990), pp. 154-60; James Wm. McClendon, Jr., *Systematic Theology: Doctrine,* Systematic Theology, vol. 2 (Nashville: Abingdon, 1994), pp. 199-213. On atonement in the early church fathers, see J. F. Bethune-Baker, *An Introduction to the Early History of Christian Doctrine: To the Time of the Council of Chalcedon* (London: Methuen & Co. Ltd., 1938), pp. 327-55.

Christ was killed, an apparent defeat of God and victory by Satan. However, Jesus' resurrection turned the seeming defeat into a great victory, which forever established God's control of the universe and freed sinful humans from the power of sin and Satan. This motif carries the designation of "classic" because it is the prevailing view found in early church theologians.

A variation of the classic or victory motif depicted Christ's death as the ransom price paid to Satan in exchange for freeing the sinners Satan held captive. With his resurrection, Christ then escaped the clutches of Satan, and sinners were freed from Satan's power. However, paying a ransom assumes that even Satan has certain rights that must be respected. Another variation denies such rights, and pictures the defeat of the devil via deception. Failing to perceive the presence of God or the deity of Christ hidden under the flesh of Christ, analogous to the way bait covers a fishhook or cheese baits a mouse trap, the devil assumes an easy prey and swallows the bait of the humanity of Jesus and is caught by the deity hidden under the human nature. In these several images, the stress on victory through resurrection identifies this motif as Christus Victor.

The Christus Victor motif faded away and lost favor after the sixth century and in more recent times has fallen under increasing criticism. Reasons for the demise of Christus Victor usually suggested by writers on the history of doctrine include: (i) aversion to the idea that God would either acknowledge certain rights of the devil, or stoop to overcoming the devil through trickery; (ii) discomfort with the motif's military and battle imagery; (iii) incompatibility of either the image of a cosmic battle or a ransom payment to Satan within a modern cosmology; (iv) lack of evidence of the victory of the reign of God in our world; (v) Christus Victor's dualistic outlook in light of a modern worldview composed mostly of "gray areas."[5] I will later suggest a quite different explanation for the demise of Christus Victor when I argue that a revised form of it commends itself to the twenty-first century.

---

5. Aulén, *Christus Victor: An Historical Study of the Three Main Types of the Idea of Atonement*, pp. 7-12; Reinhold Seeberg, *Text-Book of the History of Doctrines,* two volumes bound in one, trans. Charles E. Hay (Grand Rapids: Baker, 1961), vol. 2, pp. 67-71; Jaroslav Pelikan, *The Growth of Medieval Theology (600-1300)*, The Christian Tradition: A History of the Development of Doctrine, vol. 3 (Chicago: University of Chicago Press, 1978), pp. 136-39.

Satisfaction Motif

In his *Cur Deus Homo* (1098), Anselm of Canterbury (c. 1033-1109) explicitly rejected the idea that Satan had rights and that Jesus' death was a ransom paid to the devil. He developed the satisfaction theory to replace the ransom theory. The satisfaction motif includes several variations and emphases.

For Anselm, the sin of humankind had offended the honor of God and had brought disharmony and injustice into the universe. A debt payment was necessary in order to restore God's honor or to restore justice in the universe. Since humankind owed the debt but could not pay it, Jesus paid the debt by dying in their place. Jesus' death was a payment made to God's honor in order to restore justice and harmony in the universe. The death was "propitiation" when the image is of the sacrifice offered as compensation to the offended honor of God, and "expiation" when it concerns the sinners' guilt and penalty which are covered. Beyond atonement for individuals, Anselm understood the death of Jesus as the satisfaction of God's justice in the universe. Anselm's satisfaction atonement image likely originated as a reflection of the penitential system and the sacrament of private penance that was developing throughout the medieval era, and also reflected the image of the feudal lord who gave protection to his vassals but also exacted penalties for offenses against his honor.[6]

Anselm's image posed the death of Christ as the means to satisfy the offended honor of God. Building on the stress Martin Luther and John Calvin placed on Christ's death as penal suffering — the suffering by Christ of divine judgment on behalf of sinners — the divines of Protestant Orthodoxy in the following centuries developed the satisfaction theory within a strong legal and penal framework.[7] Christ's sufferings "were the

---

6. McClendon, *Doctrine*, p. 205; Pelikan, *Growth*, pp. 141-44; Seeberg, *Text-Book*, vol. 2, pp. 66-70; Wolfhart Pannenberg, *Jesus — God and Man*, trans. Lewis L. Wilkins and Duane A. Priebe (Philadelphia: Westminster, 1975), pp. 42-43; R. W. Southern, *Saint Anselm: A Portrait in a Landscape* (Cambridge: Cambridge University Press, 1990), pp. 221-27.

7. McClendon, *Doctrine*, pp. 206-8; Kraus, *Jesus Christ Our Lord*, pp. 154-56; Pannenberg, *Jesus — God and Man*, pp. 278-80; McDonald, *The Atonement*, pp. 181-95. For discussion of this shift in images of satisfaction atonement and its implications for the application of punishment in western systems of criminal justice, see Timothy Gorringe, *God's Just Vengeance: Crime, Violence and the Rhetoric of Salvation*, Cambridge Studies in Ideology and Religion, no. 9 (Cambridge: Cambridge University Press, 1996), pp. 126-219.

penalty of the law executed on Christ as the sinner's substitute."[8] What Christ's death satisfied was the divine law. With satisfaction aimed at the law, the role of God was conceived in the mode of the trial judge who exacted the penalty demanded by the law, or as the prosecuting attorney who charged sinners with violating the law. Versions varied on the extent of the application of the death. Did the law require payment of an exact price equal to the accumulated sins of sinners, and thus the death of Christ could cover only the sins of the elect? Those who answer this question with "yes" argue that it is the only way to prevent Jesus' death from being an eternal suffering and death. Those who answer "no" argue that Jesus' death did not meet an exact requirement of law, but rather satisfied a general condition and established the possibility of forgiveness for those who would avail themselves of the provisions. In this case, the death did not actually cover all sins of all humankind but rather provided a way for God to forgive without setting aside the provision of the law. This view is sometimes called a general atonement. A version of it was stated by Hugo Grotius (1583-1645), a Dutch legal theorist, in what he called the "governmental" theory. Picturing God not as judge but as Governor of the universe, Grotius argued that God need not exact every penalty stipulated by the law. Rather, by offering God's own son as the example of penalty exacted by the law, God would be able to pardon sinners without a relaxation of the divine law.[9]

With an emphasis on satisfying either God as an offended party or legal obligations established by God's law, this family of views can go by the name of "satisfaction theory" of atonement. Focus on Jesus' death as an action in place of or as a substitute for sinful humankind makes it the "substitutionary theory." Stress on Jesus' payment of the penalty that the law required of sinners or on Jesus' suffering the penalty which sinners deserved produces the "penal theory" of atonement. When designated as "Anselmian," this family of atonement theories is identified with the man who made the first systematic articulation of it. Common to this family of views in any of its versions is that the death of Jesus involved a divinely orchestrated plan through which Jesus' death could satisfy divine justice or divine law in order to save sinful humankind.

---

8. McDonald, *The Atonement*, p. 195, with reference to A. A. Hodge.
9. McClendon, *Doctrine*, p. 208; McDonald, *The Atonement*, pp. 203-7.

Moral Influence Motif

Writing a generation after Anselm, Abelard (1079-1142) developed the moral influence theory, also called the subjective view, as a specific alternative to Anselm's theory. Like Anselm, Abelard rejected the idea of Jesus' death as a ransom paid to the devil. But Abelard also rejected any idea of Jesus' death as debt paid to God's honor. He further disliked the stress on God's judgment required in the satisfaction theory and objected to the fact that it seemed to picture a change in God's attitude toward the sinner after he or she accepted Jesus' death on their behalf. After all, the perfect, impassible God does not change. For Abelard, the problem of atonement was not how to change an offended God's mind toward the sinner, but how to bring sinful humankind to see that the God they perceived as harsh and judgmental was actually loving. Thus for Abelard, Jesus died as the demonstration of God's love. And the change that results from that loving death is not in God but in the subjective consciousness of the sinners, who repent and cease their rebellion against God and turn toward God. It is this psychological or subjective influence worked on the mind of the sinner by the death of Christ that gives this view its name of moral influence theory.[10]

While these atonement images all talk about how Jesus' death saves, they differ significantly from each other. The motifs are easily distinguished by keeping in mind that each theory has a different object for the death of Jesus, or has the death of Jesus aimed at a different entity. For classic Christus Victor, in either the cosmic battle or the ransom versions, Satan is the object of Jesus' death; Jesus' death is directed toward the devil. In Anselm's version of the satisfaction theory, the offended honor of God is the object of Jesus' death. In Protestant Orthodoxy's version, God's law stands as the object of Jesus' death. For the moral influence theory, sinful humankind — that is, us — is the target of Jesus' death. The death is aimed at us as a way for God to get our attention. Seeing these different objects or purposes for Jesus' death makes clear that there are truly different options for explaining how the death of Christ affects those who claim the name of Christ.

Conversations between versions of the theories of Anselm and Abelard have characterized much of the atonement debate since the medi-

---

10. Pelikan, *Growth*, pp. 127-29; Finger, *Christian Theology 1*, pp. 310-17; McDonald, *The Atonement*, pp. 174-80.

eval period. Since Anselm, some version of satisfaction atonement has been the majority view for both Catholics and the communions of Protestant Orthodoxy. However, Catholicism has not accorded the status of dogma to a specific theory of atonement, while nineteenth- and early twentieth-century conservative Protestants gave creedal status to satisfaction atonement. On much the same basis articulated by Abelard, nineteenth- and early twentieth-century Protestant liberals advocated a version of moral influence theory over against the satisfaction theory of fundamentalism and evangelicalism. A primary example is Horace Bushnell's use of satisfaction terminology to argue for a moral influence theory of atonement.[11] In the twentieth century, Gustaf Aulén's *Christus Victor* initiated renewed visibility for the Christus Victor image.

This description has followed the conventional summaries of atonement images, and the discussion to follow proceeds with these general descriptions in mind. Eventually it will also become clear why it is not necessary to respond in detail to each particular version of these atonement models in making a case for narrative Christus Victor. To anticipate, every form of the satisfaction motif assumes divinely initiated or divinely sanctioned violence — the Father needing or willing the death of the Son as the basis for satisfying divine honor or divine justice or divine law. Since the logic of the satisfaction motif itself assumes that divinely sanctioned violence, a search for a different version of satisfaction does not resolve the problem. That point will become most clear in Chapter 7, which deals with the defenders of Anselm and with Anselm's *Cur Deus Homo* itself.

Narrative Christus Victor

I take an indirect route to narrative Christus Victor. It begins not with questions about the death of Jesus but with an analysis of Revelation, the last book of the Bible.

---

11. McClendon, *Doctrine,* pp. 210-13; Finger, *Christian Theology 1,* pp. 310-14; McDonald, *The Atonement,* pp. 299-302.

The Apocalypse [12]

The elements of cosmic confrontation and victory appear throughout Revelation, making the book virtually an extended, multifaceted statement of the Christus Victor image — a confrontation between good and evil, between the forces of God and the forces of Satan, between Christ and anti-Christ. For example, the victory motif appears in the unit comprised of chapters 5–7. The lion and lamb symbols of Revelation 5, which both refer to Jesus, portray one instance of a conqueror motif — with lion as a symbol of victory while the slaughtered lamb signifies the (nonviolent) manner of the victory. The victory song of the heavenly creatures (5:9-10) celebrates the subsequent joining of people of all ethnic and culture groups into a "kingdom and priests serving our God," which "will reign on earth." In other words, celebrated here is the victory of the reign of God over the rule of evil that slaughtered the lamb, Christ.

In Revelation 6 and 7, it is the nonviolent conqueror — the slain lamb — who has earned the right to open the seals, and it is the lamb's victory over the forces that oppose the reign of God that is celebrated by the two great multitudes of the second scene of seal six. Seals one through four and six progress through various kinds of oppression and destruction, culminating with the highest level of evil — utter chaos — in the first scene of the sixth seal. Here the very structure of the universe seems threatened as the sun and moon darken, stars fall, and sky vanishes, while earthquakes move mountains and islands, and the rich and poor and powerful and powerless all flee in panic together. Seal five shifts viewpoint from an earthly scene to the heavenly realm, where the souls of the martyrs under the altar somewhat petulantly bemoan the slowness of God in avenging their deaths — deaths that resulted from the oppression and death depicted in seals one to four.

But frustration at the slowness of God's vengeance and despair at great devastation are not the end of the sequence. Alongside the scene of chaos

---

12. Parts of the following interpretation of Revelation are revised and expanded versions of material in my *Keeping Salvation Ethical: Mennonite and Amish Atonement Theology in the Late Nineteenth Century*, foreword by C. Norman Kraus, Studies in Anabaptist and Mennonite History, no. 35 (Herald Press, 1997), pp. 39-43, and in "Reading the Past, Present, and Future in Revelation," in *Apocalypticism and Millennialism: Shaping a Believers' Church Eschatology for the Twenty-First Century*, ed. Loren L. Johns (Kitchener, Ont.: Pandora Press, 2000), pp. 104-18.

and destruction pictured in scene one of the sixth seal is a much longer description of celebration in the second scene of seal six. This scene of celebration encompasses the entire seventh chapter of Revelation. The first vignette of Revelation 7 displays the gathering of the 144,000 — 12,000 from each of the tribes of Israel. The second vignette portrays "a great multitude that no one could count" (7:9), drawn from all the peoples of the earth.

The two multitudes represent different aspects of the people of God. The 144,000 emphasizes the continuity of the people of God with Israel. The number 144 is 12 × 12, which is the number of tribes of (old) Israel times the number of disciples (nucleus of new Israel). After "myriad," which is 10,000, "thousand" is "the largest numerical unit in the Bible." Since the Bible uses both myriad and thousand to mean "a very large number," they should not be read with literal precision. The number 144,000 is a symbolic number that represents Israel while conveying the idea that the people of God is vast. The multitude composed of people "from every nation, from all tribes and peoples and languages" (7:9) was also vast, too numerous to count. When we think in terms of modern mathematics and computers that routinely crunch numbers with virtually countless numbers of zeros, 144,000 seems much smaller than "a great multitude that no one could count." It would have appeared much larger to first-century readers, however, and the author of Revelation no doubt intended to present two images of God's people, each indicating a huge throng comparable in size to the other.[13] Revelation 7 pictures these multitudes in celebration of the victory of the Lamb over the devastation and destruction that mounted through seals one to four and six. Juxtaposition of this celebration in seal six with the utter chaos and destruction in the scene of 5:12-17 suggests the greatness of the victory. This celebration matches that of chapter 5, which acclaimed the victory of the slaughtered lamb, the resurrected Christ.

The symbolic imagery in the scene of the throne room and the celebration that culminates the opening of the seven seals presents an awe-inspiring and thrilling message, namely that the resurrection of Jesus Christ is the ultimate and definitive cosmic victory of the reign of God over the rule of Satan and the multiple evils that he produces, including war and devastation, famine, pestilence, and natural disasters. This is the

13. See M. Eugene Boring, *Revelation,* Interpretation: A Bible Commentary for Teaching and Preaching (Louisville: John Knox Press, 1989), p. 130, including quotation.

victorious Christ, Christus Victor. With the resurrection of Jesus is revealed the true nature of reality, the universal rule of God. Jesus' resurrection marks the definitive turning point — the decisive victory — in the ultimate struggle with Satan for the fate of the universe. The vast multitude of the people of God celebrate this victory. With the resurrection of Jesus, the future reign of God has already begun in human history. While the culmination still awaits, a piece of the future exists now.

While the imagery of Revelation 5–7 clearly pictures the ultimate significance of the death and resurrection of Jesus for God's universal rule, the symbols most certainly had antecedents in the first century of Christian history that the first or original readers would have readily understood. Analysis of symbols and their antecedents reveals the correlation between the historical church of the first century and Christus Victor in the book of Revelation. The result is Christus Victor depicted in terms of first-century history, a historicized or earthly Christus Victor. However, each of these terms risks being misunderstood as limiting the scope of Christ's victory to earth or to human history. Thus I have chosen to designate this motif as narrative Christus Victor,[14] which encompasses victory in both human historical and cosmic realms, as well as emphasizing Jesus' life and ministry (in contrast to Gustaf Aulén's depiction of the motif), as is sketched in the following section.

Attention to possible historical antecedents makes it apparent that the confrontation and victory occurred in the world in which we live, and that the cosmic imagery depicts the author's interpretation of the universal and cosmic significance of events in our, historical world. While we cannot be absolutely certain of the antecedents the author had in mind, it is important to keep clearly in view that Revelation's context is the first and not the twenty-first century. I suggest that the sequence of seven seals corresponds to the reigns of Roman emperors from Tiberius (14-37 C.E., seal 1), during whose rule Jesus was crucified, through Caligula (37-40 C.E., seal 2), Claudius (41-54 C.E., seal 3), Nero (54-68 C.E., seal 4), and Vespasian (69-79 C.E., seal 6), to the short reign of Titus (79-81 C.E.) or more likely Domitian (81-96 C.E., seal 7). Seal 5 corresponds to the eighteen-month period that saw three emperors of short duration. The "silence" in seal 7, followed by the beginning of a new sequence of seven without terminating the first seven, indicates the time in which the author is writing — he is

14. Thanks to Leanne Van Dyk, who first suggested this term.

commenting on the meaning of events from the resurrection of Jesus (which he interprets as the most significant event in the history of the universe) until his (the author's) own time.[15]

When Revelation 6:2 says that the rider of seal one "came out conquering and to conquer," it means that the rider tried but failed in his effort to conquer. This mere appearance of conquering may constitute an oblique reference to the death and resurrection of Jesus. Since Jesus did not stay dead, the imagery implies, the rider — Tiberius — had only a temporary or apparent victory. Following symbols are more obvious. The blood-red horse, the sword, and taking peace from the earth in seal two correspond to the threats posed by Caligula. In addition to Caligula's provocations against Jews in particular, the symbolism seems to refer to events in 40 C.E. After decreeing that places of worship should be converted to shrines that acknowledged his deity, Caligula sent Petronius from Antioch with an army of more than two legions to march through Judea to install a large statue of Caligula on the altar in the temple in Jerusalem. When Petronius halted the march after lengthy appeals from the Jews, the threat did not fully materialize, and Caligula died before his order to kill Petronius and start the army moving again could be carried out.[16]

The symbols of famine in seal three most certainly refer to the widespread series of famines that occurred in several lands, including Palestine, during the reign of Claudius. These famines are well documented in the

15. No consensus exists on the correlation of seals and emperors. For other suggestions on the correlations of seven and ten emperors with the seven heads and ten crowns of the beast in Revelation 17, see Adela Yarbro Collins, *Crisis and Catharsis: The Power of the Apocalypse* (Philadelphia: Westminster, 1984), pp. 58-64; J. Massyngberde Ford, *Revelation: Introduction, Translation and Commentary,* The Anchor Bible (Garden City, N.Y.: Doubleday, 1975), pp. 289-91; and Jarl Henning Ulrichsen, "Die Sieben Häupter und die Zehn Hörner zur Datierung der Offenbarung Des Johannes," *Studia Theologica* 39 (1985): 1-20. None of these suggests the particular correspondence proposed in what follows, which I have adopted from Associated Mennonite Biblical Seminary professor Willard Swartley, who presented it in lectures at Bluffton College in October 1978.

16. Josephus, "Jewish War 2.184-203," in *The Jewish War, Books 1-3,* in *Josephus,* vol. 2, trans. H. St. J. Thackeray, The Loeb Classical Library (Cambridge, Mass.: Harvard University Press, 1976), pp. 395-403; Philo, "The Embassy to Gaius 197-348," in *The Embassy to Gaius,* in *Philo,* vol. 10, trans. F. H. Colson, The Loeb Classical Library (Cambridge, Mass.: Harvard University Press, 1971), pp. 101-75, also xii-xiv; Anthony A. Barrett, *Caligula: The Corruption of Power* (New Haven: Yale University Press, 1989), pp. 182-91; Emil Schürer, *The History of the Jewish People in the Age of Jesus Christ (175 B.C.–A.D. 135),* vol. 1, rev. and ed. Geza Vermes and Fergus Millar (Edinburgh: T. & T. Clark, 1973), pp. 388-92.

literature of that time, including a reference in Acts 11:28.[17] Nero followed Claudius as emperor. The double ugly riders named Death and Hades in seal four, who kill with "sword, famine, and pestilence, and by the wild animals of the earth," most certainly depict Nero, who began the first imperial persecution of Christians. Nero made Christians the scapegoat for the great fire in Rome in 64 A.D., and his cruelty to Christians and others became legendary. Among other things, he dressed Christians in the skins of wild animals to be torn to pieces by dogs, or used them as living torches to light the games and chariot races in his gardens or in the Vatican circus.[18] The bubonic plague claimed thirty thousand victims in one autumn during Nero's era.[19]

Following Nero three men ruled as emperor in a space of about eighteen months. None was able to eliminate rivals and establish a lasting hold on the office. Galba ruled seven months, from mid 68 to January 69 C.E., followed by Otho and then Vitellius. Galba was murdered by soldiers loyal to Otho, while Otho committed suicide to avoid being killed by followers of Vitellius. The shift of viewpoint in seal five from earthly to heavenly realm corresponds to this break in the succession of emperors, when none of the three claimants to the throne succeeded in fully consolidating power.[20]

After his soldiers eliminated Vitellius, Vespasian attained the crown late in 69 C.E. The next year, an imperial army under the command of

17. Josephus, "Jewish Antiquities 20.101," in *Jewish Antiquities, Book 20*, in *Josephus*, vol. 10, trans. Louis H. Feldman, The Loeb Classical Library (Cambridge, Mass.: Harvard University Press, 1981), p. 55; Tacitus, "The Annals of Imperial Rome 12.43," in *The Annals of Imperial Rome*, rev. ed., trans. and intro. by Michael Grant (London: Penguin Books, 1988), p. 271; Suetonius, "Claudius, Afterwards Deified 18," in *The Twelve Caesars: Gaius Suetonius Tranquillas*, rev. ed., trans. Robert Graves, rev. and intro. by Michael Grant (London: Penguin Books, 1989), pp. 196-97; Hans Conzelmann, *Acts of the Apostles: A Commentary on the Acts of the Apostles*, ed. Eldon Jay Epp and Christopher R. Matthews, trans. James Limburg, A. Thomas Kraabel, and Donald H. Juel, Hermeneia (Philadelphia: Fortress, 1987), p. 90; Ernst Haenchen, *The Acts of the Apostles: A Commentary* (Philadelphia: Westminster, 1971), p. 374.

18. Suetonius, "Nero 16.2," in *Twelve Caesars*, p. 221; Tacitus, "Annals 15.44," in *The Annals*, pp. 365-66.

19. Suetonius, "Nero 39.1," in *Twelve Caesars*, p. 236.

20. Suetonius, "Galba, Otho, and Vitellius," in *The Lives of the Caesars*, in *Suetonius*, vol. 2, trans. J. C. Rolfe, The Loeb Classical Library (Cambridge, Mass.: Harvard University Press, 1979), pp. 189-277.

Vespasian's son Titus sacked Jerusalem and destroyed the temple. From the perspective of Jews, the fall of David's city and destruction of the temple would produce virtually unfathomable feelings of despair and tragedy, the end of life and civilization as they knew it — precisely the mood represented by the elements of the opening scene of the sixth seal. Heavens and earth shake and shatter, while people of all levels — from the most powerful to the most lowly — flee in chaos and panic.

However, the sixth seal does not end with despair at the destruction of the city. A heavenly messenger stays damage to earth and sea until the servants of God have been identified, marked "with a seal on their foreheads." In Revelation 7, the two vast throngs in celebration mode stand juxtaposed with the destruction of the city of Jerusalem. In the midst of the worst imaginable desolation from an earthly perspective, the two multitudes are depicted in celebration. And to heighten the irony, the reader learns in 7:17 that the great, white-robed multitude consists of martyrs, "who have come out of the great ordeal [and] have washed their robes and made them white in the blood of the lamb." Robed in white, they stand before the throne on which God sits and before the lamb and they shout,

> Salvation belongs to our God who is seated on the throne, and to the Lamb! . . . Amen! Blessing and glory and wisdom and thanksgiving and honor and power and might be to our God forever and ever! Amen. (Rev. 7:10, 12)

The message to be learned from the image of the cheering throngs is that the rule of God has already triumphed for those who live in the reality of the resurrection. Even when confronted with the devastation wreaked by the rule of Rome, culminating with the destruction of the temple and the sacred city of Jerusalem, they do not face ultimate despair. Though earthly rule appears to culminate in destruction, the rule of God has already begun on earth with a victory, the resurrection of Jesus. With the scenes of cheering throngs in seal six, the writer of Revelation makes a statement about a historical event, namely the fall of Jerusalem. These celebratory scenes convey the message that in the grand scheme of things as defined by the reign of God, even the fall of Jerusalem pales in significance to the resurrection of Jesus. Here in a different form is the confrontation of reign of God and reign of evil, with the reign of God victorious in the resurrection of Jesus. This is Christus Victor depicted in the realm of history.

While correlating the seven seals with imperial reigns identifies a clear political location for Revelation in the first century, recent scholarship develops other dimensions of the social milieu in which Revelation was written and to which it speaks. Even though Revelation clearly serves to reinforce the commitment of Christians to remain strong in the face of persecution, little evidence exists to support a claim that the book was written to counter direct persecution of Christians by Domitian, the emperor when it was written.[21] Adela Yarbro Collins identified three different sources for the sense of confrontation and "perceived crisis" that runs throughout the book — a feeling of isolation that follows the recent expulsion of Christians from the synagogue, a sense of mutual antipathy with gentile neighbors, and conflicts about wealth. Collins also noted five elements of personal and communal trauma that involved the Romans as adversaries of Christians. These include the persecutions under Nero and the destruction of Jerusalem previously noted, the polytheistic imperial religious cult, martyrdom, and the deportation of John, Revelation's author.[22] J. Nelson Kraybill developed a comprehensive analysis of the economic and commercial context of Revelation that is visible in such well-known texts as 13:16-17 and 18:11-18.[23] Leonard L. Thompson provided a comprehensive sociological analysis of the political order of Rome, which John so vehemently opposed.[24] Most recently Wes Howard-Brook and Anthony Gwyther have developed a wide-ranging description of the Roman empire and imperial ethos to which Revelation provided a multifaceted and comprehensive challenge. In line with the claim that evidence does not suggest overt persecution at the time the book was written, they depict the crisis which the author of Revelation addressed as "complacency about Rome." Their analysis of imperial politics, economics, culture, and cult then shows why Revela-

---

21. J. Nelson Kraybill, *Imperial Cult and Commerce in John's Apocalypse,* Journal for the Study of the New Testament Supplement Series, vol. 132 (Sheffield, U.K.: Sheffield Academic Press, 1996), pp. 34-38, esp. 34-35, n. 37; Wes Howard-Brook and Anthony Gwyther, *Unveiling Empire: Reading Revelation Then and Now* (Maryknoll, N.Y.: Orbis Books, 1999), pp. 117-18.

22. Collins, *Crisis and Catharsis,* pp. 85-107.

23. Kraybill, *Imperial Cult.*

24. Leonard L. Thompson, *The Book of Revelation: Apocalypse and Empire* (New York: Oxford University Press, 1990).

tion's author perceived a sense of confrontation with Rome without the presence of direct persecution.[25]

These analyses of social and economic elements complement the identification of the seals with imperial epochs. The import is to identify the Christian readers of Revelation as members of a society that followed a very different lord than did Roman society. Revelation depicts the community of God's people living in but not of the world. And this clear identity over against Roman society is true whether or not, in any given epoch, the Roman ruler creates Christian martyrs and pursues a specifically anti-Christian policy. While it is not necessary to adopt my specific suggestion for understanding the historical political connotations of the text of the seven seals, it is important to locate Revelation in the first-century world. With the first-century context in mind, it is clear that the symbolism of conflict and victory of the reign of God over the rule of Satan is a way of ascribing cosmic significance to the church's confrontation of the Roman empire in the first century. The fact that some biblical scholars may disagree on the specific first-century historical antecedents to the symbols of Revelation should not detract from my argument as a whole. It is the imagery itself and not a particular historical interpretation that presents the Christus Victor motif. Most importantly, the theological message that in the resurrection of Jesus the reign of God is victorious over evil remains true even if the sequence of evils and destruction symbolized in seals one to six is interpreted only in terms of general references to war, famine, pestilence, earthquake, and other natural disasters.

The historical framework of emperors and the construct of church confronting empire — narrative Christus Victor — suggested here for chapters 5–7 fits other parts of Revelation as well. The multiple images and scenes of the book sometimes proceed in chronological order and other times loop back and present the same sequence with other imagery, including much that is drawn from the Old Testament. It is not necessary to uncover every possible historical allusion or instance of Old Testament imagery or to solve all questions of interpretation in order to make clear that this historical approach can fit the entire book.

Revelation 12 uses a different set of images to depict the clash between the forces of God and of Satan. The birth and snatching of the male child to the throne of God are an unambiguous reference to the birth, death, and

25. Howard-Brook and Gwyther, *Unveiling Empire*, pp. 87-118, quotation p. 116.

resurrection of Jesus. The beautifully clothed woman with a crown of twelve stars represents Israel, the people of God from whom the Messiah comes. The ultimate significance of the resurrection is depicted via the classic image of Christus Victor, namely cosmic battle — the war of Michael and his angels against the dragon and his angels, the forces of God versus the forces of Satan. Conquered by the death and resurrection of Jesus and the testimony of the martyrs, who "did not cling to life even in the face of death" (Rev. 12:11), the Dragon — that is, Satan, the devil — is expelled from heaven, while the heavenly announcer proclaims victory (Rev. 12:10-11). The beautiful woman also represents God's people, the church, which is pursued by Satan, the defeated dragon.

The symbols in chapter 12 function like those in chapters 5–7 to provide a cosmic dimension to events in the historical arena. The defeated, seven-headed dragon seems a transparent reference to the Satanic nature of the Roman empire, whose eponymous city was built on seven hills, while the seven heads and ten crowns correspond to the seven crowned emperors and the total number of ten emperors and short-term claimants previously noted in the discussion of the seals. Rome and its emperors stand as the earthly representation of Satan's rule over against the church, which is the earthly manifestation of the rule of God. Chapter 12 thus constitutes another depiction of the cosmic and eschatological dimension of the historical confrontation of Jesus and the Christian church with the Roman empire.

As the struggling and numerically insignificant church contemplates the might of Rome, the temptation is to despair. However, for those who perceive the resurrection of Jesus, the reign of God has already triumphed. The victory celebrated in 12:10-12 has already happened — "*now* [emphasis mine] have come the salvation and the power and the kingdom of our God and the authority of his Messiah." Though the empire still has the potential to harm the church, that damage comes from an already defeated dragon whose power is blunted and limited. Protection appears in the wings with which the church flies into the wilderness, the finite time she spends there (three and a half years), as well as the fact that the earth swallows the river that spewed from the dragon's mouth.

In chapter 13, the dragon, the first beast from the sea who receives authority from the dragon, and the beast from the sea who "makes the earth and its inhabitants worship the first beast" (13:12) constitute an unholy trinity, which mirrors God, Jesus Christ, and the Holy Spirit. Like the seven-headed dragon that symbolized the empire, the beast that received "his throne and great authority" from the dragon also resembles the dragon, or Rome, the source of its authority. The beast has ten crowns, corresponding to the total of seven crowned emperors and three pretenders identified earlier, as well as seven heads (emperors), one of which has an apparently healed, mortal wound. This wounded head no doubt refers to Nero and the myth that after his death he would return from the underworld to wreak more destruction on the earth. The healed wound would then be a later emperor who causes damage like Nero — a Nero returned to life. This beast thus features a kind of evil resurrection to shadow the resurrection of Jesus.

These various symbolic images have real historical antecedents and represent the institutions and the sources of power and authority that are followed by those who do not acknowledge the rule of God. The first beast from the sea symbolizes earthly authority that is "not Christ," hence "anti-Christ." Whatever solution one might accept for the riddle that identifies a first-century emperor with the number 666, not being able to buy or sell without the beast's mark symbolizes allegiance to an economic system and an authority that is not built on Jesus Christ. In contrast, God's people follow the slain lamb — Christ — wherever he goes. The people of God also sport a mark, namely the name of the lamb and "his Father's name" written on their foreheads (14:1; cf. Deut. 6:8). The lamb who stands on Mount Zion (14:1), and the lamb-marked 144,000 who surround him constitute the divine counterpart to the followers of the beast — the anti-Christ — and his number-marked followers.

In Revelation 20 one encounters the renowned millennium or "thousand years" for which the "Devil and Satan" are bound. Here one sees a symbolic contrast between human and divine perspectives on earth's history. Recalling that *thousand* means primarily "a very large number," this large number of years can be compared with the 1260 days or three-and-a-half years that the woman (the church) spends in the wilderness under God's protection (12:6) or the forty-two months or three-and-a-half years that the nations will trample over the holy city and the court outside the temple (11:2, 3). Since Revelation contrasts earthly and heavenly views of events of the world, the symbolic numbers of a thousand years and three-and-a-half years represent two different views of earthly history between Jesus' resurrection and his return — one from earth's perspective and the other God's.

The binding of Satan is then not a new event, encountered only here for the first time in Revelation. Rather, it constitutes another symbolic reference to the triumph by the reign of God over the evil perpetrated by the Roman empire. The binding of Satan is thus a parallel symbol to the defeat of the dragon in 12:9-10 that resulted in a celebration of the salvation that belongs to God and the Lamb in 7:10. The supposed "millennium" of Revelation 20, which occupies only a small space in the book and appears only here in the Bible, does not refer to a specific period of history yet to be inaugurated. Rather it is a symbolic way to affirm that regardless of the apparent power of evil abroad in the world, those who live in the resurrection of Jesus know that that evil has been overcome and its power limited. When one considers the power of Satan from the perspective of the reign of God, Satan's power — "three-and-a-half years" — is indeed limited within the vast scope — a "thousand years" — of God's time.

The significance of three-and-a-half years as a symbolic reference to the limitations of evil's power appears more clearly when one notes that seven is a sacred number frequently used of things related to God. We read of seven flaming torches, which are the seven spirits of God (3:5), and the Lamb with "seven horns and seven eyes, which are the seven spirits of God sent out into all the earth" (5:6). An unholy number, half a seven, then designates the earthly time that Satan harasses the church in Revelation 12:6. When compared with God's vast time of a "thousand" years, Satan's time is short and finite, just three-and-a-half years or 1260 days.

The contrast in times — one vastly expansive, the other very limited — emphasizes the limited and defeated power of the earthly representatives of Satan when seen in light of the resurrection of Jesus. During the symbolic three-and-a-half years, Satan's power is declared limited and finite by God preparing a place in the wilderness where the woman can be nourished, by the wings of the eagle with which she can fly into the wilderness, and by the earth swallowing the river that flows from the mouth of the dragon. Since the dragon represents Rome, the "millennium" text of chapter 20 proclaims yet another version of the message from the seven seals motif in chapters 5–7 and the woman and dragon of Revelation 12. It is a message of encouragement to Christians confronting the power of the Roman empire. Revelation shows that transcendent reality differs from the perceived reality. Christians therefore need not fear the suffering and destruction meted out by Rome, the earthly manifestation of Satan.

The judgment at the great white throne in Revelation 20:11-15 has been frequently accepted as the culmination of the book. This assumption is particularly true for dispensationalism and those theologies that focus on God's punishment of sinners. However, the foregoing opens the door to a quite different culmination of the argument in Revelation.

The argument thus far has displayed several vignettes of narrative Christus Victor — confrontation between church and empire, between the earthly representatives of the reign of God and the rule of Satan. In each of these cases, however, the message is that the reign of God has *already* triumphed in the resurrection of Jesus, and that the earthly representative of the reign of God — that is, the church — should take comfort in and even celebrate that triumph. The first vignette, that of the opening of the seven seals, reached a culmination of destruction with the fall of Jerusalem to the army of Emperor Vespasian, which was then counterbalanced in Revelation 7 by the scene of two vast, celebratory throngs. The vignette of woman, dragon, and heavenly battle in chapter 12 displayed a similar message of triumph in the midst of harassment. With these images in mind, it is entirely plausible that the culmination of Revelation occurs in chapter 21, with the vision of the new heaven and new earth and a new Jerusalem.[26] Throughout the book, the resurrection of Jesus was portrayed as having overcome evil in various guises. As a culmination to the book, chapter 21 presents the restoration of all things — an ultimate overcoming of evil — and a new Jerusalem, emphasizing the restoration of what was destroyed. The victory of the reign of God over the rule of evil culminates with the vision of the new Jerusalem, which needs no temple because the presence of God in the city is "the Lord God the Almighty and the Lamb" (21:22). It is a city whose light is "the glory of God" and whose "lamp is the Lamb," in which all nations will "walk by its light," whose gates never close, and into which the people of God will bring "the glory and the honor of the nations" (21:22-27). This is truly the victory won by the slain lamb, using sizes and symbolism that place the new Jerusalem in continuity with the old, but depicted in a way that both engulfs the old and overwhelms the forces that destroyed it. Finally, the New Jerusalem already exists in part, in the testimony and "alternative praxis" of those loyal to the slain lamb. "New Jerusalem is found wherever

---

26. Thanks to John Kampen for the suggestion that the culmination of Revelation occurs in chapter 21, with the vision of the new heaven and new earth.

human community resists the ways of empire and places God at the center of its shared life."[27]

Emerging from this survey of historical antecedents for the symbols of Revelation is the picture of the church as a social structure that poses an alternative to the social structure of the Greco-Roman empire. Each of these social entities solicits ultimate loyalty. The empire confronts and challenges Christians because they profess a loyalty to something other than the empire. Christians pose a contrast to the empire precisely because they are "marked" by loyalty to the resurrected Jesus rather than by the demands of the emperor and the exigencies of the empire. The symbolism of Revelation provides a cosmic dimension for this very earthly confrontation. This confrontation visible in Revelation constitutes the historical condition that is expressed in the atonement motif called narrative Christus Victor.

In light of this chapter's initial assertion that rejection of violence belongs to the essence of Jesus' life and work, it is important specifically to see that the confrontation of church and empire depicted symbolically throughout Revelation is a nonviolent confrontation. Many interpreters have missed this point entirely. We note first of all that the victory of the reign of God over the empire that represents the forces of Satan is won by the death and resurrection of Christ. Chapter 5 has both the lion and lamb as symbols of Christ, with the lion a symbol of victory and the slain lamb a symbol of the *means* of victory, namely death and resurrection. The figure of the lion appears only here in Revelation, while the slain and resurrected lamb continues as an enduring symbol throughout the book. Clearly the slain lamb indicates a nonviolent confrontation between reign of God and reign of evil, and a nonviolent victory via death and resurrection for the reign of God.

Second, Christians contribute to the victory of the slain lamb by their testimony. "But they have conquered him by the blood of the Lamb and by the word of their testimony, for they did not cling to life even in the face of death" (Rev. 12:11). Victory through testimony is clearly a nonviolent means of victory — through death and witness.

Third, the supposed battle scenes are not really battles at all. In chapter 12, the language of battle between the forces of God and the forces of Satan

27. Howard-Brook and Gwyther, *Unveiling Empire*, pp. 184, 192-95, 230, quotation, pp. 184, 192.

is really a depiction of the cosmic significance of the resurrection of Jesus. Even more important is the nonviolent character of the supposed battle in the last segment of chapter 19. Here a rider on a white horse defeats the kings of the earth and their armies. They are "killed by the sword of the rider on the horse, the sword that came from his mouth" (19:21). It is apparent, however, that no actual battle takes place. Called "Faithful and True" (19:11) and "The Word of God" (19:13), and clothed with a robe dipped in blood *before* the supposed battle (19:13), the rider is obviously a resurrected, victorious Christ. His weapon is a sword that extends from his mouth, which makes it the word of God. Ephesians 6:17 and Hebrews 4:12 also use a two-edged sword as an image of the Word of God. In the segment of 19:11-21, the beast and the kings and their armies are defeated not by violence and military might. They are undone — defeated — by the Word of God. This passage is another symbolic representation of the victory of the reign of God over the forces of evil that has already occurred with the death and resurrection of Jesus. It is by proclamation of the Word, not by armies and military might, that God's judgment occurs.[28] The supposed battle that follows the release of Satan after the millennium constitutes a parallel image.[29]

Demonstrating that Revelation presents a multifaceted image of Christus Victor in history emphasizes that Jesus Christ is the real focus of the book. That conclusion leads directly to seeing that the Gospels present a different image of narrative Christus Victor.

---

28. On 19.11-21 see Richard B. Hays, *The Moral Vision of the New Testament: Community, Cross, New Creation: A Contemporary Introduction to New Testament Ethics* (New York: HarperCollins, 1996), p. 175; Boring, *Revelation,* pp. 195-200.

29. Consider this nonviolent victory via the Word against the dependence on violence in the common dispensational premillennial reading of Revelation. Since the dispensational scheme requires a battle of Armageddon before Satan is finally defeated, the dispensational view does not understand the resurrection of Jesus as the ultimately decisive event in Revelation as well as throughout the writings of Paul. Even more significantly, when the dispensational scheme presumes Armageddon to be an actual battle between armies using nuclear weapons, the image of God is entirely different from the God of Jesus Christ depicted in Revelation as well as in the Gospels. The God of dispensationalism is a violent and vengeful god who overcomes evil and violence with greater violence. The God of Revelation is a God who overcomes nonviolently through the Word, which is Jesus Christ.

The Gospels

A brief sketch demonstrates that the narrative of Jesus as displayed in the Gospels fits within the universal and cosmic story of the confrontation of reign of God and rule of Satan depicted in Revelation. If Revelation's imagery displays the cosmic significance of that confrontation, the Gospels portray the same confrontation from the earthbound perspective of those who walked the dusty roads of Palestine as companions of Jesus. The summary here notes representative kinds of texts, with primary use of the Gospel of Luke.

In her poetic response to the annunciation, Mary's song includes reference to acts of God in lifting up the lowly and the hungry in the face of the powerful and the rich (Luke 1:52-53). Linking those acts to the promise to Abraham (Luke 1:55) in effect extends the confrontation to the beginning of Israel's history. Luke's genealogy (3:23-38) marks the continuity of Jesus with previous acts of God in history in a different way, tracing his lineage through Joseph to Adam and to God. It follows that the victory of the reign of God that attains its decisive moment in the resurrection of Jesus is the restoration of the fallenness of humankind symbolized by the story of the Fall (Gen. 3).

The temptation narrative (Luke 4:1-13) makes visible the confrontation of reigns. There is the obvious image of Jesus eye-to-eye with Satan. But Jesus' rejection of the proffered means to power — gaining approval and authority by pandering to popular opinion (turning stones to bread), attracting attention through feats of strength and daring (throwing himself from the pinnacle of the temple), and seizing power by physical and military might (gaining the kingdoms of the world) — shows that the reign of God has an entirely different basis of allegiance, authority, and power than Satan's kingdom.

At the opening of Jesus' public ministry (Luke 4:14-30), his quotation of Isaiah 61:1-2 was not spiritualized. The good news for the poor (Luke 4:18-19) had explicitly social connotations.[30] When Jesus proclaimed that this scripture was fulfilled in their hearing (Luke 4:21), he represented and made present a movement in history, namely the reign of God, that challenges the forces which threaten and enslave, whether they are economic or political. He confronted the prevailing social order with a new reality.

---

30. John Howard Yoder, *Politics of Jesus*, pp. 29, 32.

The consequent rejection of both the message and its bearer by those who heard Jesus (Luke 4:29-30) emphasized the confrontation of the competing reigns.

Following the appearance in Nazareth, Luke noted other acts of Jesus that displayed the power of the reign of God over the physical and spiritual forces that enslave individuals, as well as over the oppressive dimensions of the natural order. These included an exorcism at Capernaum (4:31-37), the healing of Peter's mother-in-law and additional healings and exorcisms (4:38-41), the miraculous catch of fish (5:1-11), and the stilling of the storm (Luke 8). In the stories on this brief list, Luke shows that the reign of God in Jesus has power over physical and spiritual forces that enslave individuals as well as over the created, natural order. And in these acts of Jesus, the presence of salvation in the reign of God is already happening as people are freed from the forces that threaten or enslave them.[31]

Jesus' teaching and preaching announce the nearness of the reign of God and describe human relationships when governed by it (Luke 4:43; 6:17-48; 8:1; 9:11). By attributing the reign of God to the "poor," and proclaiming those who "hunger" as blessed (6:20-21), Luke's version of the beatitudes made it quite clear that the reign of God has a particular, historical dimension.[32] Those governed by God's rule love their enemies, do good to those who hate them, and do not retaliate against evil with more evil (6:27-36). The reign of God does not exist in an invisible, abstract way. Those who are subject to the rule of God will show it by the way they live. "Why do you call me 'Lord, Lord,'" asked Jesus, "and do not do what I tell you?" (6:46).

The followers of Jesus also participate in the confrontation of worldly rule by the reign of God. Jesus commissioned the twelve "to proclaim the kingdom of God and to heal," (Luke 9:2) and then seventy others. When they returned and reported with considerable jubilation what they had done (Luke 10:17), their presentation of the reign of God involved a clash of competing powers. "Lord, in your name even the demons submit to us!" And Jesus replied, "I watched Satan fall from heaven like a flash of light-

---

31. Raymund Schwager, *Jesus in the Drama of Salvation* (New York: Crossroad, 1999), pp. 31-32.

32. It is not really the case that Matthew removes the specifically social dimenions of poverty and hunger by spiritualizing them. Rather Matthew's "blessed are the poor in spirit" (5:3) asserts that the reign of God provides the perspective from which to judge attitudes and behavior.

ning." (Luke 10:17-18). According to Luke's language, in the people whom Jesus commissioned, the reign of God confronted and vanquished the reign of Satan.

The teaching and the life of Jesus show that the objectives of the reign of God are not accomplished by violence. Rejection of violence, however, ought not be interpreted as passivity. Walter Wink has demonstrated that far from counseling passivity, Jesus' statements about turning the other cheek, giving the cloak, and going the second mile (Matt. 5:39-41; Luke 6:29) actually demonstrated an assertive and confrontational nonviolence that provides an opponent with an opportunity for transformation. With suggestions such as these the oppressed person has the potential to seize the initiative, shame the offender, and strip him of the power to dehumanize.[33]

Jesus said, "But if anyone strikes you on the right cheek, turn the other also" (Matt. 5:39). The only natural way for a blow to land on the right cheek, Wink wrote, was with the back of the hand. Such a blow would be an insult or an admonishment administered by a superior to an inferior. Normally one would not strike an equal in this humiliating way, and doing so carried an exorbitant fine. Since the left hand was only used for unclean tasks in that culture, hitting the right cheek with the left fist would not occur. Hitting with a right-hand, closed fist acknowledged the one struck as an equal. Thus a supposed superior — master over slave, husband over wife, parent over a child, Roman over Jew, man over woman — would specifically not want to strike an inferior with a fist. The backhand blow to the right cheek had the specific purpose of humiliation, and a blow in retaliation would invite retribution. Thus turning the other, or left, cheek showed that the supposed inferior refused to be humiliated. And with the left cheek now bared, the striker would be left with two options — a left-handed blow or a blow with a right-handed fist. Since neither option was acceptable to the supposed superior, he has lost the power to dehumanize the other.

A court of law constitutes the setting for Jesus' injunction about giving the cloak or undergarment along with the outer coat (Matt. 5:40). The law allowed a creditor to take the coat (or outer garment) as a promise of future payment from a poor person without means to pay a debt (Exod.

33. My development of the texts on nonretaliation follows Wink, *Engaging the Powers,* pp. 176-84.

22:25-27; Deut. 24:10-13, 17). Only the poorest person would have only an article of clothing to surrender as security. Since the coat was likely the debtor's sole remaining article of clothing, the (wealthy) debt holder had to return it each evening for the owner to sleep in. Further, in that society the shame of nakedness fell more on those viewing it and those who caused it than on the naked person. Thus stripping off the undergarment in the public setting of the court along with the required outer garment would have the effect of turning the tables on the wealthy debt holder; it would put the poor person in charge of the moment while exposing the exploitative system and shaming the wealthy and powerful person who takes the last object of value from a very poor person.

Going the second mile had great power to embarrass the soldier who compelled the first mile (Matt. 4:41). Roman law allowed soldiers to command at will the forced labor of carrying burdens for one mile, but limited the service to one mile. The limitation provided some protection for the occupied people. But if one followed Jesus' words and cheerfully carried a burden beyond the required first mile, it put the soldier in the awkward position of not complying with the limit posed by his superior. As a result, the soldier could end up in the embarrassing position of begging the civilian to put down the burden lest the soldier be disciplined.

In these cases, Jesus' instructions were not commands of passive nonresistance. On the contrary. He was teaching nonviolent ways for oppressed people to take the initiative, to affirm their humanity, to expose and neutralize exploitative circumstances. "He is formulating a worldly spirituality in which the people at the bottom of society or under the thumb of imperial power learn to recover their humanity."[34] Through such means the people of God can witness to the presence of the reign of God as a contrast to the social order that does not recognize the rule of God. In practicing these means of confrontation, the followers of Jesus share in the witness of the reign of God against the rule of Satan, personified as in Revelation, by imperial Rome — a theme that I have called narrative Christus Victor.

When Jesus healed on the Sabbath, the action had a deliberately confrontational element. Before he revived the withered hand, he called the man to come and stand with him in a prominent location so that those who objected to such Sabbath activity would be certain to notice. Then

---

34. Wink, *Engaging the Powers,* p. 182.

Jesus looked "around at all of them," making eye contact and drawing their eyes to him before he told the man with the crippled arm, "Stretch out your hand" (Luke 6:6-11). Other reports of healing on the Sabbath make equally clear that these acts of Jesus were not only controversial but also intentionally confrontational (Luke 13:10-17; 14:1-6). By healing on the Sabbath, Jesus demonstrated that the regulations propagated by the religious leadership were subverting and distorting the purpose of the Sabbath under the reign of God. He confronted that rule with an act of healing that displayed the character of God's reign.

In his encounter with the Samaritan woman, Jesus confronted prevailing standards in another way (John 4:1-38). He had already violated the strict purity expectations by traveling through, rather than around, Samaria. Then he surprised the woman at the well by his willingness, as a Jew, to accept a drink from her, a Samaritan. The purity code forbade contact with a menstruating woman. Since one could never be certain that a Samaritan was not in the unclean state, the practice was to assume that she was unclean, a condition that also extended to any vessel she touched.[35] In their turn, the disciples were equally surprised that he spoke to a woman (John 4:27). In fact, in recent literature it has been pointed out frequently that Jesus' interactions with women raised their standing and broke the conventions of a patriarchal society. Walter Wink, for example, stated that "we can see that in every single encounter with women in the four Gospels, Jesus violated the mores of his time."[36] Jesus' acts of healing on the Sabbath and his encounters with women are integral dimensions of his mission to make the reign of God visible over against the rule of evil in the social order.

Jesus' answer to the disciples of John the Baptist cited a lived version of the reign of God. When John sent his disciples to ask Jesus if he was "the one who is to come," Jesus referred to recent healings, exorcisms, and restorations of sight when he said, "Go and tell John what you have seen and heard" (Luke 7:22). That episode displays how the writers of the Gospels portray the mission of Jesus in terms of a visible manifestation of the reign of God, which confronts and poses an alternative to the powers of the world.

35. C. K. (Charles Kingsley) Barrett, *The Gospel According to St. John: An Introduction with Commentary and Notes on the Greek Text* (New York: Macmillan, 1962), p. 194.
36. Wink, *Engaging the Powers,* p. 129.

On the road to Caesarea Philippi, Jesus asked the disciples about his identity, and Peter replied, "You are the Messiah, the Son of the living God" (Matt. 16:16). Affirming Peter's answer, Jesus also began to explain what it really meant — "that he must go to Jerusalem and undergo great suffering . . . and be killed, and on the third day be raised" (Matt. 17:21). As Peter's protest of that scenario showed, he was not prepared for a messiah who would suffer and die, not prepared for a rule of God that confronted evil from a position of seeming weakness. In a stern dressing down, Jesus told Peter: "Get behind me, Satan! You are a stumbling block to me; for you are setting your mind not on divine things but on human things" (Matt. 16:23). The rule of God enacted by Jesus clearly posed an alternative to normal expectations, especially when it concerned the refusal to use violence as means of struggle.

In the act of cleansing the temple, Jesus confronted the established social order with the reign of God. Jesus found the temple desecrated. The debate about the exact nature of that desecration need not concern us here. Whatever the presumed desecration, of import for current purposes is that Jesus engaged in a "cleansing" action to reclaim the temple for the rule of God (Luke 19:45-48; Matt. 21:12-13). This action, along with such acts as Sabbath-day healings and civil interaction with a Samaritan woman, witness to a reality different than the one governing the social order. It also provoked Jesus' death.

Jesus was tried and executed by crucifixion in Jerusalem. His submission to the powers of evil was consistent with the portrayal of God's rule that he proclaimed in the Sermon on the Mount, gave to Peter on the road to Caesarea Philippi, and exhibited in numerous other ways. When the armed party came to arrest Jesus in the garden, his companions asked, "Lord, should we strike with the sword?" (Luke 22:49). Peter (identified in John 18:10) did pull his sword to defend Jesus and succeeded in cutting off the ear of the slave of the high priest. Jesus pointedly said, "No more of this" (Luke 22:51) or "Put your sword back in its sheath" (John 18:11). References to legions of angels that Jesus could call but did not (Matt. 26:53), or to the need "to drink the cup that the Father has given me" (John 18:11), give Jesus' rejection of the sword an ultimate dimension in the Gospel writer's view, making it an extension of God's rule. That Jesus' mission rejects the sword also seems evident in the words with which he chides the armed contingent that arrested him. Had they understood what he was really about, he said, they would have known that weapons were certainly unnecessary ("Have you come out as against a robber, with swords and clubs to capture me?" [Matt. 26:55 par.]) and that he had been freely available in the temple on a daily basis for arrest without weapons.

The rejection of the sword appeared again during his trial, when Pilate asked Jesus if he were indeed the King of the Jews as was being said. Jesus replied that

> My kingdom is not from this world. If my kingdom were from this world, my followers would be fighting to keep me from being handed over to the Jews. But as it is, my kingdom is not from here. (John 18:36)

The comment cannot mean that the rule Jesus represented had nothing to do with life on earth, otherwise he would not have been collecting disciples and teaching them how life was lived within the reign of God. The statement means that the sword belongs to the kingdoms of the world, but is not used in the reign of God.

When Jesus told Peter to put his sword away and then faced his accusers and confronted death without violence, Jesus was living out the way that the reign of God confronts evil. The resurrection of Jesus, God's act in history to overcome the ultimate enemy — death — puts God's stamp of approval on Jesus. Resurrection is God's testimony that in Jesus, the reign of God has entered into the world. The resurrection of Jesus is an advance sample of the reign of God that will become visible in its fullness when Jesus returns. To see the life and teaching of Jesus is to see how things are under the rule of God.

From a position of apparent weakness, the reign of God as present in Jesus confronted and submitted to power. His nonviolent death was not a departure from the activist pattern of confronting the social order and making the reign of God visible. In the face of active or direct evil or violence, the refusal to respond in kind is a powerful, chosen act, not a mere passive submission. Refusing to return evil for evil unmasks the violence of the evil acts, and demonstrates that the evil which killed Jesus originated with humankind and not with God.

The outcome of Jesus' arrest and trial was that brute force killed him in what appeared to be a triumph for the powers of evil. Yet that triumph of evil was limited and momentary. As the Gospels recount the story, three days later Mary Magdalene and other women, and then the disciples found an empty tomb, which they accepted as a sign that God had raised Jesus from the dead. In the living Jesus the reign of God displayed its power over the ultimate enemy — death — and thus over the worst that evil could do, namely deny Jesus his existence. With the last enemy was overcome in the person of the living, resurrected Christ, a new era had begun in the reign of God in history. This revealing of the reign of God in the resurrection of Jesus is expressed as narrative Christus Victor.

At first glance it might seem that Jesus' words at the last supper support satisfaction atonement. He gave the cup to the disciples, saying, "For this is my blood of the new covenant, which is poured out for many for the forgiveness of sins" (Matt. 26:28). These words, however, need not be read as a statement of the compensatory death featured in satisfaction atonement; in fact, a careful reading supports the interpretation that in Jesus the reign of God confronted evil and conquered it. Since Jesus' message of the reign of God was inseparable from his person, his deeds — including his nonviolent submission to death — have theological significance. Understanding the covenant sayings at the last supper involve understanding them in light of the mission of Jesus and the nature of his proclamation of grace and judgment under the reign of God.[37]

Jesus' mission was to make present and visible the reign of God. That mission meant witnessing to and presenting God's unmerited forgiveness and the reconciliation of sinners to God. Because this forgiveness was available outside the temple practices, conflict with temple authorities was inevitable.[38] In his preaching about judgment Jesus did not teach that goodness and the justice of God were two consecutive stages, as though at a point in time the goodness and mercy of God end and then the judgment of God begins. Rather, Jesus made it clear that statements about the retribution of God were really a declaration of what those who reject the rule of God bring on themselves. Their sin turns upon them, and in effect, they judge themselves. Declarations of judgment make clear the consequences of rejecting God. But God remains a God of love and grace, whose offer of forgiveness always remains open.[39]

When Jesus took the bread and the cup and gave them to his disciples as his body and blood, he was making the disciples a gift. Since his person

---

37. My interpretation of the Lord's Supper sayings of Jesus follows Schwager, *Jesus in the Drama*, pp. 93-114.

38. Schwager, *Jesus in the Drama*, p. 105.

39. Schwager, *Jesus in the Drama*, pp. 53-58.

was identified with the reign of God, the gift of bread and wine as his body was a gift fully identified with the reign of God, and presented in a form that people can fully consume and become one with. As the disciples eat, they make the kingdom of God fully their own, and are identified with the reign of God. Jesus giving himself for them was a carrying out of his mission to present the reign of God on their behalf. In this giving of himself for the reign of God, the nonviolent confrontation of his enemies has high theological significance. It displays the love of God for enemies, a making visible of the reign of God that is even willing to suffer rejection at the hands of its enemies. Jesus died for his enemies, making visible the reign of God for them while they were yet sinners. As Raymund Schwager said,

> On the one hand, the body that was given to eat emphasizes that the offering up to a violent death was far more than a noble ethical example. The fate of the kingdom of God was at stake. On the other hand, the body which was given up to death makes clear that the gift of God's kingdom in the situation of rejection was only possible thanks to a love of one's enemies which answered the violent rejection with a still greater offering up. Neither of the two forms of offering is meaningful without the other, and yet both together bring to expression how Jesus understood his decision as a death for many.

In carrying out his mission, Jesus was ready to die and he was willing to die. It was not a death, however, that was required as compensatory retribution for the sins of his enemies and his friends. It was a death that resulted from fulfillment of his mission about the reign of God.

All manner of people played roles in the rejection of the reign of God and in the killing of Jesus. Describing these roles does not dispute who had final authority with regard to the historical event. The established authority — imperial Rome — crucified him and bears ultimate responsibility for his death.[40] Evidence suggests that local religious authorities cooperated to some extent in order to deal with what they saw as a troublemaker in their midst. The rabble acquiesced in the death sentence. There were the disciples

---

40. Paul Winter, *On the Trial of Jesus,* 2nd ed., rev. and ed. T. A. Burkill and Geza Vermes (New York: Walter de Gruyter, 1974); Martin Hengel, *Crucifixion: In the Ancient World and the Folly of the Message of the Cross* (Philadelphia: Fortress, 1977); Ellis Rivkin, *What Crucified Jesus? Messianism, Pharisaism, and the Development of Christianity,* with a foreword by Eugene J. Fisher (New York: UAHC Press, 1997).

— Judas who betrayed him, those who could not remain awake to watch with Jesus in the garden, and then Peter who denied knowing him. These all played roles in the death of Jesus. All were in the power of the forces of evil and acted without knowing the role they played in rejecting the reign of God. Jesus died for them — as the manifestation of the reign of God offered to sinful humankind, while the nonviolent response to death expressed his Father's great love for sinful humankind, a love great enough to give up the Son in order to make the gift of the rule of God visible.

This story of Jesus became the orienting account for those who accepted Jesus as Messiah. In the weeks after Jesus was no longer bodily present, when the apostles and followers of Jesus were asked in whose name or in whose authority they acted, they told this story (Acts 2:14-39; 3:13-26; 4:10-12; 5:30-32; 10:36-43; 13:17-41). The last section of the story featured an invitation to the hearers themselves to join and find salvation in the story, and to participate in the life of the people of God (Acts 2:40-42; 4:12; 10:47-48; 13:43). Those who responded to and accepted the living Jesus shared in the victory and become part of the witness to the reign of God.

This survey of texts illustrates how the Gospel writers portray the mission of Jesus in terms of a visible manifestation of the reign of God, which confronts and poses an alternative to the powers of the world. This description of the teaching and life of Jesus from an earthly perspective puts the narrative within the framework of Christus Victor. Assuming that Jesus is of God and that the person of Jesus embodies the reign of God, this narrative pictures the reign of God in a confrontation or struggle with the reign of evil (Satan). In many ways the teaching and acts of Jesus pose the reign of God in conflict with the powers that oppose it. When Jesus was executed, the powers of evil enjoyed a momentary triumph — Jesus' very existence is removed. However, God raised Jesus from death, thereby revealing the reign of God as the ultimate power in the cosmos. This is an earth-centered version of the story that Revelation tells from a cosmic perspective — two complementary and overlapping expressions of narrative Christus Victor.

Is this narrative an atonement narrative? The answer is "no," if for atonement narrative one means a story that pictures Jesus' death as a divinely arranged plan to provide a payment to satisfy the offended honor of God or a requirement of divine law, or that understands Jesus as the substitute bearer of punishment that sinful human kind deserves. Narrative Christus Victor is not an atonement narrative if one requires a change in the relationship between God and sinful humankind based on the assumption of retributive justice that making right or restoring justice happens when evil deeds are balanced by punishment.

But the answer is "yes," if one envisions a reconciliation of sinful humankind to God on the basis of the life, death, and resurrection of Jesus. In discussions of dogma, the classic questions of atonement concern the nature of sin and how Jesus' death saves humankind from that sin. Narrative Christus Victor accounts for these questions. It portrays sin as bondage to the forces of evil, whose earthly representatives include the structures of imperial Rome, which had ultimate authority for Jesus' death; the structures of holiness code, to which Jesus posed reforming alternatives; and the mob and the disciples in their several roles. All participants in society down to and including ourselves, by virtue of what human society is, participate in and are in bondage to — are shaped by — the powers represented by these earthly structures. Salvation is to begin to be free from those evil forces, and to be transformed by the reign of God and to take on a life shaped — marked — by the story of Jesus, whose mission was to make visible the reign of God in our history.

In carrying out that mission, Jesus was killed by the earthly structures in bondage to the power of evil. His death was not a payment owed to God's honor, nor was it divine punishment that he suffered as a substitute for sinners. Jesus' death was the rejection of the rule of God by forces opposed to that rule. In fact, this review of Jesus' life as narrative Christus Victor exposes how incongruous it is to interpret this story as one whose ultimate purpose was to arrange a death in order to satisfy divine justice. Far from being an event organized for a divine requirement, his death reveals the nature of the forces of evil that opposed the rule of God. It poses a contrast between the attempt to coerce by violence under the rule of evil and the nonviolence of the rule of God as revealed and made visible by the life, death, and resurrection of Jesus.

When evil did its worst, namely denying Jesus his existence by killing him, God's resurrection of Jesus displayed the ability of the reign of God to triumph over death, the last enemy. The power of the reign of God over the forces of evil is made manifest in the resurrection of Jesus.

Those who believe in the resurrection perceive the true nature of power in the universe. Resurrection means that appearances can be deceiving. Regardless of what appears to be the case from an earth-limited or earth-bound perspective, such as the seeming crescendo of evil that builds through seals one to six of Revelation 6, resurrection demonstrates the power of God's rule over all evil.

The resurrection as the victory of the reign of God over the forces of evil constitutes an invitation to salvation, an invitation to submit to the rule of God. It is an invitation to enter a new life, a life transformed by the rule of God and no longer in bondage to the powers of evil that killed Jesus. For those who perceive the resurrection, the only option that makes sense is to submit to the reign of God. Christians, Christ-identified people, participate in the victory of the resurrection and demonstrate their freedom from bondage to the powers by living under the rule of God rather than continuing to live in the power of the evil that killed Jesus. Salvation is present when allegiances change and new life is lived "in Christ" under the rule of God.

Although perception of the resurrection in narrative Christus Victor has an impact on sinners, calling them to escape from bondage to the powers of Satan and to submit to the rule of God, narrative Christus Victor is no mere refurbishing of moral influence atonement. The resurrection reveals the true balance of power in the universe whether sinners perceive it or not. Sinners can ignore the resurrection and continue in opposition to the reign of God, but the reign of God is still victorious. It is this revelation of the true balance of power, whether or not acknowledged by sinful humankind, that distinguishes narrative Christus Victor from moral influence theory. This latter atonement motif lacks resurrection as an integral characteristic and features no change in the order of things until individual sinners perceive the loving death and respond positively to God. Further, in moral influence theory, the death of Jesus must be an act of God to show love to sinful humankind. In narrative Christus Victor, the death of Jesus is anything but a loving act of God; it is the product of the forces of evil that oppose the reign of God. While God loved sinful humankind enough to send Jesus to witness to the rule of God, Jesus' death is not a loving act of God, but the ultimate statement that distinguishes the rule of God from the reign of evil.

Narrative Christus Victor is indeed atonement if one means a story in which the death and resurrection of Jesus definitively reveal the basis of power in the universe, so that the invitation from God to participate in God's rule — to accept Jesus as God's anointed one — overcomes the forces of sin and reconciles sinners to God. Through identification with Jesus, sinful humankind shares in Jesus' death and in his resurrection. To identify with Jesus is to have life in the reign of God. As Gustaf Aulén wrote about the classic view, "this salvation is . . . an atonement in the full sense of the word, for it is a work wherein God reconciles the world to Himself, and is at the same time reconciled. . . . The victory over the hostile powers brings to pass a new relation, a relation of reconciliation, between God and the world."[41]

René Girard

While this interpretation of the story of Jesus — narrative Christus Victor — has been developed independent of René Girard, it is compatible with much of his theory about mimetic violence and its implications for understanding the death of Jesus and the development of atonement theology.

Human beings develop by imitating each other, and in that imitation they end up as rivals who desire the same things. Girard calls this imitative desire *mimesis*, a term that enables him to include the element of rivalry in the imitation.[42] If unchecked, this mimetic rivalry inevitably results in violence, the murder of one of the antagonists.

In Girard's hypothesis, human civilization developed from efforts to control mimetic violence.[43] At the beginning of human civilization, unchecked mimesis produced chaos, which Girard describes as the violence of all against all. At some point this violence became focused on a single individual, marked by a distinguishing weakness or characteristic. The chaos of all against all could be transformed into peace and order, it was learned, when all antagonists come to focus on a single individual as the cause of all the violence. When this individual, on whom was loaded all the blame for the chaos, was removed — murdered — peace and order reigned where previously there was chaos. This first murder then became the foundation of that human society. Culture and religion are the result of subsequent efforts to limit violence and maintain the order in the society created out of the founding murder.

41. Aulén, *Christus Victor: A Historical Study of the Three Main Types of the Idea of Atonement*, pp. 4-5.

42. René Girard, *Things Hidden Since the Foundation of the World*, trans. Stephen Bann and Michael Metter (Stanford, Calif.: Stanford University Press, 1987), p. 18.

43. This summary of Girard's thesis on violence and the origin of human culture and religion is based primarily on Girard, *Things Hidden*, pp. 3-47, and the essays in Parts I, II, and III of René Girard, *The Girard Reader*, ed. James G. Williams (New York: Crossroad, 1996).

The endeavor to limit violence and maintain peace rests on three pillars. One is prohibitions — of all actions and situations that contribute to mimetic violence. Rituals constitute the second pillar. These rituals — games, dramas, animal sacrifices — provide approved outlets for expression of mimetic rivalry within a culture, and thus limit the actual violence perpetrated. While prohibition and ritual appear as opposites — prohibiting versus acting out — their function is the same. They both limit mimetic violence and contribute to the maintenance of order. But eventually a mimetic crisis develops, when prohibitions and rituals can no longer control rivalry and maintain order. At this point, the third pillar of culture and religion comes into play, the killing of a scapegoat. As problems mount, a search begins for an individual (or a group) to blame for the problem. The chosen victim must be marginal to the society as a whole, and lack the ability to retaliate or seek revenge. On this scapegoat is then fixed the blame for the crisis. Because it is really believed that the scapegoat has caused the crisis, violence ceases for a time following the removal — the murder — of the scapegoat, and it seems that violence brings peace. To maintain order, the community formed on the basis of murdering the scapegoat continues to reenact that formative event through sacred rituals and by the substitution of "new victims for the original victim, in order to assure the maintenance of that miraculous peace."[44]

According to Girard's research, this story of the scapegoat is virtually a universal story of originary violence, found in numerous cultures and societies. The founding events of societies — the murders on which they are founded — are portrayed in myths, which contain enough historical data to locate the origins in history. At the same time, the function of the myth is to disguise the founding murder so that it does not appear as murder. The story of origins is always told from the perspective of the majority, ruling order, which enables the majority to hide the innocence of the scapegoat victim and to affix blame to it for society's problems. Removing the scapegoat then takes on the appearance of a necessary and noble deed that is done in order to preserve the society. Killing the scapegoat becomes not an act of murder but an act of salvation. Life appears to come from death. Exposing the innocence of the victim would reveal the deed as murder, and thus undercut its efficacy as a saving event. Thus the function of ritual and of religion is to limit the violence to a single victim or single group of

44. Girard, *Things Hidden*, p. 103.

victims, while simultaneously disguising the fact that it is a ritual murder and providing transcendent validation of the process. The basis of the success of scapegoat violence is its disguise. But under this veil of secrecy there continues a never-ending cycle of violence begetting more violence.

Girard's theory about the role of violence in the foundation of human culture and religion has implications for reading the Bible, both the Old Testament and the story of Jesus.[45] Beginning with the story of Cain and his founding of a city, the accounts in the early chapters of Genesis reflect the development of culture and religion on the basis of a founding murder. But the uniqueness of the Bible's stories, according to Girard, is that they consistently tell the story from the standpoint of the innocent victim, whether Abel or Joseph or the Hebrew slaves in Egypt. By focusing on the innocence of the victim, the Bible exposes the sacred justification of violence against the victim, and thus undermines the power of the scapegoat mechanism. Through the Old Testament toward the New, there is increasing awareness of the function of the scapegoat ritual, and an increasing awareness that Yahweh, the God of Israel, rejects violence.

The final revelation of human violence and of the nonviolence of Yahweh and the reign of God occurs with the crucifixion of Jesus. As the representative of the reign of God, Jesus is absolutely committed to nonviolence. As the innocent victim, he exposes the violence of those who oppose the reign of God. His death unmasks the powers of evil, and renders empty their claim that peace and order are founded on violence.

Girard finds no evidence for a sacrificial interpretation of the crucifixion of Jesus in the Gospels. "There is nothing in the Gospels to suggest that the death of Jesus is a sacrifice, whatever definition (expiation, substitution, etc.) we may give that sacrifice."[46] Interpreting Jesus' death in that way, Girard argues, is the continuation of a Christian religion in the tradition of scapegoat violence. Rather than continuing it, Jesus' death unmasks and thus ends religion based on sacrifice or retributive violence.

Narrative Christus Victor finds a great deal of support in Girard's theory of the origin of violence and human culture and in his reading of the narrative of Jesus in the Gospels. Of particular importance for my argument is his insistence on the nonviolence of Jesus and the nonviolent char-

45. For Girard's application of his theory to the Bible, see Book II of Girard, *Things Hidden* and the essays in Part V of Girard, *Girard Reader.*
46. Girard, *Things Hidden,* p. 180.

acter of God and the reign of God, and his consequent argument that the crucifixion of Jesus cannot be interpreted as a divinely sanctioned or divinely willed sacrifice. It is very important to underscore that violence originates with humans and not with God.

Narrative Christus Victor has a more broadly based understanding of the life and teaching of Jesus than does Girard's view. Narrative Christus Victor has more focus on the entire scope of Jesus' mission to make the reign of God visible, which obviously includes the rejection of violence but is not limited to it. The Jesus of narrative Christus Victor is thus more activist than Girard's Jesus, whose death unmasks the violence of the scapegoat mechanism. One specific place to see this difference is in interpretations of Jesus' sayings about turning the other cheek and surrendering the cloak along with the coat (Matthew 5:38-40). Girard interprets these as complete renunciation of retaliation, "ridding men of violence."[47] While I agree that these sayings are a renunciation of violence, narrative Christus Victor follows Walter Wink in also understanding them as posing activist ways to turn the situation against the aggressor.

Paul

Given the presence of the image of narrative Christus Victor at each end of the New Testament, it ought not surprise that this motif fits with the New Testament's most important theologian. It is frequently assumed that the apostle Paul's language about cross, sacrifice, and fulfillment of the law are the foundation of satisfaction atonement. Work by J. Christiaan Beker and Raymund Schwager renders that assumption incorrect.

Pauline scholar J. Christiaan Beker has demonstrated that the Apostle Paul's "thought is anchored in the apocalyptic world view and that the resurrection of Christ can only be understood in that setting."[48] This apocalyptic orientation is the context in which to understand Paul's thought on

---

47. Girard, *Things Hidden*, p. 197.

48. This sketch follows ch. 8, "Paul's Apocalyptic Theology: Apocalyptic and the Resurrection of Christ," in J. Christiaan Beker, *Paul the Apostle: The Triumph of God in Life and Thought* (Philadelphia: Fortress, 1980), pp. 135-81, quotation p. 135. See also J. Christiaan Beker, *Paul's Apocalyptic Gospel: The Coming Triumph of God* (Philadelphia: Fortress, 1982); Nancy J. Duff, *Humanization and the Politics of God: The Koinonia Ethics of Paul Lehmann* (Grand Rapids: Eerdmans, 1992), pp. 117-52.

the death and resurrection of Jesus and thus the compatibility of narrative Christus Victor with Paul.

Paul understood himself "to be the eschatological apostle who spans the times between the resurrection of Christ and the final resurrection of the dead."[49] For Paul hope is not just faith in God or in the possibility of an open future. Paul's hope has an apocalyptic specificity, namely the resurrection of Christ, which is both victory over evil and death in the old order and also the beginning of the transformation of fallen creation in the new order.[50] Jesus' resurrection did not simply mark the end of history. It is rather that the end (or goal) of history, namely the reign of God, is breaking into the present and beginning the process of transforming all of creation. The resurrection of Jesus cannot be merely an "intrapsychic" event; rather "it appeals to the Christian's solidarity with the stuff of creation that God has destined for 'resurrection' glory."[51]

Paul's resurrection language cannot work when it is separated from this temporal and cosmological framework.[52] Isolating or separating the resurrection of Jesus from the apocalyptic context results in various kinds of individualism or spiritualization. Beker notes, for example, "a Gnostic savior [who] leaves the scene of corrupted matter by shedding his body on the cross and by ascending to his proper heavenly abode, where Spirit conjoins Spirit,"[53] or identifying resurrection with the immortality of the individual soul after death. Such moves may result in the collapse of apocalypticism into Christology or anthropology.[54] Against these perceptions, Paul poses the "exaltation of the crucified Christ, . . . a proleptic event that foreshadows the apocalyptic general resurrection of the dead and thus the transformation of our created world and the gift of new corporeal life to dead bodies."[55] Beker shows that Paul's ecclesiology also reflects the apocalyptic. "Paul's church is not an aggregate of justified sinners or a sacramental institute or a means for private self-sanctification but the avant garde of the new creation in a hostile world, creating beachheads in this world of God's dawning new world and yearning for the day

49. Beker, *Paul the Apostle*, p. 145.
50. Beker, *Paul the Apostle*, p. 149.
51. Beker, *Paul the Apostle*, p. 149.
52. Beker, *Paul the Apostle*, p. 153.
53. Beker, *Paul the Apostle*, p. 153.
54. Beker, *Paul the Apostle*, p. 154.
55. Beker, *Paul the Apostle*, p. 153.

of God's visible lordship over his creation, the general resurrection of the dead."[56]

For most of church history, Beker said, there has been a tendency to separate resurrection from its apocalyptic environment and to resolve the tension between the yet-not-yet character of the resurrection in one of two ways — either by postponing the culmination or by collapsing the culmination into the present. The climax of this movement was in the Nicene and Chalcedonian struggles, when, via logos doctrine, the interest shifted from the resurrection status and imminent return of the Son of God at the right hand of God to incarnation and the relationship between Father and Son in preexistence.[57]

Paul lived with the tension of yet-not yet — he established churches with a long-term missionary strategy while living in expectation of an immediate or very near Parousia. Paul "persists in imminent expectation, notwithstanding his awareness of the delay of the Parousia."[58] Paul could maintain the tension because he understood that the issue was "primarily not one of chronological reckoning but one of theological necessity."[59] Chronology is important to show both the difference between Jesus' resurrection and the Parousia as well as the theological link between them. But because it was a theological necessity, and was not posited on specific chronological understanding, Paul could maintain the tension of yet-not-yet. Because it was a theological necessary, he did not speculate on dates and was not discouraged by the apparent delay of Parousia (1 Thess. 5:1-2).[60]

The apocalyptic orientation of Paul is the framework within which to read and interpret what he says about the cross, death, and resurrection of Christ.[61] While Paul used language and images of sacrifice, he reinterpreted such language radically. Beker's analysis shows that Paul's reinterpretations of this sacrificial language brings him into line with the image that this book calls narrative Christus Victor rather than with Anselm as has been frequently assumed.

Paul shared with all Christians an apocalyptic interpretation of the

56. Beker, *Paul the Apostle*, p. 155.
57. Beker, *Paul the Apostle*, p. 158.
58. Beker, *Paul the Apostle*, p. 178.
59. Beker, *Paul the Apostle*, p. 178.
60. Beker, *Paul the Apostle*, p. 178.
61. The following discussion of Paul's understanding of the cross and the death and resurrection of Christ follows the outline of Beker, *Paul the Apostle*, ch. 9.

resurrection, namely the belief that "the Christ-event had inaugurated the messianic age and the kingdom of God."[62] However, these Christians drew different conclusions than Paul from the Christ-event. Paul reinterpreted the sacrifice of Christ as an apocalyptic event.

For Paul, the death of Christ meant the end of the law. The law called anyone cursed who was hanged on a tree (Gal. 3:13). Paul established an either-or relationship between the law and Jesus. Since Paul understood the law and a crucified messiah to be mutually exclusive, accepting Jesus as Messiah meant the end of the law (Rom. 10:4). "The death of Christ signifies the great reversal, because the judgment of the Torah on Christ becomes instead the judgment of God in Christ on the Torah."[63]

Paul did not simply reject the law or declare it previously invalid. Rather, the law was not just ended; it was fulfilled. Paul accepted the confession of the Antioch church that Christ died a sacrificial death for the forgiveness of sins condemned by the law (Acts 13:38, 39), a death that was "for us" or "on our behalf" or "for our sins" (Gal. 3:13; 1 Cor. 15:3). However, Paul radicalized this confession, so it did not simply mean forgiveness under the law. The new eschatological life — the inauguration of a new age — which follows the resurrection of Jesus means the termination of the law and the end of the previous age. "Christ's death is a sacrificial death that acknowledges our just condemnation by the law, and yet the dominion of the law ceases with the sacrifice of Christ."[64] The death of Christ both confirmed the law's verdict (Rom. 8:4) and abolished it (Rom. 3:21).[65] Since the law has come to an end, the resurrection of Jesus inaugurated a new age. When Paul envisions the ending of one age and the beginning of a new, the apocalyptic orientation of his thought is clear. Beker concludes, "Paul's interpretation of the death of Christ is remarkably apocalyptic."[66]

Because the death of Christ marks the defeat of the powers of evil, it is "not merely a moral act but an apocalyptic event."[67] These powers, aligned in what Beker called a "field," are the inseparable and interrelated alliance of "death, sin, the law, and the flesh," which are "under the sovereign rule

---

62. Beker, *Paul the Apostle*, p. 184.
63. Beker, *Paul the Apostle*, pp. 183-86, quotation p. 186.
64. Beker, *Paul the Apostle*, p. 187.
65. Beker, *Paul the Apostle*, p. 186.
66. Beker, *Paul the Apostle*, p. 189.
67. Beker, *Paul the Apostle*, p. 189.

of death."[68] These powers determine the human situation within the created order. Since the law is one of these powers, it is abolished by the death of Christ. With the death of Christ, the rebellion by the powers that rule this age (that is, death, sin, the law, and the flesh) has reached its zenith. But even more than negating the powers, the death of Jesus judges the powers, a judgment that "will be confirmed in the last judgment."[69] "Paul reinterprets the traditional Christian concept of the righteousness of God as covenant renewal, of Christ as expiation or as the Paschal Lamb (Rom. 3:24-26; 1 Cor. 5:7), of the sacrificial blood of Christ (Rom. 3:24-25; 5:9), in terms of his understanding of the death of Christ as the judgment of the powers of this age."[70] For Paul, "the inauguration of new age with the resurrection is contingent on the radical end of the old age in the cross."[71] It is this apocalyptic dimension of the death of Christ that distinguishes Paul from the Antiochenes' understanding of the future resurrection of the dead and that is the distinctive element in Paul's reinterpretation of Jewish thought.[72]

Beker points out that in Paul's apocalyptic orientation, the death of Christ changed both the condition for life after death and the particularist view of Jewish apocalyptic. In Jewish apocalyptic thought, resurrection was a reward for faithfulness and obedience. While Paul has something of this element, Beker explains, it "dwindles before the knowledge that only the death and resurrection of Christ saves both Jews and Gentiles from the death sentence of the wrath and judgment of God (Rom. 1:16–3:20)."[73] While the death of Christ judged humankind, the resurrection signifies the grace of a new life for all.[74]

Beker further emphasizes the inseparable connection in Paul between the death and resurrection of Christ so that the death of Christ is drawn into the "apocalyptic-cosmic event that inaugurates the cosmic triumph of God."[75] It is the inseparable connection of these two distinct, historical

68. Beker, *Paul the Apostle*, p. 189.
69. Beker, *Paul the Apostle*, p. 190.
70. Beker, *Paul the Apostle*, p. 191.
71. Beker, *Paul the Apostle*, p. 191.
72. Beker, *Paul the Apostle*, p. 191.
73. Beker, *Paul the Apostle*, p. 193.
74. Beker, *Paul the Apostle*, p. 193.
75. Beker, *Paul the Apostle*, p. 189.

events that gives the death of Christ its eschatological significance and prevents it from being an individual theology of the cross.

Beker points out that death and resurrection are first of all consecutive events for Paul. "After the judgment of death comes the glory of the resurrection and new life."[76] While the cross accentuates the judgment of the old age, it is resurrection that announces the coming of the new age. The language of sacrifice and atonement can express judgment and forgiveness, but is "incapable of stating the new ontological state of life that succeeds the judgment of God in the death of Christ. Forgiveness means acquittal of punishment but not the destruction of the power of sin or the 'new creation' of the Christian's participation in the resurrection mode of life."[77] Resurrection constitutes the basis of the new creation, transformed life lived under the power of the reign of God.

Stated succinctly, Beker's depiction of the apocalyptic orientation of Paul's thought lines Paul up with narrative Christus Victor as seen in Revelation and the Gospels and renders Paul incompatible with satisfaction atonement. Anselm's satisfaction atonement has no necessary role for resurrection. In satisfaction atonement, the focus is on the penalty-paying death, and resurrection occurs at an entirely different place in the theological outline. In contrast, resurrection is the foundation of Paul's thought and is what gives Paul's thought the apocalyptic orientation described by Beker. Furthermore, resurrection is what gives narrative Christus Victor the apocalyptic orientation commensurate with what Beker says about Paul. It seems straightforward that since satisfaction atonement lacks a role for resurrection in salvation, it is not apocalyptic in orientation, and therefore is incompatible with Paul. Narrative Christus Victor has an apocalyptic orientation and can be shown to fit with Paul's thought. Finally, it is the apocalyptic orientation of narrative Christus Victor, with the proleptic presence of the reign of God (or the future reign of God breaking into the present) that makes narrative Christus Victor the motif that supports confrontation of the status quo by the church as representative of the reign of God. Here is the basis of the Christian's commitment to life in Christ and to continue Jesus' mission to witness to the presence of the reign of God in history. In contrast, lacking a proleptic presence of the reign of God via resurrection, satisfaction atonement features an image of

76. Beker, *Paul the Apostle,* p. 197.
77. Beker, *Paul the Apostle,* p. 197.

salvation outside history, which means that it lacks any impulse of confrontation with and witness to the social order, which orients it toward accommodation and support of the status quo.

Raymund Schwager's analysis of Paul, which is heavily influenced by René Girard, complements Beker's depiction of the apocalyptic orientation of Paul's thought.[78] After showing that Jesus' mission concerned the reign of God, Schwager dealt with certain formulations from Paul that some interpreters claim for an entirely different understanding of Jesus' mission and his death. One such text is Romans 8:3, according to which God, "sending his own Son in the likeness of sinful flesh, and to deal with sin, condemned sin in the flesh." Here, Schwager writes, "Paul describes Christ's death for sinners (atonement) as a condemnation of sin." Another important text is 2 Corinthians 5:21: "For our sake he [God] made him to be sin who knew no sin, so that in him we might become the righteousness of God." Similar to it is Galatians 3:13: "Christ redeemed us from the curse of the law by becoming a curse for us — for it is written, 'Cursed is everyone who hangs on a tree.'" Schwager notes that Martin Luther and Karl Barth, among others, understand these texts as a theology of the cross in which Jesus underwent punishment due sinful humanity, as though Jesus' death "is a judgment . . . attributed to the heavenly Father [as] a direct act of condemnation of his Son."[79] William Placher, whose view is analyzed in Chapter 7, cites 2 Corinthians 5:21 as proof par excellence of Paul's orientation toward satisfaction atonement, even if Christ's taking the place of sinners needs to be reinterpreted in light of recent feminist and womanist challenges.[80] The idea that the heavenly Father acted to punish or condemn the Son in place of punishing sinful humans, of course, fits satisfaction atonement but does not match the understanding portrayed above for the Gospels and Revelation as expressed in narrative Christus Victor.

How one understands the judgment of the cross in such texts, Schwager notes, depends on our understanding of who acts in obedience to God's will, and specifically "whether one should understand the opponents of Jesus as directly the agents of divine will."[81] In Jesus' mission on behalf of the reign of

78. This summary of Schwager's discussion of Paul follows Schwager, *Jesus in the Drama*, pp. 160-69.

79. Schwager, *Jesus in the Drama*, p. 162.

80. William C. Placher, "Christ Takes Our Place: Rethinking Atonement," *Interpretation* 53, no. 1 (January 1999): 5-20.

81. Schwager, *Jesus in the Drama*, p. 163.

God, his "human will cooperated in such a way that, in obedience, he completely followed the divine will which sent him." But, Schwager points out, if Jesus was made sin and was being condemned or punished by the Father, as is the case with the punishment (compensatory violence) of satisfaction atonement, then those who killed Jesus must also have been acting in accord with the divine will and acting in a sense as agents of God. In this case, Jesus ceased being the revealer of God, and his opponents were entrusted with the divine mission of killing him as punishment on humankind, which stands in direct contradiction to the claim that in his mission Jesus' human will cooperated in complete obedience with the divine will that sent him. Some might then make the possible argument that both Jesus and the opponents of Jesus reveal something of the will of God. That argument, however, would pit "the message and surrender of Jesus (nonviolence, love of enemies, holding back from finally judging anyone) and the actions of his enemies . . . in contradictory opposition" that extends into the idea of God. Thus Schwager concludes, "If the New Testament conviction of God's revelation is not to be destroyed, the action of God in Jesus must be clearly separated from possible 'divine' actions by his opponents."[82] Stated in different terminology, Schwager clearly wants to avoid an interpretation of a text such as 2 Corinthians 5:21 that would make God the divine agent behind the death of Jesus.

The idea that the action of God in Jesus must be separated from any possible expression of divine will in the actions of Jesus' opponents sheds a different light on the statements that God "condemned sin in the flesh" (Rom. 8:3), that Christ became a curse for us (Gal. 3:13), or that God made Christ to be sin (2 Cor. 5:21). Schwager first notes in the Old Testament that "although God brings everything about, people resist him and act against his will. But the faith of Israel never made God responsible for sin (as an act of God against God), but always only people."[83] When Paul then says three times in Romans 1:24-28 that God "delivered" them to punishment, it is not delivery to an "external authority." Rather the anger of God is a declaration that God has handed "people over to the dynamic and inner logic of those passions and of that depraved thinking which they themselves have awakened by their turning away from God." The result is that "they punish themselves (mutually)."[84] That God "condemned sin in the flesh" is then a

82. Schwager, *Jesus in the Drama*, p. 163.
83. Schwager, *Jesus in the Drama*, p. 164.
84. Schwager, *Jesus in the Drama*, p. 165.

statement of the "active and boundless force which holds people imprisoned in its own dynamic and ruins their life." And God made Jesus to become sin (2 Cor. 5:21) is a statement that "God was not the direct actor, but he sent his Son into the world ruled by sin, and thus, through the excess of sin making use of the law, he became sin and a curse."

When Paul says that Jesus became a curse for us (Gal. 3:13), that is a testament to the power of sin to corrupt the law whose intent was to save. If it was not the law, "which in itself is good" that made Jesus a curse, but rather the action of sin in corrupting the law, then quite clearly it cannot be God who makes Jesus a curse. Rather, "within the Pauline world of ideas, the utterance of Galatians 3:13 can only mean that Christ became a curse through the power of sin, which made use of the law." And then Schwager says about 2 Corinthians 5:21: "God was not the direct actor, but he sent his Son into the world ruled by sin, and thus, through the excess of sin making use of the law, he became sin and a curse."[85] The immediate actors in this curse and condemnation of Jesus must have been those proponents of the law, and Paul's "brothers in faith" who had condemned Jesus, particularly since Paul himself had persecuted Jesus' disciples, doing evil "in his zeal for the good law."[86] Concerning 2 Corinthians 5.21, Schwager concludes:

> The power of sin is so cunning that it can get completely within its grasp the good and holy law and can so distort it that it works against God and his envoy. If Jesus in the name of the divine law was condemned as a 'blasphemer' and thus was made into a curse, even into Satan (John 10:33; 19:7), it was consequently not God, the originator of the law, who cursed his Son. The power of evil rather turned back the command which came from God against the Son. Working from this insight, we are finally led to the interpretation of 2 Corinthians 5:21, that God did not himself destroy Christ in judgment. Certainly, he sent him into the world of sin, but entirely with the aim of saving humankind. However, the power of sin was so great that it was able by means of its own mechanism and dynamic to draw him into its world and thus to make him into sin.[87]

---

85. Schwager, *Jesus in the Drama*, p. 167.
86. Schwager, *Jesus in the Drama*, p. 168.
87. Schwager, *Jesus in the Drama*, p. 168.

This material from J. Christiaan Beker and Raymund Schwager demonstrates that the narrative of Jesus depicted in the Gospels and the theology of Paul are clearly in agreement. Each envisions that Jesus' mission was to save by making present the reign of God. It was not God who organized the death of Jesus but rather "human beings (the Jews and gentiles, Judas, Peter, and the other disciples)." These "acted in a strange blindness, so that in the end they did not know what they were doing (Luke 23:24)."[88] And for present purposes, it is clear that texts such as 2 Corinthians 5.21 do not constitute incontrovertible proof of satisfaction atonement. Like Beker, who understood Paul's comments about the cross in an apocalyptic context, Schwager also understands that Paul sees the death of Jesus, not in terms of compensatory violence (restore justice by punishing a Jesus made sin in place of punishing sinful humankind), but as the confrontation between the reign of God and evil powers. Resurrection then becomes the victory of the reign of God over the power of sin.[89]

Old Testament Sacrifices

The sacrificial system of ancient Israel is another biblical motif frequently assumed to supply the model for satisfaction atonement. It appears, however, that the correlation is more linguistic than substantial.

The first eight chapters of Leviticus outline procedures for a number of ritual sacrifices — burnt offerings, offerings of well-being, cereal offerings, sin offerings, guilt offerings. These ritual sacrifices are performed in times of celebration and thanksgiving (as the peace offering, Lev. 7:12, 15) and in times of unwitting sin, both when restitution is impossible and when restoration cannot be made (as in sin and guilt offerings, Lev. 4–6:7). In these varying circumstances, the ritual sacrifice is virtually the same. The worshiper — the individual making the sacrifice — brings a perfect and healthy animal to the priest from the herd or flock. Often it is a male, but on occasion can also be female. Depending on the circumstances of the worshiper, it can be a bull, goat, sheep, turtledoves or pigeons. Apparently

---

88. Schwager, *Jesus in the Drama*, p. 169.

89. Timothy Gorringe also shows that Paul's writings do not need to be read in terms of retribution and satisfaction atonement, but without developing the eschatological dimensions of Paul described by Beker and Schwager. See *God's Just Vengeance*, pp. 71-77.

for those with the fewest resources, the offering can be grain. The worshiper places his or her hands on the head of the animal. It is then killed by the priest, who scatters the animal's blood on and around the altar. Portions of the animal are then burned on the altar, with the smoke and odor rising from the fire, going "up" where God is. For the cereal offering, oil and frankincense are poured on the flour and it is burned, "a pleasing order to the Lord." These sacrifices make "atonement" for the worshiper (Lev. 1:4; 4:20, 26, 31, 35; 5:6, 10, 13, 16, 18; 6:7; 7:7).

An initial point in understanding the potential relationship of this ceremonial sacrifice to atonement images is to observe the circumstances in which the ritual sacrifice occurred. Since the ritual was performed in times of rejoicing and thanksgiving as well as in times of sin, it cannot be a simple matter of a ritualized blood payment to satisfy guilt as prescribed by the law.

A further clue to understanding the possible relationship of this sacrifice to atonement imagery comes from Leviticus 17:11, "For the life of the flesh is in the blood." (See also 17:14; Gen. 9:4; Deut. 12:23). According to the understanding of biology among the early Hebrews, the life of any creature was in its blood.[90] Put this understanding together with the worshiper's symbolic identification with the animal being sacrificed through laying on of hands. When the priest placed the blood of the animal with which the worshiper is symbolically identified on the horns of the altar where God is said to reside, it was a ritual self-dedication and self-giving of the worshiper to God. This ritual did not involve destruction of an animal in place of killing a person. Rather, the life of the animal, namely its blood, and with it the life of the worshiper, was given to God. Rather than dying in the place of the worshiper, the animal's blood goes to God, "representing the life of the person who will henceforth live for God."[91] This ritual rededication of the worshiper to God is appropriately practiced at any juncture of life, whether joyous or sorrowful. As a rededication, however, it cannot or should not be appropriated as an image of satisfaction atonement in which the blood or death is thought to satisfy a legal penalty imposed as the price of sin.[92] It is rather a blood ritual of self-dedication to God.

90. While it is obvious that modern science has long held a different view, the belief of the Hebrews is not illogical. It is true that a creature that loses all its blood will die.

91. John H. Yoder, *Preface to Theology*, p. 221.

92. For examples of this interpretation of Hebrew sacrifices, see J. S. Whale, *Christian Doctrine: Eight Lectures Delivered in the University of Cambridge to Undergraduates of All Faculties* (Cambridge: Cambridge University Press, 1961), pp. 82-84; Schwager, *Jesus in the*

There is the additional point that the sins dealt with in this ritual re-dedication are primarily sins committed inadvertently and unintentionally (Lev. 4:2, 13, 22, 27; 5:2, 14, 17; exceptions to the inadvertent sins are noted in 5:1 and 6:2-4). For the most serious and comprehensive sins, blood is not involved. Leviticus 16 describes the ritual whereby the scapegoat bear-ing "all the iniquities of the people of Israel, and all their transgressions, all their sins," is driven away into the wilderness, "bear[ing] on itself all their iniquities to a barren region" (16:20-22). It is of note that the scapegoat is not killed; rather it bears the sins away into the wilderness.

The motif of sacrifice can of course be appropriated as an image for the death of Jesus. When it becomes clear, however, that the element of sat-isfying a legal penalty is not a dimension of the Hebrew ritual sacrifice, then mere use of sacrificial terminology or imagery should not be con-strued as evidence for satisfaction atonement. As was shown via the work of J. Christiaan Beker and Raymund Schwager, sacrificial terminology can fit within a context different from satisfaction, namely that of narrative Christus Victor.

A second element of challenging the Hebrew sacrificial system as the model of atonement theology is the critique from the prophets, who called the whole sacrificial system into question. Their messages occurred in the context of the crisis and agony of Israel from the destruction of the north-ern kingdom in 721 B.C.E. through to the destruction of Jerusalem and fall of the temple in 587 B.C.E. In the face of these threats, "the prophets ex-pected no help from God through the sacrificial cult; rather they saw in it an expression of that falsehood and mendacity which was responsible for the fatal crisis."[93] Amos wrote: "I hate, I despise your festivals, . . . Even though you offer me your burnt offerings and grain offerings, I will not ac-cept them." In contrast to such empty activities, what is desired is to "let justice roll down like waters, and righteousness like an everflowing stream" (Amos 5:21-22, 24). Other prophets wrote similar calls for love or justice to reign in place of sacrifices. Hosea said: "For I desire steadfast love and not sacrifice, the knowledge of God rather than burnt offerings" (6:6), and Isaiah wrote: "What to me is the multitude of your sacrifices? says the

---

Drama, pp. 177-82; John H. Yoder, *Preface to Theology,* p. 221; Donald Joseph Selby and James King West, *Introduction to the Bible* (New York: Macmillan, 1971), pp. 153-55 [OT]; Gorringe, *God's Just Vengeance,* pp. 34-57.

93. Schwager, *Jesus in the Drama,* p. 180.

LORD; I have had enough of burnt offerings of rams and the fat of fed beasts; I do not delight in the blood of bulls, or of lambs, or of goats. . . . learn to do good; seek justice, rescue the oppressed, defend the orphan, plead for the widow" (1:11, 17; see also Jer. 6:20; Mic. 6:6-8; Ps. 40:7-8; 51:16-17). Jeremiah even questioned whether sacrifices originated with God at all. "For in the day that I brought your ancestors out of the land of Egypt, I did not speak to them or command them concerning burnt offerings and sacrifices. But this command I gave them, "Obey my voice, and I will be your God, and you shall be my people; and walk only in the way that I command you, so that it may be well with you" (Jer. 7:22-23).[94]

This critique of sacrifice by preexilic prophets undercuts the claim that the Hebrew sacrifices pictured in the Old Testament constitute necessary support for Anselmian, satisfaction atonement imagery. This argument gains even more potency when one sees, in the following section, that the writer of Hebrews places this prophetic critique of sacrifice in the mouth of Christ.

Hebrews

With its image of Jesus as the high priest and language of sacrifice, the letter to the Hebrews seems intrinsically to support sacrificial and satisfaction images of atonement. This section challenges that assumption.

René Girard described the theology of Hebrews as a kind of halfway station between Old Testament sacrifices and Jesus' ending of sacrifice. Girard interpreted Hebrews in the same category as the Servant Songs of Second Isaiah, which place the primary responsibility for the death of the Servant on humankind, but still retain some responsibility for Yahweh in the Servant's death. In the same way, Girard believes, Hebrews calls into question the validity of sacrifice, but because the letter does not state explicitly that the mob killed Jesus, it still enacts the sacrificial form with a place for divine as well as human responsibility in the death of the victim.[95]

However, other scholars have argued that Girard's analysis of mimetic violence also fits Hebrews, and that it in fact has a nonsacrificial understanding of the death of Jesus. While Hebrews obviously uses the language

---

94. Schwager, *Jesus in the Drama*, p. 180.
95. Girard, *Things Hidden*, pp. 227-31.

of sacrifice, the important questions concern how the rhetoric of sacrifice in Hebrews functions and "which elements of the discourse of sacrifice are assumed, tolerated, modified, or embraced is another question."[96] Or as Michael Hardin wrote, "using sacrificial language and accepting the victimage mechanism are two different things."[97]

Hardin argued that the author of Hebrews subverted sacrificial language under the cover of sacrificial language. Since he shares human flesh with all of humanity, Jesus is mediator between God and humanity. But the significant aspect of this mediatory role, Hardin writes, is that "the mediating function of Jesus is not compared to that of the sacrificial lamb but of the high priest. Jesus is not so much offering as offerer." This difference is significant. If Jesus were compared to the "passive lamb," he would be a victim and join the victimage of which Girard spoke. But by comparing Jesus to the high priest, Jesus is neither victim, nor "is he in collusion with the mob in his death." Instead, he is in control of his destiny and choosing to give up — sacrifice — his life rather than to kill and perpetuate the cycle of violence. "For Jesus to share in common humanity specifically means that he puts an end to the sacrificial system: he 'dies once for all' (9:26, 28). . . . Jesus' incarnation and death is not to be repeated. Repetition is indigenous to the sacrificial mechanism, where ritual repetition of sacrifice recalls the originary murder which originally founded the community. . . . It is precisely the repetitive character of the sacrifices in the Hebrew cultus which is deemed one of its major liabilities (7:27; 9:25)."[98]

The author of Hebrews thus understands the death of Jesus, Hardin argued, as a surrender of life without a quest for vengeance. "Jesus does not repay humanity with violence, which it dealt him. By not participating in violence, Jesus breaks the mechanism of violence and opens the way for a new obedience. Vengeance is not part of the high priestly work of Christ." This refusal to exact vengeance by Jesus is contrasted to Abel, whose death was the founding murder of the biblical tradition. Where Abel's blood cries from the ground for vengeance (Gen. 4:10), the author of Hebrews

96. Loren L. Johns, "'A Better Sacrifice' or 'Better Than Sacrifice?' Michael Hardin's 'Sacrificial Language in Hebrews,'" in *Violence Renounced: René Girard, Biblical Studies, and Peacemaking*, ed. by Willard M. Swartley (Telford, Pa.: Pandora Press U.S., 2000), p. 121.

97. Michael Hardin, "Sacrificial Language in Hebrews: Reappraising René Girard," in *Violence Renounced*, p. 106.

98. Hardin, "Sacrificial Language in Hebrews," p. 107.

wrote that Jesus' blood "speaks a better word than the blood of Abel" (Heb. 12:24). Rather than crying for vengeance, Jesus' blood speaks "a word of mercy and forgiveness."[99]

Following the discussion of Jesus' death as a refusal to use violence, Hardin developed the use of Psalm 40 in Hebrews 10:1-18 to place rejection of the system of sacrifice "on the lips of the pre-incarnate Christ."[100] Building on this interpretation of the use of Psalm 40, Hardin says that it is in taking on human flesh and doing the will of God that "Jesus becomes the author of salvation." In rejecting sacrifice — the "religion grounded in violence" — Jesus "plays the only role available to him in the incarnation process: he becomes the ultimate victim." And in doing the will of the Father, Jesus models "Christian life as a self-offering."[101] Christian life is "modeled on that of Jesus who gave his life for the world." The demands mentioned in Hebrews — being at peace with all (12:14), mutual encouragement to good deeds (10:24), hosting strangers (13:1-2), and remembering the unjustly imprisoned (13:3) — "all reflect a community whose sacrifices consist not in the taking of the life of another, but of self-giving." This giving rather than the taking of life "is a fundamental reorientation that takes place when one comes to the knowledge of the sacrifice and the self-giving of the Son of God."[102] Thus Hardin concludes, "The Christian life calls one to intentionally care for victims and if necessary to become the victim." And while Hebrews uses "the language of sacrifice, [it] rejects all connections between violence and the sacred. Instead Hebrews offers a new paradigm of what real self-giving (human and divine) is all about."[103]

In his response to Hardin, Loren Johns emphasized arguments that challenge a sacrificial theology in Hebrews. With Hardin, he noted that the author of Hebrews is much more interested in portraying Jesus as high priest than as sacrifice.[104] Further, when Jesus' death is referred to as a sacrifice, the emphasis is on his *self*-offering rather than "a reification of sacrifice theology." This emphasis "avoids blaming God or some cosmic mecha-

99. Hardin, "Sacrificial Language in Hebrews," p. 111.

100. Hardin, "Sacrificial Language in Hebrews," p. 112.

101. Hardin, "Sacrificial Language in Hebrews," p. 114.

102. Hardin, "Sacrificial Language in Hebrews," p. 115.

103. Hardin, "Sacrificial Language in Hebrews," p. 116.

104. Relevant texts include 2:1; 3:1; 4:14, 15; 15:1, 5, 10; 6:20; 7:26, 27, 28; 8:1, 3; 9:11; 13:11. Johns, "'Better Than Sacrifice,'" p. 122.

nistic 'need' for propitiation by identifying the will of God and the will of Christ as one. When it does speak of sacrifice, Hebrews treats Jesus' death as exemplary rather than substitutionary."[105]

Schwager noted that by identifying Jesus with the order of Melchizedek, Hebrews separates Christ from the broad sacrificial tradition of Aaron and Levi. However Christ's priestly action is understood, it inaugurates a new covenant and puts him in a new priestly order rather than continuing the daily sacrifices of the old covenant order.[106] The new sacrifice makes clear that the old ones purified only in an external cultic sense, but did not bring about inner healing. Thus in Hebrews 10:1-18 and its use of Psalm 40, there is a repudiation of a sacrificial hermeneutic. Hebrews 10:5-7 has Christ quote Psalm 40:6-8, noted above, about God not desiring sacrifice and offering and not taking pleasure in burnt and sin offerings. The writer of Hebrews notes that these undesirables were "offered according to the law," then gives an additional quotation from Christ that "See, I have come to do your [God's] will" (10:8), and concludes "he [Christ] abolishes the first [the law] in order to establish the second [God's will]" (10:9).[107] In other words, the writer of Hebrews puts in Christ's mouth words that abolish the sacrificial system and replace it with obedience to the will of God.[108] Finally, one can juxtapose this repudiation of the sacrificial hermeneutic with the Christus Victor imagery in Hebrews 2:14-15: "Since, therefore, the children share flesh and blood, he himself likewise shared the same things, so that through death he might destroy the one who has the power of death, that is, the devil, and free those who all their lives were held in slavery by the fear of death." Johns suggests that this text

---

105. Johns, "'Better Than Sacrifice,'" p. 23.

106. Schwager, *Jesus in the Drama*, p. 182.

107. Schwager, *Jesus in the Drama*, p. 183; Johns, "'Better Than Sacrifice,'" p. 123.

108. Alongside the argument that ritual sacrifice was an act of self-dedication rather than of penal killing, Schwager also noted arguments for seeing sacrifice as a penal killing. And he noted that the prophets' sharp repudiation of sacrifice is mitigated by the important role that the sacrificial cult came to play in postexilic Israel. Thus Schwager called the meaning of the sacrificial cult in the Old Testament an "unsolved problem," which by itself cannot become the starting point for an interpretation of the death of Christ. Schwager then allows Hebrews 10:8 to solve the problem of the supposed contradictory evidence in the Old Testament. He concludes: "The continuity of content between the Old and New Testament runs not through the cultic line, but through the line of criticism of the cult, which emphasizes obedience" (*Jesus in the Drama*, pp. 179-83, quotation from p. 183).

"clearly repudiates a sacrificial hermeneutic," and "at the very least" that "the author's atonement theology is not singularly substitutionary."[109]

After noting the overt abolishment of the sacrificial cult, Schwager engages in an extended discussion about whether in a different way there might be "continuity of content between Old Testament sacrifices and the death of Christ" on the basis of sacrificial blood. That would be the case, Schwager suggests, if Jesus participated in his own death — indirectly killing himself as a sacrifice — by acquiescing to the violence of his enemies and voluntarily placing his own blood on the altar.[110] This would be "self-aggression in the service of a higher good."[111] Ultimately this could not be the case, Schwager concludes. It would contradict God's nonviolence, whereas Jesus' will was fully unified with and obedient to the will of God.[112] Further, since Christ's will is identified with the new law, which repudiates violence and results in a life of completeness with God, his death cannot be self-aggression.[113] Still further, such self-aggression is "totally at odds with the working of [the] Spirit," who is a "Spirit of freedom (2 Cor. 3:17), of love (1 Cor. 13), of joy, of peace, of forbearance, and of gentleness (Gal. 5:22ff.)." Jesus could nonetheless identify with the actions of his enemies without destroying himself by transforming their violence. Those who killed Jesus really did not know what they were doing. When Jesus submitted to them rather than exercising violence, both Jesus and those who killed him became victims (although obviously in different ways) to the power of evil that kills. "At this deeper level, Jesus no longer stood over against his opponents, but he underwent together with them the blows of a destructive power, but in such a way that he alone experienced this suffering for what it was."[114] Jesus' submission to the death was in fact a surrender of his will to God's will. This surrender to the will of God was an infiltration of the world of sin in a way that once again opened it to the heavenly Father.

What at first seemed to be something purely negative, as the rejection of love and closing in on oneself, was transformed by Christ into a surren-

---

109. Johns, "'Better Than Sacrifice,'" p. 123.
110. Schwager, *Jesus in the Drama*, p. 183.
111. Schwager, *Jesus in the Drama*, p. 184.
112. Schwager, *Jesus in the Drama*, p. 185.
113. Schwager, *Jesus in the Drama*, p. 186.
114. Schwager, *Jesus in the Drama*, p. 187.

der which bursts all dimensions of earthly existence. He is therefore both scapegoat and lamb of God; he is the one who is the one slain and the bread of life; he is the one made into sin and the source of holiness.[115]

As was the case for the writings of Paul, this discussion demonstrates interpretations of Hebrews that overturn rather than support satisfaction atonement and are compatible with narrative Christus Victor.

Israel's History

If narrative Christus Victor does not appeal to the tradition of sacrifice in the Old Testament, does it have a connection to the Old Testament? In fact, it does. The articulation of narrative Christus Victor does not limit itself to New Testament data collected from Revelation, the Gospels, and some writings of Paul and Hebrews. It is actually a continuation of a reading of the story of ancient Israel. In the call of Abraham the words of Yahweh are "I will make of you a great nation, . . . and in you all the families of the earth shall be blessed" (Gen. 12:2-3). So begins the mission of God's people, eventually called Israel, to make God's rule visible on earth and in history. The story of Israel is the history of that mission. That history is the story of those who represent God's rule in witness against the forces of the world that do not yet recognize the rule of God. The story features multiple failures as well as some successes in witnessing to the presence of the rule of God in history. The exodus from Egypt is the paradigmatic event of God's rule on behalf of God's people. The just noted challenge by the prophets to the emptiness of the sacrificial system and attendant calls for love, justice, and obedience testify to failure in carrying out that mission. Meanwhile, in exile and without political apparatus and a national monarchy, Israelites continued as the witness to the presence of the rule of God.

Jesus both continues this story and constitutes a new stage in its development. Jesus not only witnesses to the presence of the rule of God in history but is also of God so that his life and teaching are the presence of

115. Schwager, *Jesus in the Drama,* p. 189.

the reign of God in history. Jesus' confrontation of evil and his eventual victory through resurrection thus do not appear as completely novel events in the history of God's people. It is rather the continuation and culmination of a mission that began with the call of Abraham.

John H. Yoder's essay, "See How They Go with Their Face to the Sun,"[116] makes clear this link between Israel and Jesus and then the early church. The key motif for the essay comes from Jeremiah 29:7, in which the exiles are told to

> seek the welfare of the city where I have sent you into exile, and pray to the LORD on its behalf, for in its welfare you will find your welfare.

In Babylon, the exiles lived without trying to take charge of the social order. Canonization was an aspect of maintaining Jewish identity in the Diaspora. Stories of Joseph, of Daniel and his three friends, and of Esther portray the risk of faithfulness to their people and to the will of God "when civil disobedience could have cost them their lives."[117] But as exiles, the Israelites also learned and worked with and became at home in the language and the culture and the skills of the host society, and as such they contributed to the welfare of the host society. This was a continuation of their witness as the people of God when they no longer had the political apparatus of a national monarchy.

It is widely recognized that for most of the first two centuries of Christian history, Christians were pacifists. Yoder points out that they held that stance not because they had suddenly discovered a new orientation in Jesus. Rather, "the ethos of the early Christians was a direct prolongation and fulfillment of the ethos of Jewry."[118]

> Jesus' impact in the first century added more and deeper authentically Jewish reasons, and reinforced and further validated the already expressed Jewish reasons, for the already well-established ethos of not being in charge and not considering any local state structure to be the primary bearer of the movement of history. The second generation of

116. John Howard Yoder, "'See How They Go with Their Face to the Sun'," in *For the Nations: Essays Public and Evangelical* (Grand Rapids and Cambridge: Eerdmans, 1997), pp. 51-78.

117. Yoder, "See How They Go," p. 57.

118. Yoder, "See How They Go," p. 68.

witnesses after Jesus, the "apostles," added another layer of further reasons, still utterly Jewish in form and substance, having to do with the messiahship of Jesus, his lordship, and the presence of the Spirit.[119]

So Yoder concluded, "Until the messianity of Jesus was replaced by that of Constantine, it was the only ethos that made sense."[120]

At no point in this trajectory from Babylonia to Constantine were the people of God defined by a national, political structure nor by whether their culture was accepted by or made sense to the Babylonians. Although the Jews were at home in the culture of Babylonia, they nonetheless maintained a "loyalty to their own culture" in a way that "was not only transparent but even attractive to Gentiles."[121] And "since God is sovereign over history, there is no need for them to seize (or subvert) political sovereignty in order for God's will to be done."[122] Their life as a Jewish culture in the midst of Babylon thus constituted a witness to the polytheistic religions of their neighbors[123] and a witness to the presence of the rule of God on earth.

It is this stance and status of the people of God in exile in Babylonia that Jesus, as a Jew, filled out, that was continued in the church as God's people by the generation of the apostles, and that was eventually abandoned in the epoch of Constantine. And when the church assumed the role of managing the social order in the time after Constantine, it was a return to the policy of David, the rise of whose dynasty was "a disappointment not only to Samuel but to God."[124] What this book has called narrative Christus Victor thus finally becomes a reading of the history of God's people, who make God's rule visible in the world by the confrontation of injustice and by making visible in their midst the justice, peace, and freedom of the rule of God. The life, death, and resurrection of Jesus constitute the culmination of that rule of God, and also the particular point in history when God's rule is most fully present and revealed.

119. Yoder, "See How They Go," p. 69.
120. Yoder, "See How They Go," p. 70.
121. Yoder, "See How They Go," p. 72.
122. Yoder, "See How They Go," p. 67.
123. Yoder, "See How They Go," p. 71.
124. Yoder, "See How They Go," p. 60; see also p. 65.

Summary

Seeing narrative Christus Victor in this long historical context underscores how completely outside of history satisfaction atonement is. In fact, satisfaction atonement appears to reduce the life of Jesus to an elaborate scheme whose purpose was to produce his death. Narrative Christus Victor is a way of reading the entire history of God's people, with the life, death, and resurrection of Jesus as the culminating revelation of the reign of God in history, whereas the various versions of satisfaction atonement concern a legal construct or an abstract formula that functions outside of and apart from history. Seeing the long historical context of narrative Christus Victor underscores the extent to which satisfaction atonement is separated from ethical involvements and allows oppression (as will be pointed out in different ways by black, feminist, and womanist theologies) to continue without challenge.

This presentation of narrative Christus Victor has ranged across the New Testament, but also connects with the Old Testament. While the survey of biblical material has not been exhaustive, it does establish a clear pattern. Narrative Christus Victor fits the Bible from one end to the other. A minimalist conclusion is that the survey has demonstrated that satisfaction atonement is neither the only reading nor the required reading of the Bible. Beyond that minimalist reading, I believe that the biblical survey establishes narrative Christus Victor as the dominant and preferred reading of atonement in the Bible.

Narrative Christus Victor is not the classic image of cosmic beings in conflict. It is rather the event of Jesus and the church around Jesus unfolding in the realm of history as depicted in the biblical story. The following chapter places narrative Christus Victor more explicitly in conversation with other atonement images, both historical and contemporary. And through analysis of the fate of narrative Christus Victor in the history of the church, it focuses in a different way its status as a nonviolent atonement motif.

3 Narrative Christus Victor: Some Comparisons and Its Demise

Chapter 2 presented narrative Christus Victor as a motif that reflects biblical material from one end of the Bible to the other. This chapter examines narrative Christus Victor in relation to two sets of traditional understandings. First, answers to a series of questions compare and contrast narrative Christus Victor to the traditional atonement motifs. Then the discussion considers narrative Christus Victor in terms of the history of doctrine.

Distinguishing Narrative Christus Victor

The Object of the Death of Jesus

It is very instructive to consider narrative Christus Victor in light of the questions about the object of the death of Jesus used in Chapter 2 to distinguish the families of atonement theories from each other. For the ransom theory, it will be recalled, the death is an item of exchange whose object is Satan. Satan is also the object of the death when Jesus' humanity disguises deity and tricks Satan. For satisfaction atonement, it is the offended honor of God or a stipulation of the divine law toward which Jesus' death is directed. For the moral theory, sinful humankind is the object of the death. For narrative Christus Victor, the powers of evil appear as the apparent answer to the query about the object of Jesus' death. But this question and these answers do not disclose the complete picture.

The Accomplishment of the Death of Jesus

Developing nuances implied by the question about the object of Jesus' death brings out significant differences between narrative Christus Victor and other atonement motifs. Consider the question, "Who needs or needed the death of Jesus?" Or to arrive at the some point from another side, one might ask, "What does the death accomplish?" or "What would remain unaccomplished without the death?" In the classic ransom motif, Satan needs the death as payment on his side of the agreement reached. In this case, "needs" refers to an obligation in a contract to which God agrees. Satan requires the death as a right granted by covenant with God; without the death to meet the agreement, souls of sinners remain in bondage. That formulation seems offensive in its acceptance of rights for the devil. That offense is somewhat blunted by the version of classic Christus Victor that pictures God as tricking the devil when the deity of Jesus is hidden under the humanity of Jesus. But, as was noted, the idea of defeating the devil by trickery was also deemed unworthy of God.

For Anselm's satisfaction theory, which replaced classic Christus Victor, the query about what the death of Jesus accomplishes has a clear answer. God — or perhaps better stated, the offended honor of God — needs the death of Jesus as payment for the offense that sinful humankind committed against God. In the later penal version, the divine law needs the death to satisfy the legal penalty required for sin. In either case, without the death, the divine entity would remain unsatisfied and thus sinners would remain unsaved.[1]

Focusing on what is accomplished by the death of Jesus points to the assumption in any of the versions of satisfaction atonement that doing justice or making right means to punish and is based on the assumption that an offense is balanced by punishment equal to the offense. Satisfaction atonement assumes that the sin of humankind against God has earned the penalty of death, but that Jesus satisfied the offended honor of God on their behalf or took the place of sinful humankind and bore their punish-

---

1. In *Cur Deus Homo*, Anselm's problem was to depict this "need" for the incarnation and the death of Jesus to satisfy divine honor but without implying obligation on the part of God. Chapter 7 will consider Anselm's particular argument, as well as why narrative Christus Victor provides a better answer than Anselm's. Meanwhile, the discussion in this chapter proceeds on the basis of the logic of the atonement motifs apart from Anselm's answer.

ment or satisfied the required penalty on their behalf. Sin was atoned for because it was punished — punished vicariously through the death of Jesus, which saved sinful humankind from the punishment of death that they deserved. The death accomplished that punishment or it accomplished the payment to God's honor demanded as compensation for sin. The death of Jesus accomplishes this satisfaction because all versions of Anselmian atonement rest on the assumption that making right depends on punishment. Without Jesus' death serving as punishment to balance sin, there is no salvation.

Asking who or what needs the death or what the death accomplishes is quite different for the moral theory. Since the death of Jesus reveals God's love for sinners, one might say that sinners needed the death. One might also say that God the Father needed the death as the way to demonstrate the Father's love for sinful humankind. In either case, without the death, humankind would lack the supreme example of God's love.

Asking who needs the death of Jesus or what the death of Jesus accomplishes for narrative Christus Victor brings a revealing point to the foreground. For this image, the closest thing to a need for Jesus' death is that powers of evil need his death in order to remove his challenge to their power. And if this is the need, it accomplishes nothing for the salvation of sinners, nor does it accomplish anything for the divine economy. Since Jesus' mission was not to die but to make visible the reign of God, it is quite explicit that neither God nor the reign of God *need* Jesus' death in the way that his death is irreducibly *needed* in satisfaction atonement. As will be developed in more depth in following chapters, this contrast of Jesus' death as *needed* and *not needed* indicates one of the most profound differences between narrative Christus Victor and satisfaction atonement.

The Agent of Jesus' Death

The nuances of the discussion change once again when one moves from asking who needed the death of Jesus to ask, "Who was responsible for the death of Jesus?" or most provocatively, "Who killed Jesus?" These questions focus on the agency behind the death of Jesus. In an Anselmian approach to atonement, God obviously did not directly kill Jesus. In some lights, however, God seems implicated in Jesus' death. It will be recalled that Anselm removed the devil from the equation and made sinful humankind responsible directly to God. It is God's honor or God's law that was violated and had to be satisfied. Most obviously, sinful humankind cannot arrange its own satisfaction of God's offended honor, and Satan certainly does not orchestrate the death of Jesus in order to satisfy God's honor. For satisfaction atonement, it appears that the only remaining option is that God is the agent behind Jesus' death. It would appear that God is ultimately the one who arranged for the death of Jesus as the payment that would satisfy divine honor or as the compensatory punishment required by the divine law. Although the traditional language has focused on Jesus' death for sinners, asking about the agent behind the death points to God as both the author of the process or the agent behind the transaction that requires the death of Jesus as innocent victim, as well as the recipient of the death as payment to God's honor. And Jesus' earthly life appears to become an elaborate process whose purpose is accomplished when he is killed.[2] In Chapter 2, Schwager pointed to the apparent disjuncture in understandings of God's will that results when those who kill Jesus carry out the divine purpose of killing Jesus so that his death can become the satisfying penalty payment while simultaneously, by submitting to death, Jesus is fully submitted to the will of God the Father. As Schwager indicated, it appears to make both Jesus and those who killed Jesus the bearers of God's will.[3]

For the moral theory, God appears quite specifically as the agent of Jesus' death. In this motif, God the Father sent his most precious possession to die in order to display an ultimately loving act. Apparently the death of Jesus has no salvific purpose in this motif if it is not God-intended.

On the question of the agent of Jesus' death, narrative Christus Victor is clearly distinguished from other atonement motifs. Quite obviously not God but the evil powers killed Jesus, whether these powers are understood as Satan, or in terms of earthly structures such as Rome, which is the sym-

---

2. At this point, some readers will already be arguing that appeals to the Trinity and understandings of additional or different emphases turn away the conclusion that God is the agent or the cause behind the death of Jesus. Chapter 7 deals explicitly with these arguments and with writers who make that case, including Anselm himself, who sought to defend God against the idea that God needed or required anything. In the meantime, following chapters will refer to the logically derived conclusion that satisfaction atonement appears to place God behind the death of Jesus.

3. Raymund Schwager, *Jesus in the Drama of Salvation* (New York: Crossroad, 1999), p. 163.

bolic representative of Satan in Revelation, or as the powers of death, sin, the law, and the flesh. While Jesus' mission for the reign of God may have made his death inevitable in narrative Christus Victor, neither the purpose nor the culmination of the mission was to die. God did not send Jesus to die, but to live, to make visible and present the reign of God. It is obvious that for narrative Christus Victor, the agent of Jesus' death was not God but the powers of evil.[4]

This comparison of atonement motifs points to the conclusion that satisfaction and moral motifs depend on an image of God in which by implication God saves via divinely sanctioned or divinely willed violence against Jesus. The divine economy has a need for a death penalty to balance the sin of humankind as the basis for restoring justice. Narrative Christus Victor avoids this problem. In this motif, Jesus' mission was not to die but to witness to the reign of God. Jesus died not via divinely instigated violence but at the hands of those who represented the powers opposed to the reign of God. Rather than cooperating with divinely sanctioned violence, Jesus countered the violence of the powers. And as he submitted to the evil of the violent powers rather than meet it on its own terms, he made visible the fact that the rule of God does not depend on violence. The God revealed by Jesus, and the rule of God revealed by Jesus, do not respond to violence with violence. They respond to violence with its opposite. The resurrection showed the power of God to overcome even the annihilation of death that comes from the powers' exercise of violence. Narrative Christus Victor is an atonement motif that does not depend on the divinely sanctioned violence that is implicit but real in satisfaction and moral atonement motifs. Narrative Christus Victor is atonement from a nonviolent perspective.

Our Role in Jesus' Death

Additional dimensions of the question about the agency for the death of Jesus appear when one asks about the sinner's role in the drama in which the reign of God in Jesus confronted the powers of evil. Since all human-

---

4. A primary point made by René Girard is that Jesus was a victim of mimetic rivalry and the scapegoat mechanism and that his death was not an expression of the will of God. See René Girard, *Things Hidden Since the Foundation of the World*, trans. Stephen Bann and Michael Metter (Stanford, Calif.: Stanford University Press, 1987), pp. 141-223.

kind is sinful, to ask about the sinner's role is to ask about our own participation in this story.

The story of Jesus is a drama of salvation. The good news (gospel)
from this story is that sinful humankind is the beneficiary of the story: as a
result of Jesus' saving act, sinners are saved. The seemingly obvious leap is
to identify with Jesus who saves and to claim the salvation offered. However, in a collective haste to identify with Christ and to accept the salvation
offered, the Christian theological tradition seems to have bypassed a prior,
necessary, and important point of identification.

Before participating in the saving act of Jesus, we (sinners) need to acknowledge participation and identification at another point. In the drama
of salvation, we need first to identify with sin. And that identification is
more than an abstract confession of sinfulness and guilt. In particular, we
need to acknowledge our enslavement to the powers that killed Jesus, to
confess our place on the side of those who opposed the reign of God. We
are identified with the Roman imperial leaders who had ultimate authority
for his death, with Jewish leaders who cooperated to condemn Jesus, with
the rabble who acquiesced to his condemnation, with the disciples who
slept rather than praying with him as he struggled in the garden, with Judas who betrayed him, and with Peter who denied him. To confess to being
a "sinner" is not merely an abstract concept involving a debt owed to the
divine honor. Being a sinner means to acknowledge our identification with
those who killed Jesus and our bondage to the powers that enslaved them.
Every human being, by virtue of what human society is, participates in and
is in bondage to those powers and is therefore implicated in the killing of
Jesus. What Paul said about the law applies to us — Jesus' death judges us
for not fulfilling the law and for being enslaved to sin. And when Jesus died
"for us," on "our behalf," we are implicated in his death as partners with
and as captives to the forces of evil that killed him.

When our identification with the powers that killed Jesus becomes
clear, it is evident that Jesus' death really was "for us" while we were yet sinners; and that it was "costly" — both to God the Father and the Jesus the
Son. It cost Jesus his life to make God's rule visible, and it cost God the Father the death of the Son, Jesus. It was in fact a vicarious sacrifice "for us"
(if one wants to retain the term "sacrifice"), since Jesus died "for us" while
we were still identified with and in bondage to the powers of death. But
this vicarious sacrifice is not a payment to God nor a payment to a plan established by God nor a scheme to punish Jesus instead of punishing us.

Rather, this sacrifice of Jesus' life revealed the full character of the powers that enslave sinful humankind and that oppose the rule of God. Through the resurrection, God in Christ has in fact defeated these powers "for us." And it is only when we acknowledge our complicity with and bondage to these powers — that is, confess our sin — in their opposition to the reign of God that we can start to envision liberation (salvation) from them.

Grace and Forgiveness

Visualizing our identity with the powers that killed Jesus leads into the concepts of "grace" and of "forgiveness." When God invites us to identify with Jesus and to participate in the victory of the reign of God over the powers of evil, it is certainly not because we have earned God's favor. On the contrary, rather than earning God's favor, we are complicitous with those who participated in the murder of the Son of God; and it is impossible to undo or to compensate for the sin committed. There is absolutely no question of human beings earning any kind of status or standing with God. Yet God offers forgiveness and acceptance while we are still under the sway of the forces of evil — and that acceptance is truly grace. We certainly have no power to undo the evil committed — from our side, the only way that we are part of God's reign is because God has in fact forgiven us and by grace invited us to be part of God's reign. Because we cannot earn the right to participate in the reign of God, our only option is to accept by faith the loving offer of God, who invites us to be part of the reign of God in spite of having participated in the death of God's Son. Accepting Christ, coming under the rule of God does require something of us, namely repentance for the evil we have committed against the reign of God. Repentance is not something that we can do in order to earn the favor of God, it is rather how we respond to the grace of God. Such repentance is manifested by a new life, a life now lived in the resurrected Christ. This new life, which has already begun, will in God's future reach culmination with the restoration of all things, what the author of Revelation called a new heaven and new earth (Rev. 21:1).

From the earthly side, this forgiveness offered and the subsequent repentance and transformed life of narrative Christus Victor reflect Jesus' words to the woman taken in adultery to go and refrain from future sin (John 8:11); or his words to Zacchaeus, following his declaration of intent to make restitution of ill-gotten wealth, that "Today salvation has come to this house" (Luke 19:9). This grace and forgiveness does not depend on a penalty payment; it is not predicated on balancing sin and evil with punishment. It is rather a transformation of life that follows forgiveness.

Free Will versus Predestination

Upon discussion of grace and forgiveness, one can see that narrative Christus Victor entails both the responsibility of humankind (free will) and God's predestining grace (predestination of individuals), whichever side of that paradox one wants to emphasize. It is obvious that human initiative and human effort alone have no impact on the reign of evil, and that human effort alone cannot withstand the forces of evil. The victory is of God through the Lamb, apart from human beings. Only the Lamb has conquered and ransomed "saints from every tribe and language and people and nation" (Rev. 5:9). Only with the Lamb do human beings participate in the victory. That seems tailor-made to say that only those whom God invites and transforms can actually become members of God's reign and participate in the victory that culminates in the New Jerusalem.

On the other hand, Revelation also states that the victory occurs in two ways — by the blood of the lamb "and by the word of their [that is, martyrs'] testimony, for they did not cling to life even in the face of death" (12:11). The faithful witness of the believing church participates in the victory of the Lamb. By giving their lives in faithfulness to the Lamb, they demonstrate faith in the victory of the Lamb and thereby participate in and extend that victory. Sinners experience the power of the reign of God when they accept the invitation of Jesus to "follow me." Choosing to accept the invitation of Jesus and follow him, choosing to give one's life as a witness to the risen Christ, are decisions and commitments of individual volition. It is a witness to the truth of the reign of God when individuals submit to it because they freely choose to do so rather than being coerced into it. Participation in this story of victory expressed as narrative Christus Victor sits astride the paradox of predestination and free will; it clearly fits Paul's words, "But by the grace of God I am what I am, and his grace toward me has not been in vain. On the contrary, I worked harder than any of them — though it was not I, but the grace of God that is with me" (1 Cor. 15:10).

Justice and Mercy of God

This contemporary reconstruction of narrative Christus Victor avoids splitting the justice of God from the mercy of God as does Anselmian atonement. Stated differently, God's mercy and God's justice are not consecutive events in narrative Christus Victor. God's role does not change from mercy to judgment in narrative Christus Victor nor is there a contrast between God's wrath and God's mercy, as it is for Anselmian atonement. What changes in narrative Christus Victor is where we stand in the drama of Jesus' life, death, and resurrection. In terms of our identity with and confession of sin, we stand with the forces enslaved to sin and the law who killed Jesus. We stand with the evil that is revealed and condemned by his death. In the previous chapter reference was made to Raymund Schwager's comment that biblical statements of God's judgment actually refer to turning people over to their own wickedness, which continues to bind them. But as Christ-identified people, we have been invited by God to change sides and to stand with Christ, on the side of the reign of God that confronts and is ultimately victorious over the forces of evil that killed Jesus. In Christ we are indeed free from sin, free from death, free from the law that Jesus brought to an end. But while we continue in bondage to sin, God remains merciful, holding open the opportunity for a transformed existence. The wrath of God and the love of God represent the two stances from which we view the salvation drama, the two perspectives from which we view the act of God in Christ — as an act of judgment as long as we continue in bondage to the powers of evil that enslave us, and as an act of love that frees us from the powers of evil. These are not consecutive stages in God's attitude toward humankind, but differing stages in humankind's perception of God.

Ethics

The sinner's complicity with the powers that oppose the reign of God and the sinner's repentance, the genuineness of which is identified by active participation in the reign of God, is in contrast with the passive role for humankind in satisfaction atonement. The paradox of free will and predestination also involves the active participation by the individual in a transformed (saved) life, which is again unlike the passive role of human-

kind in satisfaction atonement. Narrative Christus Victor pictures humankind actively involved in history as sinners against the rule of God, and as
actively involved in salvation as the transformed individual participates in
witnessing to the presence of the reign of God in history.

In contrast, for satisfaction atonement, the sinner is a passive observer
of a divine transaction between Father and Son that occurs outside history.
As a result of the transaction, the sinner's legal status before God changes,
but beyond that change in status there is no transformation of the life of
the sinner qua sinner who lives in history. This contrast of active and passive stances of the sinner in narrative Christus Victor and satisfaction
atonement has implications for understanding ethics as it relates to atonement theology.

In the satisfaction images, the question that the death of Christ answered was how to satisfy the honor of an offended God or pay (satisfy)
the penalty required by God's law or reestablish justice in God's universe.
This satisfaction was made by the death of a perfect human, while the divine nature of Jesus gave that perfect death efficacy for the sins of all humankind. For the penal version, the question for sinners was how to escape
the penalty of death merited by their sin; and the answer was that Jesus
bore the penalty as a substitute for, or in the stead of, sinners. Those solu-
tions picture the relationship between God and humankind in terms of a
legal construct. The point about ethics is that these atonement images that
assume a legal framework say nothing about ethics. Satisfaction atonement in its several forms features an essential separation of salvation and
ethics. The atonement image changes the sinner's legal status before God
but says nothing about a transformed life. As we will see in the following
chapter on black theology, some theologians even argue that atonement
formulas devoid of ethics actually contribute to sinful living since they
provide a means to maintain a proper legal status before God without
speaking about transformed life under the rule of God.

The passive character of salvation and an atonement motif void of
ethics is noteworthy when juxtaposed with the image of narrative Christus
Victor, in which identifying with Jesus Christ (or being Christian) and the
discussion of ethics (or how Christians live) are two dimensions of the
same question. As narrative Christus Victor has been developed, when the
sinner is "saved," he or she changes loyalty from the rule of evil to the reign
of God by accepting the call of God to new life in the reign of God. It is not
a mere change of legal status before God, but a change in character and al-

legiance that means nothing — in fact, has not occurred — if there is no life lived according to the reign of God. And since Jesus is of God, Jesus' life is a witness to the way the reign of God looks in the world. The sketch in Chapter 2 of narrative Christus Victor in the Gospels outlined the life of Jesus as it made the rule of God present and visible in the world. Without elaboration, I note here for emphasis that the nonviolent character of the ethics of the reign of God is of particular significance.

Atonement in History

The legal paradigm of the satisfaction atonement images is ahistorical. The transaction between Father and Son pictured in satisfaction atonement is outside the historical world in which we live. But it is precisely in the historical world that we discuss how to live in ways shaped by the reign of God. And it is in that historical arena that the reign of God is victorious in narrative Christus Victor. Stated another way, atonement defined in terms of a legal paradigm does not make use of what is learned about Jesus from the narrative-shaped and story-based depiction of Jesus' confrontation of evil. The satisfaction theory does not make inherently necessary any specific or particular knowledge of the way Jesus was human or divine, nor does it require any particular knowledge of Jesus' teaching. In contrast, without the narrative depiction of Jesus in narrative Christus Victor, one does not know what the reign of God looks like nor how those who would be Christian would orient themselves in the world. Pointing to the ahistorical character of satisfaction atonement is thus another way to show the ethical void of satisfaction atonement.

This first section of this chapter has developed some theological characteristics of narrative Christus Victor by means of comparison and contrast with satisfaction and moral influence atonement motifs. For several reasons, this is a first round of such comparisons. For one thing, the comparison with narrative Christus Victor has used summaries of the prevailing motifs and has not dealt in detail with Anselm's *Cur Deus Homo* itself. Further, the discussion has not yet considered the modern proponents of Anselm, who defend him against the challenges just raised. These considerations appear in Chapter 7. And most importantly, there are additional dimensions of narrative Christus Victor to develop and further challenges to traditional atonement motifs to observe before reaching the climactic discussion in Chapter 7. The next section of this chapter develops one set of additional learnings about narrative Christus Victor derived from understanding its fate in the history of the church.

The Demise of Christus Victor

While I have referred to the construction of narrative Christus Victor, it is first of all a biblical motif to which a name has been attributed for ease of reference. This biblical image recounts the narrative of Jesus in a way that focuses on the reign of God made visible by Jesus within the history in which we live, and it is a model that attributes cosmic meaning to events in the realm of history.

But what happened to this biblical motif? What accounts for its apparent demise, and its eventual replacement by Anselm's satisfaction theory, with Abelard's moral approach as the minority counterpart to the satisfaction images? My answers are not those found in the standard treatments of the history of doctrine. Providing the answers will also bring to the fore another dimension of narrative Christus Victor as an atonement image that assumes nonviolence.

A first step in understanding the fate of narrative Christus Victor is to recognize that it is also an image of ecclesiology. Pointing out likely historical antecedents for the symbolism of Revelation locates this telling of the biblical narrative in history and shows clearly that the narrative is about the church of the first century. According to this biblical construction, the church was the earthly instrument that continued Jesus' mission of making visible the reign of God. Since the Roman empire of the first century did not acknowledge the reign of God or confess Jesus as Messiah, it is hardly surprising that the church differed from the empire. By the majority of accounts, one of the most easily perceived differences concerned the use of the sword. Whereas the empire had armies, and emperors consolidated their authority with military power, the early church rejected use of the sword and was pacifist.

It is the social relationship of early church and empire that corresponds to what I have called narrative Christus Victor. This motif assumes that the structure that makes visible the reign of God poses a contrast to or a witness to the social order that does not know or acknowledge the reign of God. That was the case for the church in the time of Revelation, and it continued on in the post–New Testament era. This reconstituted, narrative Christus Victor makes sense of and depends on this social context.

Constantinian Synthesis

Beginning in mid-second century and continuing for more than two centuries, the church underwent a series of changes that had far-reaching consequences.[5] The evolutionary character of the changes does not belie their significance. Because of the Emperor Constantine's legalization of Christianity with the Edict of Milan (313 C.E.), his own adoption of Christianity, and his apparent favoring of Christianity in his policies, his name has come to symbolize the new status of the church. However, the changes had begun before him and the new status was fully achieved only after him. Thus Constantine is not so much cause as one who reflects and reacts to the direction in which the situation was evolving.

The early church's feelings about harassment, estrangement, and potential extinction, which are visible in Revelation, reflected its lack of legal standing in the empire and the potential for hostile actions by imperial authority against the church. In this pre-Constantinian context, it was the beleaguered church that represented divine providence or God's working in the world, and this church clearly stood over against the empire. Church confronted empire. The church was uncomfortable with the structures around it.

What Constantine has come to symbolize was a change in status of the church in the Greco-Roman empire — from an illegal and sometimes persecuted minority to the favored and eventually established religion of the empire. The end result of the changes associated with Constantine but ac-

---

5. For the story of these changes and Constantine's role in them, see H. A. Drake, *Constantine and the Bishops: The Politics of Intolerance* (Baltimore: Johns Hopkins University Press, 2000). The following description of the theological significance of these changes is shaped by John Howard Yoder, "The Constantinian Sources of Western Social Ethics," in *The Priestly Kingdom: Social Ethics as Gospel* (Notre Dame: University of Notre Dame, 1984), pp. 135-47; John H. Yoder, "The Otherness of the Church," in *The Royal Priesthood: Essays Ecclesiological and Ecumenical,* ed. Michael G. Cartwright (Grand Rapids: Eerdmans, 1994), pp. 53-64. An earlier version of my description of the Constantinian shift appeared in J. Denny Weaver, "Atonement for the NonConstantinian Church," *Modern Theology* 6, no. 4 (July 1990): 309-11.

tually enacted by Theodotius was that the church came to identify with the social order and to make use of and express itself through the institutions of the social order. The empire became identified with the cause of Christianity, and the success (or failure) of the empire corresponded to the success (or failure) of Christianity.[6] Rather than posing a contrast or a challenge to the social order, church officials could now use imperial structures as allies if political authorities sided with the particular officials on the issue in question. And of course they opposed them when the political authorities disagreed with churchly officials. The church no longer confronted empire and society; instead, the church supported and was supported — established — by the empire. While church and government officials still engaged in disputes, Christianity (or the church) was no longer a minority, oppressed structure. The fact that church and civil authorities also opposed each other sharply on occasion does not challenge the fact that each assumed that both civil authorities and churchly authorities had roles in ecclesiastical affairs; their disagreements concerned the manner of intervention and which of the competing authorities had power over the other rather than being an argument about the principle per se of civil interven-

---

6. Constantine continued in the well-established imperial belief that the emperor sought divine favor and support for the conduct of imperial affairs, and that success — particularly success in battle — showed divine favor. Where Constantine differed from previous emperors was in substituting the Christian God for pagan deities. Constantine had noted the failure of Diocletian's policy to suppress Christianity. In the belief that religious belief could not be coerced, Constantine adopted a policy of toleration under a vaguely defined monotheism. His policy was to allow Christians and pagans to coexist, and then to find a formula that would allow followers of Athanasius and Arius to coexist under the umbrella of monotheism. What has been perceived as Constantine's waffling in support of orthodox Christology after the Council of Nicea (his switching support back and forth between Arians and followers of Athanasius) were his efforts to support whichever side(s) seemed to be moving under the broadly defined umbrella of monotheism. Constantine's consensus policy ultimately came apart, and in the course of the fourth century, the Christian forces of coercion won out. The culmination of the centuries-long evolution of the church from outside to inside the empire came at the end of the century, when Theodotius declared Christianity the only true religion of the empire and also sided with the party of Athanasius against the Arians. While Constantine's name has come to symbolize these changes, Theodotius was the emperor who actually implemented them. Thus one might say that Theodotius was more "Constantinian" than Constantine! For this interpretation, see Drake, *Constantine and the Bishops*. Still useful are analysis and comments throughout A. H. M. Jones, *Constantine and the Conversion of Europe* (New York: Macmillan, 1948; reprint, Toronto: University of Toronto, 1978); Ramsay MacMullen, *Constantine*, reprint, 1969 (London: Croom Helm, 1987).

tion in church affairs. With emperors and lesser political officials now taking sides in theological disputes and backing the decrees of church councils, the church came to encompass the social order as a whole. A kind of culmination was reached when Emperor Theodotius made the results of the Council of Constantinople the official theology of the empire. This fusion of church and social order is anachronistically called a "Christian society."

With civil rulers assuming authority in churchly issues and treating the church as an institution of the empire, the rulers of the social order became presumed agents of God, and the political entities then became the bearers of God's providence.[7] This change concerns the identity of the institution that carries and makes visible God's providence or God's rule in history. Prior to Constantine, it was the church — the people of God — that witnessed to God's rule in history. Since the church that consisted of a small, minority voice in a relatively inhospitable world could always feel itself in a precarious position and on the verge of extinction, it took faith to say that God was in control of history and that the reign of God had already triumphed in the resurrection of Jesus. It was very clear, however, that church existed over against the social order or in a state of confrontation with the world. That relationship reversed itself in the course of the changes symbolized by Constantine. It now seemed self-evident that God controlled history (Was it not the case that the empire claimed to embrace Christianity?), while it required faith to believe that an invisible but faithful church existed within the mass of nominal faith of the supposedly Christian society.

Parallel to the shift from church to empire as the institutional bearer of God's providence was the shift from Jesus to the ruler or emperor as the norm by which to judge the behavior of Christians. Stated in oversimplified fashion, the pre-Constantinian church looked to Jesus the Lord as the norm of faith and practice, and faithfulness to that norm constituted the decisive aspect of judgment.[8] Being Christian meant to live the life modeled by Jesus, the head or lord of the church. On the other hand, the emperor symbolized

---

7. John Howard Yoder, "Constantinian Sources," p. 138; John H. Yoder, "Otherness," pp. 57, 60.

8. The relationship between church and civil authorities did develop in different fashions in east and west, with the bishop in the west maintaining more independence vis-à-vis civil authorities than in the east. Nonetheless, albeit in different ways, both traditions came to assume that it was the political institutions that carried God's providence in history. The debate concerned not whether God worked through these political institutions but whether civil rulers or bishops had the most immediate divine authority over the political sphere.

the empire. Once Christianity became the religion of the empire and of the social order, and the continuation of Christianity was linked to the success of the empire, preservation of the empire or the institution of the social order became the decisive criterion for ethical behavior, and the emperor or ruler became the norm against which the rightness of a behavior such as killing or truth-telling was judged.[9] In other words, as the leader of the civil order that protected the Christian church, the appropriateness of the "Christian" emperor's behavior was judged not with reference to Jesus' teaching and example but by how it furthered the cause of the empire or governing structure that protected the church. As a result of the shift in view from Jesus to the emperor, there was a marked change in the ethical orientation of the church. The norm of "Christian" behavior became that which everyone could perform, with the emperor in the role of everyone. Being Christian came to mean adherence to a minimum standard of social behavior in the "Christian" empire. The idea was abandoned that the so-called hard sayings of Jesus (e.g., Matt. 5:38-44, par.) applied to all Christians, and the teaching and example of Jesus were not thought to apply to the lives of ordinary Christians.[10] What would happen to the empire and thus the church if everyone, starting with the emperor, acted by Jesus' teaching?

The exercise of the sword shows most clearly the change in the status of the church from contrast to accommodation of the social order. Whereas before, Christians did not wield the sword and pagans did, now Christians wielded the sword in the name of Christ. The claim was that "Christian" concerns required use of the sword in order to defend the society and the empire, which is now a defender of church and Christian faith. In a manner of speaking, *not* applying the teaching of Jesus became the "Christian" thing to do.

While one could indicate a number of other changes parallel to the shift from church to empire as the institutional bearer of God's providence, the important point for the present discussion concerns the change in the church's relationship to its surrounding society. The church moved from a position outside society to a position within society. It shifted from

---

9. John Howard Yoder, "Constantinian Sources," p. 138.

10. Two differing institutional objections to the evolution of the church toward identification with the social order were the Donatist movement and the monastic movement. Donatism came to uphold a higher standard as a separatist movement. From a position within the church, monasticism gave visibility to a standard of Christian conduct higher than the minimal behavior of ordinary Christians.

a stance of estrangement and confrontation to one of support for the social order and its governing structures.

Ecclesiology and Atonement

While Christus Victor imagery gradually faded away, the motif of Jesus' defeat of the devil survived so that Anselm of Canterbury could refute it in his *Cur Deus Homo*. Although not immediately accepted, the satisfaction motif that Anselm put in place of Christus Victor eventually became the dominant motif, with Peter Abelard's "moral influence" theory as the primary alternative. The traditional reasons given for the demise of Christus Victor are several: objection to the idea that God would either recognize certain rights of the devil or stoop to overcoming the devil through trickery, objection to its dualistic worldview, the seeming lack of evidence of the victory of the reign of God in the historical realm in which we live, incompatibility of the imagery of cosmic battle with our modern worldview, and distaste for the battle imagery. None of those reasons is adequate.

With reference to atonement images, the important point is that narrative Christus Victor is an atonement motif that assumes — even depends on — an imagery of confrontation, a church that witnesses to the social order. In fact, it does not make sense without it. At the level of cosmic imagery, the forces of God confront the forces of Satan. In its demythologized and historicized form, the confrontation occurs between the social structure created by Jesus and extended by his followers on the one hand, and the structures of the first-century social order and Roman empire on the other. The real reason that narrative Christus Victor fell out of the theological matrix, I suggest, was not so much because of its imagery of demons or objections to tricking the devil, but because the church had lost its sense of confrontation with the world.[11] One element of this shift from confronta-

---

11. The only earlier scholarship that has anticipated this correspondence of atonement images and ecclesiology is George Huntston Williams, *Anselm, Communion and Atonement* (Saint Louis, Mo.: Concordia Publishing House, 1960), which is a lightly revised reprinting of George H. Williams, "The Sacramental Presuppositions of Anselm's *Cur Deus Homo*," *Church History* 26, no. 3 (September 1957): 245-74. Williams argued that Christus Victor corresponded to the once-for-all sacrament of baptism in the early church while Anselm's satisfaction atonement was developed within the understanding of the eucharist as the repeated, sacramental mode of entry into the body of Christ.

tion to accommodation was losing track of the possible historical antecedents of the symbolism in the book of Revelation.[12] With the church no longer confronting the empire, but rather accepting the intervention of political authorities in churchly affairs and looking to political authorities for support and protection, the actual historical, social situation of church-state cooperation and fusion of church and social order no longer matched the cosmic imagery of confrontation. And when the cosmic imagery of Revelation no longer matched the historical context, the cosmic imagery lost much of its meaning. The atonement motif that used such imagery could be refuted and abandoned.

This shift in the social context for atonement imagery took place gradually. It was not the case that the theologians of the time perceived immediately a new ecclesiology and then set out to develop a different theory of atonement to match it. Rather, the change in ecclesiology happened gradually, in an evolutionary manner. The shift in atonement images also happened gradually. The idea that God defeated the devil through trickery was still prominent enough to be specifically refuted by Anselm in *Cur Deus Homo* of 1098 and continued, since Anselm's view was not immediately accepted.[13] But although the change was gradual,

12. In his discussion of the canonization of Revelation, Eugene Boring notes varying attempts at interpretation that already in the second century did not tie it to first-century historical figures and events (M. Eugene Boring, *Revelation,* Interpretation: A Bible Commentary for Teaching and Preaching [Louisville: John Knox Press, 1989], pp. 2-5). That the church lost track of such historical antecedents of Revelation by the third century ought not surprise us. For a contemporary example, note the historical symbolism of Negro spirituals forgotten in a shorter period of time and recovered in James H. Cone, "Black Spirituals: A Theological Interpretation," *Theology Today* 29, no. 1 (April 1972): 54-69; and James H. Cone, *The Spirituals and the Blues: An Interpretation* (Maryknoll, N.Y.: Orbis Books, 1992). As an informal example, I recount my own experience with students. To illustrate the use of symbols to depict historical figures, for a contemporary parallel to Revelation's four horsemen, I often describe a number of figures on horseback — a headless rider, one with a large scar on a potbelly, one who falls off his horse, and one with a big grin wearing an Angels' baseball cap. My twenty-year-old students need explanations before recognizing allusions to U.S. presidents John F. Kennedy, Lyndon Johnson, Richard Nixon, and Jimmy Carter.

13. Gustaf Aulén, *Christus Victor: A Historical Study of the Three Main Types of the Idea of Atonement,* trans. A. G. Herbert (New York: Macmillan, 1969), pp. 38-39; J. N. D. Kelly, *Early Christian Doctrines,* rev. ed. (New York: Harper & Row, 1978), pp. 375-89; Darby Kathleen Ray, *Deceiving the Devil: Atonement, Abuse, and Ransom* (Cleveland: Pilgrim Press, 1998), pp. 123-25; R. W. Southern, *Saint Anselm: A Portrait in a Landscape* (Cambridge: Cambridge University Press, 1990), pp. 210-11.

there did come a time when discussing atonement in terms that assumed confrontation between church and social order no longer made sense. Narrative Christus Victor disappeared from the picture when the church came to support the world's social order, to accept the intervention of political authorities in churchly affairs, and to look to political authorities for support and protection.

Beyond this correlation of narrative Christus Victor with pre-Constantinian ecclesiology, several additional arguments also suggest that Anselm's motif belongs specifically to the medieval rather than early church ecclesiological context. For one, historians of doctrine have observed that Anselm's motif is at home in the medieval penitential system[14] and that it reflects the backdrop of feudalism and the feudal lord to whom the vassals owe service and honor.[15]

Second, the satisfaction motif deals only with individuals, and it says little if anything about structural or systemic problems. The significance of this point becomes evident only after one recalls that Christus Victor envisions a confrontation of reigns and the structures that represent them — reign of God versus reign of evil in cosmic perspective, church versus empire in the earthly, historical realm. While the sin(s) of individuals are certainly included within the evil/sin confronted by narrative Christus Victor, this motif is also much more than a way to deal with individuals or individual sin. Narrative Christus Victor envisions structures confronting structures, even as the structures clearly include individuals. This structural dimension is hardly surprising when one recalls that Christus Victor addressed a world in which it was not assumed that the social order was governed by the church. In contrast, Anselm wrote in a time when church was assumed to encompass the social order, and God's providence (the reign of God) was assumed to be expressed through the course of the social order. Thus, in Anselm's imagery, with the social order under control

14. Reinhold Seeberg, *Text-Book of the History of Doctrines,* two volumes bound in one, trans. Charles E. Hay (Grand Rapids: Baker, 1961), vol. 2, p. 69; Jaroslav Pelikan, *The Growth of Medieval Theology (600-1300),* The Christian Tradition: A History of the Development of Doctrine, vol. 3 (Chicago: University of Chicago Press, 1978), p. 143; George Huntston Williams, *Anselm.*

15. H. D. McDonald, *The Atonement of the Death of Christ in Faith, Revelation, and History* (Grand Rapids: Baker, 1985), pp. 163-64; Carl E. Braaten, "The Christian Doctrine of Salvation," *Interpretation* 35, no. 2 (April 1981): 124; Southern, *Saint Anselm: A Portrait in a Landscape,* pp. 221-27.

of God and no longer confronted by the church, it is quite understandable how Anselm's imagery deals only with components of the sin of individuals and does not deal with the structural (systemic) dimensions of sin. These observations constitute a second way that Anselm's motif fits the particular conditions of the medieval church rather than the context of the early church.

Third, Anselm's *Cur Deus Homo* says almost nothing about the particulars of the life and the deeds of Jesus. Anselm depicted Jesus as the God-man, using the categories of humanity and deity from Nicea and Chalcedon. Aside from the obvious references to Jesus' death, *Cur Deus Homo* contains no reference to the life or the deeds of Jesus other than to state that in addition to the satisfying death, there were also "many other reasons" for Jesus

> to be like men and to dwell among them without sin, but these are more easily and clearly seen by themselves in his life and actions than by rational demonstration alone before any experience. For who can set forth how necessarily, how wisely, it was done, when he, who was to redeem men and to lead them back by his teaching from the way of death and ruin to the way of life and blessedness, moved among men, and, in that very association, presented himself as an example, while by word he taught them how to live? But how could he give himself as an example to the weak and mortal, to teach them not to draw back from justice on account of injuries or insults or sufferings or death, if they did not recognize that he himself felt all these things?[16]

George Williams cites this passage as evidence that Anselm did not neglect imitation of the obedient Christ "even before his death," "while His death itself is taken as the climax of a life of utter obedience."[17] I must observe, however, that whatever the teachings or example of Jesus were that Anselm had in mind, they were not integral to the atoning work of Jesus. It seems that this kind of non-reference to the particularity of Jesus fits the specific

16. Anselm, "Why God Became Man," in *A Scholastic Miscellany: Anselm to Ockham*, ed. and trans. Eugene R. Fairweather, The Library of Christian Classics (Philadelphia: Westminster, 1956), p. 161 (II.xi).

17. George Huntston Williams, *Anselm*, p. 52.

context of the imperial church, in contrast to the early church, whose orientation by the narrative of Jesus distinguished it from world.

When the church comes to accept the social order and to see the structures of the social order (such as political authority) as a means of furthering the church and expressing church concerns, then ethics are derived more from the social order than the specific narrative of Jesus. Returning to the sword as the primary example, rather than opposing the sword, the church came to rationalize the sword as a means to defend or extend Christ's church or the now Christianized social order in which the church was at home. It is in the context of this church that Anselm's atonement imagery replaced Christus Victor. The point is that if one wanted to construct an ethic for the church of how the church looked in contrast to the world, Anselm's atonement imagery would be of little help. It simply does not supply the specifics of Jesus that would guide the church in posing a significant contrast to the world. Since narrative Christus Victor sketched above as a biblical and early church construct does supply the basis of that contrast, it appears once again that Anselm's atonement imagery is specific to the medieval church and virtually irrelevant to the early church.

Another way to talk about the absence of the specifics of Jesus in Anselmian atonement is to say that it separates salvation from ethics. Except for the idea of innocent suffering, which will be dealt with in the chapters on feminist and womanist approaches to atonement, satisfaction atonement separates salvation from ethics. Understanding the relationship of the sinner to God in terms of a legal transaction whose conditions require a once-for-all death provides little if any guidance for the ethics — the *Christ*ian life — of the sinner whose debt has been paid. That is, when salvation means to have one's debt paid that was owed to God, salvation is understood apart from any effect or impact that it has on the subsequent life of the saved individual.[18] Salvation in terms of a legal transaction is salvation separated from ethics involved in the concrete, historical life of the saved individual.[19] In fact, it might even be argued that this motif assumes

18. One point sometimes argued to defend satisfaction atonement against the charge that it poses an abusive image for women is to argue that as the divine Son, Jesus' actions are not to be imitated because he had a mission that is not our mission. I suggest that that argument makes even more clear the separation between salvation and ethics that exists in the satisfaction atonement motif.

19. This separation of salvation from ethics is also true in the penal version of satisfaction atonement that was developed by later Protestantism.

the ongoing sinfulness (failure) of the sinner and provides an understanding of atonement where grace covers the penalty of that sin. This approach to atonement reflects a church that has reached accommodation of violence within the social order, a church in which the Christian life of ordinary lay people resembles the minimal expectations of polite society. It is the "religious," who follow the councils of Jesus' teaching, from whom more is expected than normal life in society.[20]

These observations about satisfaction atonement imagery in no way mean that Anselm or these formulas oppose ethics, or are incompatible with attempts to articulate a Christian ethic. It is rather that the ahistorical, legal transaction allows ethics to appear in another part of the theological outline, where it is intrinsically separated from what one says about Jesus' life and teaching. The formulas are compatible with an ethic that expresses the exigencies of the social order.

The atonement construct that I have called narrative Christus Victor clearly has roots in the New Testament in general, and in the narrative of Jesus in particular. Further, it reflects the specific ecclesiological context of the early church into the second century. That atonement theology in the post–New Testament era did not develop along the lines of narrative Christus Victor but instead followed the path that passed through Anselm is in part due, I submit, to the church's evolutionary shift toward accommodation of the social order, in particular its accommodation of violence. The theology of Anselm is a theology specific to a church that has separated ethics from salvation and the saving work of Jesus.

Connecting narrative Christus Victor to a pre-Constantinian ecclesiology heightens the contrasts previously indicated between it and the satisfaction images. It is in the church fused with the social order, in which ethics became detached from Jesus, that satisfaction atonement the-

---

20. While some version of Anselm's satisfaction theory has been the majority view of both Catholics and Protestants, it has engaged in a long-running conversation with the moral influence theory that Abelard (1079-1142) posed as an alternative to it. In the moral influence theory the problem concerns the distorted image sinners have of God, as they perceive God more as a harsh Judge than a loving Father. When the Father gives his Son to die, the death of Jesus then demonstrates God's supreme love for sinners, who consequently cease rebelling and turn toward God when God's love is perceived. Although more intrinsically inclined toward an ethical dimension than the satisfaction theory, the moral influence motif also focuses on the death of Jesus and fails to make use of any particular aspect of the life or teaching of Jesus.

ories came to the fore. The sword provides perhaps the most easily understood example of this separation of ethics from salvation. When the church accepted the sword and acquiesced to the imperial army fighting in the name of Christ and under a banner bearing the cross, in essence the church had shifted the orientation of its ethics from Jesus to the exigencies of the social order. On the other hand, narrative Christus Victor corresponds to an ecclesiology of church whose mission is to make visible the reign of God within the social order. Since the social order presumably does not reflect the nonviolence of Jesus, this church functions as a countercultural movement, whose ethics display the difference between the reign of God and the social order.

The observations in this section are the first round of the discussion of satisfaction atonement as a function of post-Constantinian, medieval ecclesiology. A second round of this discussion appears in Chapter 7.

Christology

The forgoing analysis of atonement theology has a counterpart in Christology. Anselm's satisfaction motif draws on Chalcedonian Christology, which also emerged in the church after Constantine.

In the phrase that represents the heart of the Nicene creed, Jesus is called *homoousios*, that is, "one substance" or "one being," with the Father. Chalcedon's key phrase identifies Jesus as "fully God and fully man." These formulas have been granted the status of being general or universal, above-the-exigencies-of-history confessional statements that all right-thinking Christians everywhere should espouse as the foundation of Christian faith. It is Chalcedon's terms of "God" and "man" that are in the title of Anselm's *Why the God-man*. However, as was the case for satisfaction atonement, I suggest that rather than stating a universal view, these formulas reflect the particular context of the church in which they achieved the status of dogma.

A first point concerns the philosophical categories and world picture of Nicene-Chalcedonian Christology. These formulas assume Greek philosophical, ontological categories and a world picture of a hierarchical universe. Our world picture does not assume the philosophical categories and world picture of Nicea-Chalcedon. Such categories and world picture do not make Nicea and Chalcedon intrinsically wrong as statements about Jesus or invalidate their historic contribution to our understanding of Jesus. However, identifying the Greek philosophical categories which they assume and indicating that the fourth-century world picture differs from our own already points to their particular historical specificity and the particular — not universal or general — character of those conciliar statements.

While our worldview does not generally use the categories and world picture of Nicea and Chalcedon, another dimension of these formulas actually presents a more problematic feature. Recall that Nicea's central claim is that Jesus is "one substance" or "one being" with the Father. Recall that the formula of Chalcedon proclaimed Jesus as "fully God and fully man." With awareness of the nonviolent character of the reign of God made visible in the narrative of Jesus and expressed in narrative Christus Victor, I simply ask, "What is there about the formulas of Nicea and Chalcedon that expresses the character of the reign of God, in particular its nonviolent character?" "What is there about these formulas that can shape the church that would follow Jesus in witnessing to the reign of God in the world?" Answer: virtually nothing. If all we know of Jesus is that he is "one substance with the Father," and that he is "fully God and fully man," there is nothing there that expresses the ethical dimension of being Christ-related, nothing there that would shape the church so that it can be a witness to the world. When these formulas serve as the summary touchstone of Christian faith, there is nothing of the particularity of Jesus to enable the Christ-related person to shape the church as an extension of Jesus' presence in the world. Rather, the would-be disciple of Jesus, who envisions a church that reflects the reign of God in contrast to the world, must turn elsewhere, to the narrative of Jesus as it is depicted in the Gospels. As seems self-evident, that narrative constitutes the basis of narrative Christus Victor.

But beyond recognizing that the classic formulas do not further a non-violent perspective, there is also a positive ecclesiological correlation. Similar to the case argued for satisfaction atonement, the formulas of Nicea and Chalcedon specifically reflect the ecclesiological context in which they emerged as the presumed general touchstone of Christian theology. Although the Council of Nicea promulgated the Nicene Creed in 325, the Creed did not become widely held until sometime after the Council of Constantinople repeated it in 381. The Council of Chalcedon did not issue its formula until 451. The important point to note is that both of these formulas follow the legalization of Christianity by the Emperor Constantine.

By the time Constantine legalized Christianity, the church was far along in the series of evolutionary changes that eventuated in its identification with the social order. These changes included the transition from a church that was a dissident and persecuted minority, clearly distinct from the empire, to a church that identified the success of its affairs with the course of the social order, and the consequent participation in the sword of the emperor.

I suggest that it is the church which no longer specifically reflected Jesus' teaching about nonviolence and his rejection of the sword that can proclaim christological formulas devoid of ethics as the foundation of Christian doctrine. The abstract categories of "man" and "God" in these formulas allow the church to accommodate the sword and violence while still maintaining a confession about Christ at the center of its theology. Keeping the narrative-oriented description of Jesus from the New Testament as the foundation of belief would challenge rather than accommodate the church symbolized by Constantine.[21]

A narrative Christology that made visible Jesus' life and teaching would challenge rather than support the church that proclaimed the formulas of Nicea and Chalcedon as the foundation of faith. Narrative Christus Victor based on the Gospels and sketched above is such a Chris-

---

21. It has been argued that the existence of preliminary versions of Nicene terminology well before 325 and the fact that the Creed was not widely accepted as normative orthodoxy until well after 325 absolve the Creed from the link to the imperialization of the church that I have described (Daniel H. Williams, "Constantine, Nicaea and the 'Fall' of the Church," in *Christian Origins: Theology, Rhetoric and Community,* ed. Lewis Ayres and Gareth Jones [London and New York: Routledge, 1998], pp. 124-31; Thomas Finger, "Christus Victor and the Creeds: Some Historical Considerations," *The Mennonite Quarterly Review* 72, no. 1 [January 1998]: 33-40). I counter that the evolutionary changes by which the church became associated with the imperial order began already in the second century and that changes in theology were also gradual and evolutionary. Thus finding what became Nicene terminology before 325 and a protracted process of acceptance after 325 merely points to the evolutionary character of the changes. And the further along one places the full acceptance of Nicene Christology, the more evident it becomes that that theology reflects a church that accepts it as normative. As a parallel modern argument, I would ask whether any historian or philosopher would argue that Adam Smith's capitalism did not reflect the social context of eighteenth-century England, that Karl Marx's economic theology did not reflect his nineteenth-century English context, or that twentieth-century liberation theology is not shaped by the Latin and South American context in which it emerged. It should be no less evident that for Christological formulas of the fourth and fifth centuries, we should ask "how" rather than "whether" they are shaped by and reflect their social context.

tology. It identifies Jesus as the one who makes present the reign of God, and characterizes God's rule in terms of the acts and the teaching of Jesus. If rejection of violence is genuinely a concern, then the place to begin envisioning and articulating a Christology for the church committed to nonviolence is not Christendom's formulas developed after the church had come to accommodate the sword and after it had come to identify the course of its affairs and God's providence with the cause of the Roman empire. Rather, the theological beginning point for a Christology that makes clear Jesus' rejection of the sword is the New Testament narrative of Jesus. It is here that one finds such things as Jesus' teaching about loving enemies, his challenges to the wealthy and his concern for the poor, his acts and teaching that raise women toward equality with men and raise the status of racially mixed Samaritans, his nonviolent confrontation of oppressive structures and conditions, his chastisement of Peter after he hacked off the ear of the high priest's servant, and ultimately his nonviolent confrontation of death. This New Testament narrative, which corresponds to narrative Christus Victor, is common to all Christians. Might reluctance to espouse it as an ecumenical formula, rather than the creed of Nicea, stem from the narrative's rejection of the sword, whose exercise has been so central to Christendom's experience?

The difference between the ontological definitions of the fourth- and fifth-century statements and a narrative-oriented identification of Jesus is more than a choice of methodology or of worldviews, and it is not just an assertion of the Bible over tradition. The difference really concerns the nature of Christian faith and what it means to be a Christian, a Christ-identified person. The New Testament's narrative of Jesus is where one learns that rejection of violence is intrinsic to Jesus' mission and to the reign of God, which his person and work made visible.[22] While the formulas from the councils of the fourth and fifth centuries do not deny this element of Jesus' teaching and life, they do render it invisible.

Does specifying the absence of ethics and their capacity to accommodate the sword in and of itself render the Nicene and Chalcedonian formulas invalid or intrinsically wrong? No, certainly not. These formulas pro-

---

22. A recent, short statement on the intrinsically nonviolent character of Jesus and the reign of God is Richard B. Hays, *The Moral Vision of the New Testament: Community, Cross, New Creation: A Contemporary Introduction to New Testament Ethics* (New York: HarperCollins, 1996), pp. 317-46.

vide answers to the important questions of whether Jesus is of God and of humanity. In fact, if one is asking these christological questions in terms of Greek philosophical, ontological categories and wants the answer shaped within a fourth-century worldview, then the answers of Nicea and Chalcedon are valid answers, and perhaps the best answers within the assumed categories. Any discussion of Christology must eventually address these considerations. The important points, however, are two. Recognition of their capacity to accommodate the sword renders them an inadequate foundation for a Christology that is cognizant of Jesus' rejection of the sword, while recognizing their particular location in time and history makes it inappropriate to elevate them to the status of a universally recognizable and uncontestable foundation that presumes to transcend all issues of time and historical context. As was the case for atonement, recognition of the particular character and orientation of the christological formulas then opens the way to envisioning other possible, and potentially more appropriate answers.

Conclusion

These observations on ethics and ecclesiology reflect an agenda focused by nonviolence at several levels. At the most obvious level, it is apparent that the story of Jesus depicted in the Gospels is a story of nonviolence and nonviolent resistance. If Jesus makes the reign of God present and visible, the Gospels' narratives of Jesus show that the reign of God confronts the rule of evil nonviolently. The same point emerges from Revelation's depiction of the confrontation between church and empire, and reign of God versus rule of Satan. In Revelation, the reign of God conquers through the death and resurrection of Jesus, not through the sword and military power. This observation is true whether one looks at the historical level of church and empire or the cosmic, apocalyptic imagery of reign of God and rule of Satan. The supposed battle scenes were not military battles, but symbolic statements about the meaning of the resurrection of Jesus, namely that in the resurrection the reign of God is revealed as already victorious over the forces of evil that harassed the church.

The nonviolent assumption of narrative Christus Victor appeared in yet another way when we observed that it eventually faded from view when the church began to identify with the social order and to accommodate the sword. It is evident that narrative Christus Victor corresponded to the church that was pacifist and would challenge the church that espoused the sword. In contrast, Anselm's satisfaction atonement reflects the church that accommodated the emperor's sword.

An assumption of nonviolence also shapes interpretations of the history of doctrine for both atonement and christological imagery. Church history has long described the evolution of the early church from persecuted minority to majority religion of a Christian empire and the accompanying change in the church from a pacifist stance to one that accommodated the sword in defense of church and social order fused with the church. Observing this process from a perspective that assumes the appropriateness of accommodating violence, the standard account of these developments is accepted as a self-evident statement of gain and maturation of the church. However, from the perspective of the nonviolence of Jesus as depicted in the Gospels and Revelation, it becomes evident that the standard account is one that opts to accommodate violence. The nonviolent perspective then also makes one aware of the extent to which developments of doctrine, such as the emergence of formulas of Christology and atonement devoid of ethics, reflect the assumptions of the church that accommodated violence rather than those of the church of narrative Christus Victor, which is nonviolent.

Together, these biblical, historical, and theological observations all point to the conclusion that narrative Christus Victor is an atonement image that has nonviolence as an intrinsic characteristic and that reflects the ecclesiological stance of the church prior to the events symbolized by Constantine. In contrast, the satisfaction motif given articulate form by Anselm does not assume nonviolence. It reflects the church that became fused with the social order, and it accommodates violence. It is not that satisfaction motif promotes violence per se.[23] Rather, this motif lends itself to easy accommodation of violence, and projects little that specifically opposes violence.

These considerations point to the need for a theology that takes seriously Jesus and his work but renders much more difficult the accommodation of violence so evident in the theology of Christendom. This book offers narrative Christus Victor as such an approach to atonement and to

---

23. The exception to this statement is the image of passive, innocent submission to violence, which is dealt with in Chapter 5.

Christology — one that emerges directly from the New Testament's narrative but does not pass through the violence-accommodating formulas and motifs of traditional theology of atonement and Christology.

It is also the case that we have only begun to see the unique dimensions and the nonviolent dimensions of narrative Christus Victor in contrast to the violence-accommodating dimensions of other atonement images. These dimensions will be clear when narrative Christus Victor is put in conversation with other theologies in following chapters. The discussion of violence and nonviolence relative to atonement motifs in this chapter has presumed primarily the overt violence of the sword. The next chapter introduces racism, a form of systemic violence, and underscores the importance of social location in the discussion of atonement theology. It will become apparent that the nonviolent atonement motif of narrative Christus Victor finds some brothers and sisters in black theology.

4 Black Theology on Atonement

Introduction

The formal beginning of black theology as a theological movement can be dated to a full-page ad that the National Committee of Negro Churchmen placed in *The New York Times* of July 31, 1966. This theological manifesto "was the first attempt in U.S. history to relate the gospel of Jesus to the black community's need for power."[1] Three years later James Cone published the first book-length statement of black theology, his now classic *Black Theology and Black Power*.[2]

When it first emerged in the late 1960s, black theology developed out of the black church and it spoke to the black church with a two-pronged agenda. It was a response to black power militants, who rejected Christianity because they saw it as the oppressive religion of white folks. Black theology provided an answer to black power. Black theology took black power's critique of white society and showed how the story of Jesus was a story that challenged the white status quo and supported the confrontations provoked by civil rights marches. But black theology also challenged the black church, which had generally accepted the gospel of white theology that

---

1. Dwight N. Hopkins, *Introducing Black Theology of Liberation* (Maryknoll, N.Y.: Orbis Books, 1999), p. 7. Hopkins provides a good, book-length introduction to black theology.

2. James H. Cone, *Black Theology and Black Power* (New York: Seabury, 1969; reprinted Maryknoll, N.Y.: Orbis Books, 1997).

supported the continued marginalization of African Americans.[3] These two agenda items meant, in effect, that black theology wedded Malcolm X's militant critique of white American society to Martin Luther King, Jr.'s Christian gospel.[4]

But black theology addresses more than the black church. It also speaks to white Christians, presenting a profound critique of white theology that does not yet recognize its whiteness. Black theology challenges the presumed general or universal theology inherited from European history to acknowledge its whiteness — its accommodation and support of both the overt violence of slavery and the systemic violence of racism and presumed white supremacy throughout United States history.

Black theology brings a new, particular perspective to the discussion of atonement. This perspective makes apparent the significance of social location, namely whether one is identified with the prevailing social order or stands in opposition to it. Second, it makes the element of racism, a form of systemic violence, an integral dimension of the atonement discussion.

First-Generation Black Theology: James Hal Cone[5]

The name most often connected with the founding of the black theology movement is James Heil Cone. Cone's development of theology grows directly out of his location in the black community, and its profound difference from white society.

---

3. James H. Cone, *For My People: Black Theology and the Black Church* (Maryknoll, N.Y.: Orbis Books, 1984), pp. 10-18, 32-39, 54-62, 79-84, 101-5; Hopkins, *Introducing Black Theology,* pp. 15-48.

4. James H. Cone, *For My People,* pp. 5-10; Hopkins, *Introducing Black Theology,* pp. 5, 8-10, 38-41.

5. Different versions of the discussion of James H. Cone appeared in J. Denny Weaver, "Theology in the Mirror of the Martyred and Oppressed: Reflections on the Intersections of Yoder and Cone," in *The Wisdom of the Cross: Essays in Honor of John Howard Yoder,* ed. Stanley Hauerwas, Chris K. Hauerwas, Harry J. Huebner, and Mark Thiessen Nation (Grand Rapids: Eerdmans, 1999), pp. 409-29, and in Chapter 5 of my *Anabaptist Theology in Face of Postmodernity: A Proposal for the Third Millennium,* with a foreword by Glen Stassen, The C. Henry Smith Series, vol. 2 (Telford, Pa.: Pandora Press U.S.; copublisher Herald Press, 2000).

African American Particularity

In *God of the Oppressed*,[6] Cone's construction of a comprehensive black theology, he described his theological roots in the African-American experience, particularly in the soil of the Macedonia African Methodist Episcopal Church in Bearden, Arkansas. One dimension of the black experience was exclusion from Christianity as practiced by white folks. The white church in Bearden affirmed faith in Jesus Christ (the same Jesus worshiped in the black church), but excluded blacks socially as well as from Sunday morning worship. Since they did not engage in rape and lynchings of African Americans, these white folks considered themselves good people, and many attended church regularly and considered themselves faithful servants of God. Yet they did everything in their power to define black reality. They taught that "God created black people to be white people's servants," which meant that blacks were "*expected* [emphasis Cone's] to enjoy plowing their fields, cleaning their houses, mowing their lawns, and working in their sawmills." Black people were also expected to attend segregated schools, sit in the balcony at the movies, drink from a "colored" water fountain, and much more. When blacks got out of their "place," that is, objected to their subservient status, it meant being beaten by the town cop and spending time in jail.[7]

In contrast to the exclusion and suppression experienced from the white church, the Macedonia A.M.E. Church filled Cone with feelings of and aspirations for freedom. "Through prayer, song, and sermon, God made frequent visits to the black community in Bearden." They received reassurance of God's concern for their well-being and safety. And as God's Spirit visited their worship, they "experienced a foretaste of their 'home in glory,'" a sample of the eschatological reality of the otherworldly home identified with heaven.[8] Quite obviously, the experiences of African Americans in the African-American community differed from the experiences of Anglo Americans who lived in a predominantly white society. Cone's experience as a black theologian began in the black community and in the black church, so that black theology is shaped by the reality of what it

---

6. James H. Cone, *God of the Oppressed*, rev. ed. (Maryknoll, N.Y.: Orbis Books, 1997).

7. James H. Cone, *God of the Oppressed*, pp. 2-3. See also James H. Cone, *For My People*, ch. 1.

8. James H. Cone, *God of the Oppressed*, p. 1.

means for the black church to live in a "society dominated by white people."[9] The ground on which Cone stands to write black theology as Christian theology is very different from the ground of those who produced what the predominantly white church calls Christian theology.

The shared history and culture of the black church provide a sense of community and make it determinative for black theology. The black church provides a worship tradition, a music tradition, and a preaching tradition, all of which shape black theology and find expression in it both in form and in content. For obvious examples of the black church as a resource in Cone's theology, note the "testimony" of *My Soul Looks Back*[10] and the development of perspective between his *A Black Theology of Liberation*[11] and the later *God of the Oppressed.* In making the argument that liberation belonged to the essence of the gospel, *A Black Theology of Liberation* quoted frequently from Neo-Orthodox theologians, particularly Karl Barth, Rudolph Bultmann, and Paul Tillich. As some black critics pointed out, and as Cone came to agree, quoting all these Europeans fostered the idea that black theology depended on white and European theology for its credibility, and even that it was "white theology that was merely painted black."[12] In response, Cone wrote *God of the Oppressed,* a black theology of liberation whose sources came almost exclusively from African-American history and tradition. *God of the Oppressed* is Christian theology shaped by Cone's experience in the black church and his knowledge of African-American history. This experience in the black church is clearly a particular perspective from which to read the Bible and do theology.[13]

But naming that African-American perspective then does something to white folks and to the presumed neutral and general or universal theol-

9. Cone, *God of the Oppressed,* p. 4.

10. Maryknoll, N.Y.: Orbis Books, 1986.

11. C. Eric Lincoln Series in Black Religion (Philadelphia: Lippincott, 1970).

12. James H. Cone, *My Soul,* pp. 60-61, quote p. 60; James H. Cone, *A Black Theology of Liberation: Twentieth Anniversary Edition* (Maryknoll, N.Y.: Orbis Books, 1990), p. 200.

13. For another example of the black church as a formative theological resource and shaper of vision, see Cone's description of how the black church shaped the vision of Martin Luther King, Jr. and was the foundation for his embrace of nonviolence as the way to resist evil (James H. Cone, *Martin and Malcolm and America: A Dream or a Nightmare* [Maryknoll, N.Y.: Orbis Books, 1991], pp. 121-31). See also Lewis V. Baldwin, *There Is a Balm in Gilead: The Cultural Roots of Martin Luther King, Jr.* (Minneapolis: Augsburg Fortress, 1991).

ogy inherited from European Christendom. White people begin to see precisely that their experience is *white* experience. And there then begins the process of identifying white experience and the white church as a particular perspective — rather than a presumed neutral or general or universal perspective — within which to read the Bible and to do theology. And one can start to ask how and when white experience is reflected in theology.

Reading the Bible Differently

Given the difference between black and traditional white history, it should not come as a surprise that when black people and white people read the Bible, they perceived it differently. As described by Cone, white theologians built logical and abstract systems and debated abstract issues like infant baptism, predestination versus free will, or the existence of God. They developed abstract systems like satisfaction atonement, which bases salvation on a legal transaction outside of history. White preaching and white theology defined Jesus as a "spiritual Savior," who delivered people "from sin and guilt," with salvation largely a "spiritual" matter and separated from the concrete realities of this world. This salvation was compatible with slavery, and continues in the faith that accommodates assumptions of white superiority. For most white theologians oppression of black people is not an important theological issue. With a few notable exceptions, they have debated abstract issues such as the relationship of Jesus' humanity to his deity, but have failed to describe relationships between Jesus, salvation, and concrete problems such as oppression or hunger. This theology reflects a society that does not perceive color — or the social conditions of people of color — as an important point of departure for theology.[14] Stated another way, much of theology by white theologians has separated or marginalized theology from ethics.

In contrast to an abstract idea of God and a spiritual savior, when African Americans read the Bible from within their history, Cone said, they saw a God involved in history, a God who liberated the slaves from Egypt and raised Jesus from the dead. With the exodus, "Yahweh is disclosed as the God of history, whose revelation is identical with his power to liberate the oppressed." The stories in the Bible reveal that "Yahweh is the God of

---

14. James H. Cone, *God of the Oppressed*, pp. 42-52.

justice who sides with the weak against the strong." Blacks believed that since God the liberator had delivered Israel from Egypt, then God would one day also deliver blacks from slavery and oppression. If God is a liberator, then Jesus, who reflects the God of Abraham, Isaac, Jacob, and the exodus, can be nothing other than liberator. When blacks read the Bible, they did not find a docile Jesus teaching a spiritual salvation. Rather they discovered Jesus the liberator, calling his people to freedom and working for their liberation. The salvation Jesus brought was not merely a spiritual transaction or an inner feeling. It was actual liberation from the conditions of oppression in which African Americans lived. Thus Cone called *liberation* the essence of black religion, both in its content (the Bible's stories of liberation) and its form (as the preacher's sermon calls the congregation into moments of actual liberation in the spirit). Christian theology as interpreted by Cone's black theology specifically envisions salvation in concrete social terms, and is always a word about liberation of the oppressed.[15]

Critique of Classic Theology

In Cone's analysis, the white reading of the Bible rests comfortably on the christological formulations of Nicea and Chalcedon and Anselm's satisfaction atonement. "What are we to make of a tradition," Cone asked, "that investigated the meaning of Christ's relation to God and the divine and human natures in his person, but failed to relate these christological issues to the liberation of the slave and the poor in the society?" Whether or not one believes that the supposedly universally applicable theology of the Nicene-Chalcedonian tradition lost the essence of the gospel, Cone said, it is clear that African Americans have a different history and a different theological orientation, both as Africans and as Christians.[16]

According to Cone's analysis, in themselves the generic categories of "humanity" and "deity" of classic Nicene-Chalcedonian theology lacked an explicit ethical content. This absence clearly set the stage for development of a theology that supported the "church's position as the favored religion of the Roman State," and did not address the conditions of the poor and the oppressed.

15. Cone, *God of the Oppressed,* pp. 57-76.
16. Cone, *God of the Oppressed,* pp. 104-5.

Few, if any, of the early Church Fathers grounded their christological arguments in the concrete history of Jesus of Nazareth. Consequently, little is said about the significance of his ministry to the poor as a definition of his person. The Nicene Fathers showed little interest in the christological significance of Jesus' deeds for the humiliated, because most of the discussion took place in the social context of the Church's position as the favored religion of the Roman State.[17]

In consequence, "Christology is removed from history, and salvation becomes only peripherally related to this world." Cone located this Nicene Christology in the social and political context of the church at the time of the Arian controversy. The Nicene Fathers in the time of Emperor Constantine were not slaves. Thus "it did not occur to them that God's revelation in Jesus Christ is identical with the Spirit of his presence in the slave community in the struggle for the liberation of humanity. They viewed God in static terms and thus tended to overlook the political thrust of the gospel."[18] This theology finds its modern continuation in the spiritualized salvation previously noted. Stated another way, this theology clearly separated theology from ethics. White theologians could claim Jesus as defined by the abstract formulas of Nicea and Chalcedon, thus claiming — correctly — to stand in the orthodox theological tradition, but at the same time own slaves or continue to participate in the oppression of slavery.

The link between liberation and reconciliation, which is clearly found in the New Testament, Cone said, has been cut for most of the history of Christian thought. He identified a twofold cause of the separation: "the influence of Greek thought, and the Church's political status after Constantine." Greek thought led to "rationalism." The church's status after Constantine "produced a 'gospel' that was politically meaningless for the oppressed. Reconciliation was defined on timeless 'rational' grounds and was thus separated from God's liberating deeds in history." Definitions of atonement developed "that favored the powerful and excluded the interests of the poor."[19]

Cone applied the critique specifically to both Anselm and Abelard.

17. Cone, *God of the Oppressed,* p. 107.
18. Cone, *God of the Oppressed,* p. 181.
19. Cone, *God of the Oppressed,* p. 211.

Anselm's soteriology built on the divine-human Jesus of Chalcedonian Christology, depicting salvation in terms of a spiritual transaction with God that spoke neither to the social conditions of African Americans in slavery nor to the oppressive character of racism in modern society. As Cone said, Anselm answered the question about the necessity of the God-man "from a rationalistic viewpoint that was meaningless for the oppressed." It was "a neat rational theory but useless as a leverage against political oppression. It dehistoricizes the work of Christ, separating it from God's liberating act in history."[20] A similar critique applied to Abelard. Cone wrote that what Abelard called an act of love "de-emphasized the objective reality of divine revelation," at the same time that Abelard "apparently failed to grasp the radical quality of evil and oppression."[21]

James Cone on Atonement

James Cone's critique of the abstract formulas of Anselm, Nicea, and Chalcedon had specific parallels to my critique of these formulas, except that where I said that they accommodated the violence of the sword, Cone said that they accommodated slavery and oppression. Given that perspective, it should not surprise us that Cone's approach to atonement features a reformulated Christus Victor, the atonement motif that was the dominant motif in the pre-Constantinian church.

Cone's treatment of atonement noted the absence of ethics in the classic formulas, namely Anselmian satisfaction or substitutionary atonement and the moral influence theory attributed to Abelard. In contrast to these formulas, Cone emphasized that reconciliation is "primarily an act of God." As an act of God, it embraces the entire world, changing sinful human beings into new creatures. Former slaves, alienated from God, now have a new relationship to God — they are free and reconciled to God. "Fellowship with God is now possible, because Christ through his death and resurrection has liberated us from the principalities and powers and the rules of this present world."[22] Cone stresses that reconciliation has an objective reality that is linked to "divine liberation." Reconciliation with

---

20. Cone, *God of the Oppressed*, pp. 211-12.
21. Cone, *God of the Oppressed*, p. 212.
22. Cone, *God of the Oppressed*, p. 209.

God happens "in history." It is "not mystical communion with the divine" nor a "pietistic state of inwardness bestowed on the believer." Thus "God's reconciliation is a new relationship with *people* [emphasis Cone's] created by God's concrete involvement in the political affairs of the world, taking sides with the weak and the helpless."[23] Israel is God's people because God "delivered them from the bondage of political slavery and brought them through the wilderness to the land of Canaan. . . . Liberation is what God does to effect reconciliation, and without the former the latter is impossible. . . . Reconciliation is that bestowal of freedom and life with God that takes place on the basis of God's liberating deeds." Thus for Cone, "the objective reality of liberation is a precondition for reconciliation," and it is clear that "God's salvation is intended for the poor and the helpless, and it is identical with liberation from oppression."[24]

Cone's reconstruction of an atonement motif anchored in the concrete reality of history builds on Christus Victor, the classical theory given renewed visibility by Gustaf Aulén. Cone noted that Christus Victor focused upon the "objective reality of reconciliation as defined by God's victory over Satan and his powers."[25] While Aulén's method was "nonpolitical," Cone said, the classical theory itself offers an opportunity for contemporary theology "to return to the biblical emphasis on God's victory over the powers of evil." The classical theory serves modern theology when it is "radicalized politically," and liberation and reconciliation can be "grounded in history and related to God's fight against the powers of enslavement." That is, the powers confronted and ultimately defeated by the resurrected Christ include not only the powers of evil mythically expressed in the figure of Satan but "earthly realities as well." Such powers confronted by Christ in cross and resurrection include "the American system," symbolized by government officials who "oppress the poor, humiliate the week, and make heroes out of rich capitalists"; "the Pentagon"; and the system symbolized in "the police departments and prison officials, which shoots and kills defenseless blacks for being *black* and for demanding their right to exist."[26]

23. Cone, *God of the Oppressed*, p. 209.
24. Cone, *God of the Oppressed*, pp. 209-10.
25. Cone, *God of the Oppressed*, p. 212.
26. Cone, *God of the Oppressed*, pp. 212-13.

Qualifying Christendom's Theology

James Cone's awareness that he does theology from within a particular so-cial location sheds a different light on the received theology of western Christendom. Its components of particular concern in this book are the Anselmian and Abelardian atonement images and the christological for-mulations of Nicea and Chalcedon. It has been frequently assumed that these formulations constitute the universal foundation or core "givens" for all Christian theology. In other words, they have served as the unques-tioned givens in Christology and atonement, as the accepted mainstream formulas that every Christian theology should acknowledge. This theol-ogy, as the assumed general theology for all Christians, would not have a qualifier such as "black" — precisely because it was assumed to be the general theology that applied to all Christians. Cone's analysis from an African-American perspective reveals the particularity of these formulas and therefore challenges their claim to universality.

Cone demonstrated that Nicene-Chalcedonian Christology, accompa-nied by Anselmian (or Abelardian) atonement, were formulations devel-oped by churchmen who belonged to the ruling class. And these formula-tions developed by the ruling class separated theology from ethics and allowed ethics to have a foundation other than Jesus. These formulations thus accommodated the dominance of the ruling class and neglected con-sideration of the oppressed. From Cone's perspective, that theology con-tinues in more recent times in the assumed mainstream theology that ac-cepts the status quo of the white power structure, the theology of those who claim to be Christian but who also rationalize white superiority. It is the theology that accommodated the violence of slavery and still continues with a spiritualized salvation that does not challenge racism and oppres-sion. From Cone's perspective, the presumed general theology of Christen-dom is not general. It has qualifiers. It is white theology or an oppression-accommodating theology or ruling-class theology or theology of the status quo. From the perspective of the nonviolent narrative Christus Victor of Chapter 2, it is violence-accommodating theology. Its assumed status as the general theology that made it the theology of the numerical majority of western adherents of Christianity served to camouflage its qualifiers or its particularity as the theology of the dominant class and the status quo.[27]

27. In spite of the supposed theology-in-general's link to the dominant class, Cone

To use the contemporary idiom of postmodernity, Cone's identifica-tion of the particularity and the qualifiers of Nicene, Chalcedonian, Anselmian theology and his dedication to developing black theology that is not dependent on Christendom's theology make his black theology a postmodern product, when postmodernity acknowledges the particularity of every theological claim to truth. In this sense, modernity is character-ized by the assumption that there is a universally accessible and uncon-testable, objectively verifiable common truth — if only we could locate its foundation.[28] Until the Enlightenment that foundation was sought within the church. With the Enlightenment, what has been called the seculariza-tion of western and North American society, there was a shift from looking for this uncontestable foundation within the church to seeking it outside the church. What is now currently called postmodernity is a recognition of the impossibility of obtaining an objectively verifiable, universally recog-nizable, uncontestable foundation of common truth. Although alarmists have decried this realization as mere relativism, the strident warning misses the mark. Postmodernity is not so much abandonment of the idea of universal truth as it is abandonment of the assumption that such truth will be readily apparent and thus accepted by anyone of right mind. Cone's black theology thus states the truth of Jesus the liberator in terms of African-American experience and in a way that lays bare Christendom's theology as a theology of the oppressors. This black theology is not relativ-istic, nor is it theology that claims to stand on a universally recognizable platform. It is rather theology with universal import, namely to express how people of any color, who reflect the story of Jesus the liberator, will challenge domination and oppression and seek to live justly in the world.

---

does not reject the traditional language outright. He believes that "Athanasius' assertion about the status of the *Logos* in the Godhead is important for the church's continued christological investigations." While it is clear, he said, that the "*homoousia* question is not a black question," the Nicene assertion that Jesus is one with the Father and Chalcedon's claim that Jesus is both human and divine are both "implied" in black theological language. But had Athanasius been a black slave in America, Cone continued, "I am sure he would have asked a different set of questions. He might have asked about the status of the Son in relation to slaveholders" (James H. Cone, *God of the Oppressed*, p. 13).

28. For a more extended discussion of my take on postmodernity, see the Introduction to my *Anabaptist Theology in Face of Postmodernity*.

James H. Cone and Narrative Christus Victor

Several parallels emerge between the approach to atonement sketched in Chapter 2 and Cone's analysis of Christology and atonement. One parallel is related to social location. The analysis of historical development and the construction of alternatives from a nonviolent (or peace church) perspective in Chapter 2 and James Cone's analysis of and posing an alternative to received European theology both have roots in religious traditions that were marginal with respect to the supposed normative, mainstream European theological tradition. Cone's roots are evident in the experiences of slavery, oppression, and racism that African Americans endured in North America. His black theology of liberation is theology from "the underside," theology from the side of the oppressed. Cone's view from the underside put the received theology in an entirely different light. It revealed how inherited European theology fit the context of the developing imperial church in which it emerged, and how it has functioned as the theology of the oppressors. Cone's black theology is a reconstruction of Christian theology that emerged from the "underside," the side of the oppressed, and offers critique of the tradition received from the dominant side.

The Mennonite peace church tradition that has nurtured my religious identity has roots in the Anabaptist reformation of sixteenth-century Europe. Anabaptists rejected the established church and through a variegated series of efforts developed a voluntary ecclesiology that rejected the intervention of civil authorities in churchly affairs.[29] By no means were all early Anabaptists pacifists,[30] but Anabaptism eventually developed a clear identity as a nonviolent movement. Since Anabaptists posed a theological and religious alternative to established political authority, they were a movement from the "underside." Rejecting the established or state church and posing an alternative church made Anabaptists a perceived, and in some cases an actual, threat to the social order. Several thousand Anabaptists be-

29. Since the 1970s the prevailing paradigm of Anabaptist origins has been one of multiple origins or "polygenesis." For a history from this perspective, see J. Denny Weaver, *Becoming Anabaptist: The Origin and Significance of Sixteenth-Century Anabaptism* (Scottdale, Pa.: Herald Press, 1987). Recently, Abraham Friesen has provided a convincing argument that Erasmus was the intellectual father of the Anabaptist movement. See Abraham Friesen, *Erasmus, the Anabaptists, and the Great Commission* (Grand Rapids: Eerdmans, 1998).

30. James M. Stayer, *Anabaptists and the Sword* (Lawrence, Kans.: Coronado Press, 1972).

came martyrs for their faith, often cruelly tortured and then executed by burning, drowning, or beheading at the hands of established church authorities, both Protestant and Catholic. Stories of these martyrs were preserved in *The Martyrs Mirror.*[31]

Martyrdom is no longer a reality for the contemporary heirs of the radical reformation in Europe and North America, and even the ill treatment experienced by conscientious objectors during the Civil War and in World War I are only fading memories.[32] These contemporary heirs of Anabaptism, now standing on the doorstep of the twenty-first century, have long since ceased to act like an underside movement and have imbibed deeply of modern culture and technology. Only the "plain" groups — such as Old Order Amish and Old Order Mennonites — continue to dress differently, reject aspects of modern culture, and retain some cultural distinctives as a sign of their faith commitment.

However, in my case the memory of a social location on the underside proved theologically significant. Although I am one of the heirs of Anabaptism thoroughly immersed in modern culture, awareness of free church ecclesiology, the pacifism that emerged, and the martyr tradition from sixteenth-century Anabaptism spurred me to ask whether these experiences might result in a different perspective on the theology of Christendom inherited from the churchly tradition that suppressed Anabaptists.[33] Chapters 2 and 3 display the results — a nonviolence-based critique of satisfaction atonement doctrine and construction of narrative Christus Victor as a nonviolent alternative.

James Cone's black theology of liberation developed from a very different underside and has a different agenda from my nonviolent atone-

---

31. Thieleman J. Van Braght, *The Bloody Theater or Martyrs Mirror of the Defenseless Christians,* trans. Joseph F. Sohm (Scottdale, Pa.: Mennonite Publishing House, 1950).

32. For Civil War experiences, see Theron F. Schlabach, *Peace, Faith, Nation: Mennonites and Amish in Nineteenth-Century America,* The Mennonite Experience in America, vol. 2 (Scottdale, Pa.: Herald, 1988), pp. 177-82, 189-93. On World War I, see James C. Juhnke, *Vision, Doctrine, War: Mennonite Identity and Organization in America 1890-1930,* Mennonite Experience in America, vol. 3 (Scottdale, Pa.: Herald Press, 1989), pp. 208-10, 218-41.

33. An initial beginning of an answer to this question came from John Howard Yoder's "relativizing" of the Nicene and Chalcedonian Christology and his systematic critique of Anselmian atonement in his *Preface to Theology: Christology and Theological Method* (Elkhart, Ind.: Goshen Biblical Seminary; distributed by Co-op Bookstore, 1981), pp. 120-58, 206-43. "Relativizing" is Yoder's own term for his treatment of Nicea and Chalcedon in *Preface.* See John H. Yoder, "That Household We Are," unpublished paper (1980).

ment theology. But from these twin critiques, which were marginal in different ways and to different degrees, there emerged a perspective with significant parallels regarding the mainstream theological tradition of Christendom. Both Cone's critique and my own were explicitly Christian and, as such, they made use of the particularity of Jesus in the New Testament.[34] I stressed the particularity of Jesus' rejection of the sword; Cone described the particularity of Jesus' acts as liberator. And from that use of the particularity of Jesus, both critiqued the categories of the classic formulas. When they are viewed from stances in the "margins," it is clear that the classic formulations use abstract categories, which separate theology from ethics and enable adherents to claim Jesus on the one hand while acting out an ethics that is not based on the particularity of Jesus. The nonviolent critique made explicit how the classic formulas accommodated the sword; the critique from black theology showed their accommodation of slavery and racism. Both supposedly marginal analyses linked the loss of the New Testament narrative and the emergence of the abstract categories of classic thought to the changes in the church symbolized by Constantine. And in their reconstruction of an alternative to the classic theology, both of the new theologies stressed the narrative about Jesus, and both anchored their new understandings of atonement in a reformulation of the Christus Victor atonement motif that was the dominant motif in the pre-Constantinian church.[35]

34. There is a common root for this christocentric emphasis in the parallel reconstructions made by Cone and myself. I reflect the influence of John H. Yoder, who studied with Karl Barth, while James Cone wrote his doctoral dissertation on Karl Barth. On the other hand, Cone also makes clear that since the original publication of *God of the Oppressed*, a "radical development" has taken place in his christological reflections. He no longer sees Jesus as "God's *sole* revelation. Rather he is an important revelatory event among many" (James H. Cone, *God of the Oppressed*, p. xiv).

35. Alongside these important parallels and points of agreement, the concept of violent resistance in the contemporary world is one important point of potential disagreement between narrative Christus Victor and black theology. African Americans and black theology have not spoken unanimously on this issue any more than have adherents of the peace churches. For response and dialogue with James H. Cone on the question of violence and resistance, see Weaver, *Anabaptist Theology in Face of Postmodernity*, pp. 138-40.

Second Generation Black Theology:
Garth Kasimu Baker-Fletcher[36]

Dwight N. Hopkins marks the rise of the second generation of black theology with the appearance in 1979 of articles by Jacquelyn Grant and Cornell West. "Both scholars," Hopkins said, "affirmed the groundbreaking role, vital necessity, and theological creativity of the first generation. But, at the same time, Grant and West raised strong criticisms and challenges."[37] Grant's "Black Theology and Black Women" challenged the invisibility of black women in black theology, while West's "Black Theology and Marxist Thought" pointed to a lack of social and economic analysis in black theology.[38] Thus the second generation of scholars in black theology both continue the agenda of the first generation but also claim their own distinct approach. "In a word, the second generation are both heirs to the black theological founders and groundbreakers in their own right."[39]

The constructive theology of Garth Kasimu Baker-Fletcher's *Xodus*[40] belongs to the second generation of black theology. It draws on popular culture as a source for liberation ethics.[41] In *My Sister, My Brother*,[42] written by Karen Baker-Fletcher and Garth Kasimu Baker-Fletcher, Xodus enters conversation with womanist theology. While the agenda of Xodus differs significantly from my work, with less clear parallels in construction than was true for James Cone, I still share some common concerns with Baker-Fletcher's Xodus. These include calling attention to the accommodation of violence (whether racism and slavery or war) in classic formulations, and a strong impetus to construct an alternative that is not dependent on the formulations of European Christendom as a presumed

---

36. A different version of this discussion of Garth Kasimu Baker-Fletcher's exodus appeared in Chapter 5 of my *Anabaptist Theology in Face of Postmodernity*.

37. Hopkins, *Introducing Black Theology*, p. 87.

38. These articles of Jacquelyn Grant and Cornell West are available in James H. Cone and Gayraud S. Wilmore, eds., *Black Theology: A Documentary History: Vol 1: 1966-1979* (Maryknoll, N.Y.: Orbis Books, 1993), pp. 418-33, 552-67.

39. Hopkins, *Introducing Black Theology*, p. 88.

40. Garth Kasimu Baker-Fletcher, *Xodus: An African American Male Journey* (Minneapolis: Fortress Press, 1996).

41. Hopkins, *Introducing Black Theology*, p. 91.

42. Karen Baker-Fletcher and Garth Kasimu Baker-Fletcher, *My Sister, My Brother: Womanist and XODUS God-Talk*, Bishop Henry McNeal Turner/Sojourner Truth Series in Black Religion, vol. 12 (Maryknoll, N.Y.: Orbis Books, 1997).

universal theology, and that reflects specifically the concerns for justice, liberation, and peace that are visible in the New Testament's narrative of Jesus.

Contextual Affinities

The X with which Xodus begins honors Malcolm X and articulates a parallel between biblical exodus and the modern exodus of African Americans from the "yoke of Eurocentricity." The word "Xodus" is a verbal linking of the critique of white society from Malcolm X with a Christian outlook. Xodus is Christian theology that expresses the liberating gospel of Jesus in terms of African and African-American expression, experiences, and tradition. Garth Kasimu Baker-Fletcher's agenda for Xodus journeying is "psychospiritual liberation," the "exodus of many peoples from the yoke of Eurocentricity," the search for "a place to stand that is not dependent on Euro-definitions of what is true, authoritative, and right."[43] Xodus is an emphatic answer to the rhetorical query, "Is our future that of complete and utter assimilation into Euro-Americanness, or are we to stand firm as a distinct 'Black' culture in the midst of the 'White' United States of America?"[44]

From its use of newly coined terms like "Xodus," or "disillragedeterminassion" or "remythification," and its expressive use of capitalized words, quotation marks, italics and boldface, the writing style itself of Xodus displays this independence of Eurocentric conventions. Written Xodus is "designed with the intent to bring to the *WRITTEN WORD*, something of the salty, tangy, pungent urgency and expressiveness which *is* BLACK ENGLISH."[45] "I will CAPITALIZE and *italicize* freely, all with the visual purpose of *demonstrating the inadequacy of English in its "standard" form.*"[46] This linguistic dimension of nurturing an identity independent of Eurocentric Christianity plays like the joyously flamboyant jazz version of my presumed standard academic English effort to construct narrative

---

43. Baker-Fletcher, *Xodus,* pp. 5, 6, 17.
44. Baker-Fletcher and Baker-Fletcher, *My Sister, My Brother,* p. 9.
45. Baker-Fletcher and Baker-Fletcher, *My Sister, My Brother,* p. 15.
46. Baker-Fletcher, *Xodus,* p. 6.

Christus Victor as a theology of atonement that poses an alternative to the violence-accommodating theology of European Christendom.

As was true for James Cone's black theology, the Xodus assertion of independence from Eurocentricity makes it a postmodern product. The exodus from Eurocentricity of which Baker-Fletcher's Xodus speaks is postmodern "because it seeks to overthrow the negative cultural imprisonment and imperialism of Europe and American while retaining (and this is often not noted) the positive aspects of democracy, personal autonomy, and technological advancement." Within postmodernism, one thus recognizes that the "tolerance" advocated by the authors of the Enlightenment applied only to Europeans — and barely even to them — and that the ideals proclaimed were spread to the rest of the world "wrapped in garments of deceit, hypocrisy, and cruelty."[47] The truth proclaimed by Xodus is very pointedly postmodern in its reflection of an African and African-American perspective, which simultaneously exposes the heretofore presumed universal truth as any of several European, North American, white perspectives.

But Xodus theology and Baker-Fletcher's passion and mission both to maintain and develop an African-American identity over against the European-derived culture of white America is much more than the mere preservation of a cultural and historical identity. Xodus is theology that matters. Theology articulates what we are committed to. *Xodus* constructs a theology that expresses how people who are "followers of Jesus"[48] should live justly in an unjust world, living as though the justice of God's reign is present in the world. In particular, Baker-Fletcher calls on black churches to become "holy Spaces of Xodus liberation."[49] Their mission is to nurture "both the spiritual life of individuals and communities, as well as the physical welfare of individuals and communities," who "teach everything that Jesus had commanded." That teaching includes

> the Sermon on the Mount (Matthew 5–7) and the Sermon on the Plain (Luke 7:17-49); any number of different "parables of the Kingdom"; the encounters with Nicodemus (John 3) and the rich young man (Matt.

47. Baker-Fletcher, *Xodus*, pp. 6, 7.
48. A part of Garth Kasimu Baker-Fletcher's self-designation is "follower of Jesus." Baker-Fletcher and Baker-Fletcher, *My Sister, My Brother*, p. 203.
49. Baker-Fletcher, *Xodus*, p. 182.

19:16-29); and that unforgettable prophetic passage about the sheep and the goats (Matt. 25:31-46). Jesus commanded a holistic gospel centered in intimate adoration and trust in God and expressed by loving actions of service to the spiritual and bodily needs of human beings.[50]

Xodus theology makes clear that ethics and theology are two different ways to express the same beginning assumptions. As Karen Baker-Fletcher and Garth Kasimu Baker-Fletcher say in the introduction to *My Sister, My Brother,* "This book is a Creative Space where systematic theology dances with ethics, the two intertwining and flowing into each other," and they appeal to comments of Katie Cannon in saying that the methodology "makes it possible for African American religious folk to see the tasks of theology and ethics as both fundamentally united and necessarily inseparable."[51]

This volume's impulse to develop a nonviolence-shaped theology of atonement that does not pass through the theological juncture of the violence-accommodating theology of satisfaction atonement finds a brother's voice in Garth Kasimu Baker-Fletcher's compulsion to develop an Xodus theology that speaks independent of presumed general, Eurocentric theology. Although in very different ways, these two projects both reflect an assumption about the intertwined and inseparable nature of theology and ethics, and have produced parallel observations concerning classic Christology and atonement.

Christology and Atonement

The constructive theology of Xodus spends little time dealing with the emphases of classic christological and atonement discussions. What discussion there is, however, makes clear the need to restructure Christology and atonement in ways that free these concepts from the capacity to accommodate injustice that characterizes the classic formulas.

Xodus requires developing an understanding of blackness. James Cone had written that blackness symbolizes "all victims of oppression who realize that their humanity is bound up with liberation from whiteness."[52]

---

50. Baker-Fletcher, *Xodus,* pp. 182-83.
51. Baker-Fletcher and Baker-Fletcher, *My Sister, My Brother,* pp. 2, 3.
52. James H. Cone, *Black Theology,* p. 7.

Baker-Fletcher deepens that definition to include "the ancient Kemetic notions of blackness as the primal symbol of the deep unconscious, the Universal Mind, Maat, Amenta (the underworld), and wisdom." Making more profound the concept of blackness in this way means that it is not limited to victims, but "is a positive spiritual force operating in all of humanity, nature, and the cosmos."[53]

Sin in Xodus understanding "means becoming aware of the ways in which Afrikans (male and female, rich and poor) are engulfed in a demonic system of whiteness/Euro-domination/oppression that has colonized both their bodies and their innermost thoughts, desires, and feelings." Consequently, following Jesus Christ in Xodus mode results in a twofold conversion. Baker-Fletcher described a first deliverance for himself and others that "came through hearing the word of Jesus Christ, accepting it, and becoming Christians." The second deliverance was to hear "the word of Blackness, which is a cry to leave Euro-dominated Space and return to God's affirmation of your Afrikan self. The second deliverance is a message of liberation."[54]

With this emphasis on blackness and deliverance from Euro-domination, it comes as no surprise that Jesus and God of Xodus are both black. In Xodus, resurrection represents the liberation of the "self from the shackles of Euro-dominated death" and "release of our inner captive so that we might rise to new life as self-affirming Afrikans." Baker-Fletcher calls this a "particularizing of traditionally Christian language,"[55] which impacts the image of both Jesus and God. "Jesus Christ embodied God. For Christians we embody Jesus. That means, for Afrikans, that Jesus and God are 'Black.'"[56]

At first glance, Baker-Fletcher implies, this particularizing of Christian salvation in terms of Xodus does seem "to negate the purported universal significance of Christian salvation and resurrection teachings."[57] He points

53. Baker-Fletcher, *Xodus*, p. 83 This assertion of the positive force and character of blackness does not demonize white. Whiteness is not cast as the opposite of blackness. What is being rejected is the attribution of negative connotations to black and positive connotations to white in western consciousness. In contrast, Baker-Fletcher forcefully develops positive connotations of black. See, for example, Baker-Fletcher, *Xodus*, pp. 83-85.

54. Baker-Fletcher, *Xodus*, p. 86.

55. Baker-Fletcher, *Xodus*, p. 88.

56. Baker-Fletcher, *Xodus*, pp. 88, 89.

57. Baker-Fletcher, *Xodus*, p. 88.

out, however, that for the early followers of Jesus, the real scandal was "the notion that the almighty, high, and omnipotent God would take on the limitation, weakness, and frailty of human flesh." When Christian salvation and resurrection thus take on an "Xodus flavor," that theology is "more in the spirit of the early Christian scandal of God embodying God-self (the doctrine of incarnation), than are any long-winded, boring dissertations of the universal significance of Christ."[58] Stated differently, Xodus Christology has no use for a supposed universal Christ that is actually like no one. Such a "universal Christ" would be a fundamentally unembodied Christ. Rather Xodus Christology focuses on the universal significance of the particular Christ who is black. The particular Christ who is black makes clear that liberation — including physical, material liberation — belongs to the gospel of Jesus Christ, and it condemns all exploitation, domination, and oppression carried out in the name of Christ. This particularizing of Christ as black does not "negate God for white folks, red folks, brown folks, or yellow folks. It is simply to affirm something that Euro-dominated Christianity refuses to entertain even to this day — that God can be, must be, and indeed is Black."[59]

Atonement in Xodus brings liberation. The cross reminds Christians of the "victory of Jesus of Nazareth over the power of death." "Within us should be an honoring of that sacrifice, of the kind of love that is willing to see a healing-salvific cause through to the end, even recognizing that the end might include death."[60] Xodus atonement rejects assumptions about the redemptive power of unmerited suffering. Jesus' work does not consist of unmerited suffering but rather is to open the possibilities for human beings to become new creatures. Referring explicitly to atonement, Baker-Fletcher states that

> our Afrikanity is theologically based on an Xodus doctrine of Atonement, which affirms God's color-fullness as an aspect of spiritual joy. Christ's death and resurrection were not to display the redemptive power of unmerited suffering, but to open up the possibilities for human beings to become 'God's new creation' (2 Cor. 5:17), for peace to be made between formerly warring peoples (Eph. 2:11-22), and for genu-

---

58. Baker-Fletcher, *Xodus*, pp. 88-89.
59. Baker-Fletcher, *Xodus*, p. 89.
60. Baker-Fletcher, *Xodus*, p. 82.

ine reconciliation to occur. Christians ought to be joyful about *these things*, not the suffering, pain, torture, and death of Jesus on a cross![61]

One of the particular dimensions of Xodus Christology is Jesus' rejection of violence. "If we [black churches] actually believe in the love of Jesus Christ, then it is time for us to demonstrate how God's Agapic love can produce a spirit of antiviolence" as a counter to the "plague of violence" that threatens life on earth. "As Martin Luther King, Jr., developed a program of nonviolence that combined the teachings of Jesus' Sermon on the Mount with the *satyagraha*-strategy of Mahatma Gandhi, so we must encourage *antiviolence*."[62] This antiviolence would occupy people with "refocusing energies and time on producing rather than destroying. More an attitude than a philosophy, antiviolence is an ethos and praxis. It is imperative to proclaim that the gospel of Jesus Christ is antiviolent, and that following Jesus confronts the plague of violence with this powerful medicine."[63]

In *My Sister, My Brother,* Garth Kasimu Baker-Fletcher appropriates Delores Williams's critique of sacrifice in traditional atonement doctrine, which has been linked to enforced surrogacy roles for African-American women.[64] Baker-Fletcher adds that "it seems to be a particularly 'male' construction within our community that one must be willing to 'die' for something in order for it to be valuable."[65] But "in XODUS," he writes, "we JOURNEY toward the future *following a living Jesus,* not tied to a Cross of death."[66] A part of his reconstruction of Christology included "Jesus as Conqueror," an image taken from the book of Revelation. This is an image of Jesus as the one who conquers evil, in contrast to the "nonviolent [that is, passive] Jesus of orthodoxy."[67]

The agenda of *Xodus* differs significantly from my work, and the parallels in construction are less clear than was true for the black theology of James Cone. Garth Kasimu Baker-Fletcher does not spell out a theory of atonement on the order of the project in hand. Yet Baker-Fletcher and I

61. Baker-Fletcher, *Xodus,* p. 188.
62. Baker-Fletcher, *Xodus,* p. 190.
63. Baker-Fletcher, *Xodus,* pp. 190-91.
64. Chapter 5 to follow discusses Delores Williams.
65. Baker-Fletcher and Baker-Fletcher, *My Sister, My Brother,* p. 103.
66. Baker-Fletcher and Baker-Fletcher, *My Sister, My Brother,* p. 104.
67. Baker-Fletcher and Baker-Fletcher, *My Sister, My Brother,* p. 106.

share some common concerns. These include calling attention to the accommodation of violence (whether racism and slavery or war) in classic formulations of atonement and Christology, and constructing an alternative that does not pass through the violence-accommodating answer inherited from the European theological tradition, and that does make ethical questions about justice, violence, and just peace integral to formulations of Christology and atonement. Narrative Christus Victor resonates with Baker-Fletcher's identification of the "imperative to proclaim that the gospel of Jesus Christ is antiviolent, and that following Jesus confronts the plague of violence with this powerful medicine."[68]

James H. Evans, Jr.'s *We Have Been Believers* lacks the Xodus insistence to create black theology free of European-derived culture. But it nonetheless expresses the central claim of black theology that theology and ethics are two forms of the same truth and that atonement and Christology should both reflect the liberating themes of the gospel.

> African-American Christians have claimed Jesus Christ as both liberator from social and political oppression and as mediator of the goodness of God and as victor over the cosmic forces of evil. . . . Black theologians have attempted to define the person and work of Christ so that black Christians might be able to claim both their personhood and their faith. Too often, however, the person and the work of Jesus Christ have been framed as opposites between which one must make a choice. A more fruitful approach is to see both the person and the work of Christ pointing to the demand to live the Christian life or to 'abide in him.'[69]

Conclusion

This brief engagement with black theology has expanded the discussion of violence and atonement considerably beyond the issues of the sword and war, which were the primary concern of narrative Christus Victor in Chapter 3. It has also changed our view of the inherited theology of Christendom. Pointing to black theology reveals how "white" and how "European"

68. Baker-Fletcher, *Xodus,* pp. 190-91.
69. James H. Evans, Jr., *We Have Been Believers: An African-American Systematic Theology* (Minneapolis: Fortress Press, 1992), pp. 96-97.

the presumed mainstream theological tradition has been, and reveals that it belongs to and has social location in a particular historical context rather than existing as an above-history, unquestioned, general or universal theology. Black theology points out that the atonement and christological formulas of Christendom's theological tradition accommodate not only violence of the sword but also slavery and the systemic violence of racism. To talk about atonement or about who Jesus is and what he did without specifically confronting those forms of violence is to continue an atonement and Christology that accommodate them. It is not a deviation from truth to point out the violence-accommodation and the whiteness of the inherited, presumed general theology of Christendom. Making that critique is actually a necessary part of the search to be more true to the gospel of Jesus Christ.

The discussion of violence in atonement theology is not complete with the discussion of black theology. The following chapter considers issues raised in feminist theology.

5 Feminist Theology on Atonement

Introduction

If black theology indicates that supposed general theology inherited from Christendom is actually white theology, it should not surprise us that feminist theology reveals that same theology's male-oriented character. Much of Christian theology has supported the superior status of men, and the dominance of men over women. After nonviolent and black theological analysis have demonstrated the way that classic atonement images and christological terminology have accommodated violence of the sword, slavery, and racism, in this chapter we will observe how those images have accommodated and supported violence against women.

Working from the context of the specific experiences of women, including recent recognition of the serious problem of physical abuse, theology in feminist perspective rejects the dominance of men over women, and advocates equality of women and men and shared authority between men and women. Feminist theology thus gives voice to and is shaped by the experiences of women who reject a subservient status vis-à-vis men. The feminist responses to male-dominated theology range along a broad spectrum of views, from evangelicals who argue from a high view of scripture that the Bible teaches the equality of women, to the rejection of Christian faith as irreformably patriarchal and male. Among those who remain Christian, there are multiple challenges to and rejections of the overwhelmingly male, patriarchal, and hierarchical characteristics ascribed to

God, as well as the general patriarchal and hierarchical character of western theology. These challenges engage both classic Christology and the accompanying dominant atonement motifs. This chapter considers a selection of such challenges. Since they arise from concerns about the systemic violence of patriarchy and male dominance as well as about physical violence against women, it is important to put nonviolent, narrative Christus Victor in conversation with the pointed concerns about atonement raised by feminists.

Feminist Theology on Atonement

Rosemary Radford Ruether

In a well-known essay on Christology, Rosemary Radford Ruether asks, "Can a Male Savior Save Women?"[1] The messianic mission of Jesus, Ruether wrote, focused on the coming reign of God, with a particular emphasis on "the vindication of the poor and the oppressed."[2] She then shows how this mission and the church's reflections about Jesus were transformed into what is now identified as "orthodox Christology" during the first five centuries of Christian history, when the Christian church evolved from a marginal sect within the Jewish renewal movements "into the new imperial religion of a Christian Roman Empire."[3] As a response to the original charismatic nature of Christian leadership, an institutional ministry of bishops developed to control those who spoke in the name of Christ. The decisive step in the "patriarchalization of Christology" occurred in the fourth century "with the establishment of the Christian Church as the imperial religion of the Christian Roman Empire." A political and religious hierarchy of being was put in place. "Just as the *Logos* of God governs the cosmos, so the Christian Roman Emperor, together with the Christian Church, governs the political universe; masters govern slaves and men govern women. . . .

1. The title of the chapter is "Christology: Can a Male Savior Save Women?" in Rosemary Radford Ruether, *Sexism and God-Talk: Toward a Feminist Theology* (Boston: Beacon, 1983), pp. 116-38. For a more popular version of the same discussion see Rosemary R. Ruether, *Introducing Redemption in Christian Feminism,* Introductions in Feminist Theology, no. 1 (Sheffield, U.K.: Sheffield Academic Press, 1998), ch. 6.

2. Ruether, *Sexism and God-Talk,* pp. 120-21, quotation from p. 120.

3. Ruether, *Sexism and God-Talk,* p. 122.

Christ has become the Pantocrator (All-Ruler) of a new world order." In this hierarchy, women are "regarded as humble members of the Christian body," but they cannot represent Christ because Christ is now understood as "founder and cosmic governor of the existing social hierarchy and as the male disclosure of a male God whose normative representative can only be male." And "only the male represents the fullness of human nature, whereas woman is defective physically, morally, and mentally." In consequence, the incarnation of God's word into a male is "an ontological necessity," and then, of course, only a male priest can represent Christ.[4]

This Christology described by Ruether, which developed as the church became the imperial religion of the Roman empire, is the previously encountered Nicene-Chalcedonian Christology that has been accorded supposedly general or universal status in the Christendom tradition. In Ruether's analysis, however, this Christology is not general or universal. It is theology that specifically reflects the hierarchical and patriarchal social order in which it developed. Identifying with this theology, Ruether believes, means acquiescing to its assumptions that the male is the normative human being while the female is somehow defective.

Ruether's answer is to return to the Jesus of the Gospels, whom she finds "remarkably compatible with feminism." Her depiction also bears strong similarity to the Jesus of narrative Christus Victor. As Ruether depicts Jesus, he spoke on behalf of marginalized and despised groups, he revised God language to use the familiar *Abba* name for God, he spoke of the Messiah as servant rather than king, he rejected the idea of dominant-subordinate relations among social groups, leaders, and followers. Women play important roles in Jesus' "vision of the vindication of the lowly in God's new order." And more. The important christological point, however, is that "theologically speaking, . . . the maleness of Jesus has no ultimate significance." But within the framework of the society shaped by patriarchal privilege in which Jesus lived, his maleness is significant. By his liberation of humanity and uplifting of the oppressed and lowly, he announced and displayed a "lifestyle that discards hierarchical caste privilege and speaks on behalf of the lowly." Similarly, "the femaleness of the social and religious outcasts who respond to him has social symbolic significance as a witness against . . . patriarchal privilege."[5] Thus "Jesus becomes paradig-

4. Ruether, *Sexism and God-Talk*, pp. 123-26.
5. Ruether, *Sexism and God-Talk*, pp. 135-37.

matic by embodying a certain message . . . good news to the poor, the confrontation with systems of religion and society that incarnate oppressive privilege, and affirmation of the despised as loved and liberated by God." With Jesus paradigmatic in this way, Ruether then suggested, "we must cease to isolate the work of Christ from the ongoing Christian community. . . . While Jesus is the foundational representative of this way of the cross and liberation, he is not its exclusive possibility. Each Christian must take up this same way and, in so doing, become 'other Christs' to one another. The church becomes redemptive community."[6]

Concerns about patriarchy and hierarchy and the presumed normativeness of the male in classic Christology have their counterparts in atonement theology. Ruether's brief remarks on atonement build on writings of several feminists, including Joanne Carlson Brown and Rebecca Parker, who are treated in this chapter, and Delores Williams, who is a subject of the following chapter. Ruether accepts the analysis of these writers, who argue that in traditional atonement doctrine, Jesus' death appears as a model of passive obedience to the Father's need to impose a mission of suffering, and who argue that unjust or innocent suffering can never be redemptive or salvific. Thus Ruether concludes that "Jesus did not 'come to suffer and die.' Rather Jesus conceived of his mission as one of 'good news to the poor, the liberation of the captive,' that is, experiences of liberation and abundance of life shared between those who had been on the underside of the dominant systems of religion and state of his time." Jesus' means was not killing the powers, "but rather to convert them into solidarity with those they had formerly despised and victimized." That mission was not focused on Jesus' death. While he realized that this mission would likely result in his death, "this is quite different from conceiving of crucifixion as something to be sought and accepted as a means of redemption. Rather we should say that redemption happens through resistance to the sway of evil, and in the experiences of conversion and healing by which communities of well-being are created."[7] Suffering and death are not redemptive. Rather, suffering is "the risk that one takes when one struggles to overcome unjust systems whose beneficiaries resist change. The means of redemption is conversion."[8]

6. Ruether, *Introducing Redemption*, p. 93.
7. Ruether, *Introducing Redemption*, pp. 104-5.
8. Rosemary Radford Ruether, *Women and Redemption: A Theological History* (Minne-

Rosemary Radford Ruether and Narrative Christus Victor

Ruether's observations concerning the evolving character of the church in the first five centuries, and the reflection of these changes in the christological formulas of Nicea and Chalcedon, have their clear counterparts in our earlier chapters. In Chapter 3 it was pointed out how the formulas of Nicea and Chalcedon accommodated the acceptance of the sword by Christians. Chapter 4 contained James Cone's assessment of the way these formulas reflected the ruling-class status of their authors and have acquiesced to racism and slavery throughout the history of Christianity.

Ruether's conclusions about atonement images and unjust suffering find a ready echo in narrative Christus Victor. Following sections develop in more depth these feminist challenges to classic atonement doctrine.

Joanne Carlson Brown and Rebecca Parker

One of the sharpest challenges to traditional atonement images is Joanne Carlson Brown and Rebecca Parker's well-known essay, "For God So Loved the World?"[9] According to Brown and Parker, women in North American society are conditioned to accept abuse. This acculturation has caused women to remain "silent for years about experiences of sexual abuse, to not report rape, to stay in marriages in which we are battered," and much more.[10] Brown and Parker claim that Christianity has been a central force in shaping this acceptance of abuse. In their view, the image of Christ on the cross teaches that suffering is redemptive, and that for women to be of value, they should likewise sacrifice themselves. If women pursue their own needs, it seems, they are in conflict with what it means to be a faithful follower of Jesus.[11]

---

apolis: Fortress Press, 1998), p. 279. Parallel comment on suffering as risk in Ruether, *Introducing Redemption*, p. 102.

9. Joanne Carlson Brown and Rebecca Parker, "For God So Loved the World?" in *Christianity, Patriarchy and Abuse: A Feminist Critique*, ed. Joanne Carlson Brown and Carole R. Bohn (New York: Pilgrim Press, 1989), pp. 1-30. A shorter version of this essay appears as Joanne Carlson Brown, "Divine Child Abuse?" *Daughters of Sarah* 18, no. 3 (Summer 1992): 24-28.

10. Brown and Parker, "For God So Loved," p. 2.

11. Brown and Parker, "For God So Loved," p. 2.

The situation is further complicated because Christian theology states that Jesus suffered in obedience to his Father's will. Brown and Parker use the image of divine child abuse to depict this suffering by Jesus at the behest of the Father. "Divine child abuse is paraded as salvific and the child who suffers 'without even raising a voice' is lauded as the hope of the world."[12] This interpretation of Jesus has persuaded many that lives of "self-sacrifice and obedience" are "the definition of faith identity," with resurrection as the promise that "persuades us to endure pain, humiliation, and violation of our sacred rights to self-determination, wholeness, and freedom."[13] Since women have been assigned the "suffering-servant role," this worldview of divinely sanctioned, innocent suffering contributes to the victimization of women in both church and society.[14] And according to Brown and Parker, it is the patriarchal and hierarchal component of Christian theology analyzed by Rosemary Radford Ruether that provides theological underpinnings for putting women into the role of suffering-servant, subservient victims.[15]

Brown and Parker show how the image of divinely sanctioned abuse (violence) appears in each of the three families of atonement images. In Christus Victor, God hands over the Son for Satan to kill, in exchange for the souls of humanity. In this view, "suffering is a prelude to triumph and is in itself an illusion." Jesus is imagined as "bait for Satan," in a mythic drama in which Jesus "gains entrance to the underworld" and the "divine light" of God "chases darkness from the throne." By incorporating the actual death of Jesus into this myth, his suffering and death become mere "divine trickery" in a plot to "deceive the deceiver."[16] Other versions of Christus Victor spiritualize the struggle against evil, so that "the journey to the underworld becomes the believer's journey into the dark night of the soul." Jesus' death then becomes the "paradigm for a stage in a psychological process that is to be patiently endured," while "God is pictured as working through suffering, pain, and even death to fulfill 'his' divine purpose."[17]

Such imagery upholds a divine model of submission to victimiza-

---

12. Brown and Parker, "For God So Loved," p. 2.
13. Brown and Parker, "For God So Loved," p. 2.
14. Brown and Parker, "For God So Loved," p. 3.
15. Brown and Parker, "For God So Loved," p. 26.
16. Brown and Parker, "For God So Loved," pp. 5-6.
17. Brown and Parker, "For God So Loved," pp. 6-7.

tion, which can have dangerous consequences for those who live in abusive and oppressive situations. "Victimization never leads to triumph," say Brown and Parker, while "it can lead to destruction of the human spirit through the death of a person's sense of power, worth, dignity, or creativity. . . . By denying the reality of suffering and death, the Christus Victor theory of the atonement defames all those who suffer and trivializes tragedy."[18]

In their discussion of Anselm, Brown and Parker refer to his statement that "the Father desired the death of the Son, because he was not willing that the world should be saved in any other way." Only God's Son could pay the debt that humanity owed to God. As has been pointed out previously, Anselm's atonement assumes what in modern terminology is called retributive justice. Brown and Parker point out that Anselm's "view of justice is not that wrong should be righted but that wrongs should be punished." "God's demand that sin be punished is fulfilled by the suffering of the innocent Jesus, whose holiness is crowned by his willingness to be perfectly obedient to his Father's will"[19] as he bears the punishment that sinful humankind actually deserved.

Brown and Parker further indicate that Anselm's satisfaction atonement sanctions suffering "as an experience that frees others." One who would imitate Jesus, a designation that applies to every faithful Christian, "can find herself choosing to endure suffering because she has become convinced that through her pain another whom she loves will escape pain." This theology can be particularly harmful in a society that conditions women to accept abuse. "This glorification of suffering as salvific, held before us daily in the image of Jesus hanging from the cross, encourages women who are being abused to be more concerned about their victimizer than about themselves."[20]

Children are also vulnerable. A child suffering at the hands of an abusive parent is caught "between the claims of a parent who professes love and the inner self which protests violation." If it makes children conflicted and vulnerable, this theology supports the abusive parent.

---

18. Brown and Parker, "For God So Loved," p. 7.
19. Brown and Parker, "For God So Loved," pp. 7-8.
20. Brown and Parker, "For God So Loved," p. 8.

When parents have an image of a God righteously demanding the total obedience of "his" son — even obedience to death — what will prevent the parent from engaging in divinely sanctioned child abuse? The image of God the father demanding and carrying out the suffering and death of his own son has sustained a culture of abuse and led to the abandonment of victims of abuse and oppression.

Not surprisingly Brown and Parker conclude, "Until this image is shattered it will be almost impossible to create a just society."[21]

Brown and Parker similarly discover abusive imagery in Abelard's moral influence theory. The problem that moral influence theory seeks to answer is how sinners can be persuaded to believe in God's mercy. The evidence, supplied by God, "is that Jesus was willing to die for us." This evidence should persuade us of "our forgiven and loved condition," with the result that we "commit ourselves to obedience like his."[22]

For Brown and Parker, the moral influence theory is one more image of divinely sanctioned abuse. "The moral influence theory is founded on the belief that an innocent suffering victim and only an innocent, suffering victim for whose suffering we are in some way responsible has the power to confront us with our guilt and move us to a new decision." On the basis of this image, "races, classes, and women have been victimized" around the world while at the same time "their victimization has been heralded as a persuasive reason for inherently sinful men to become more righteous." The suffering of victims is held up as a means for inducing the powerful to repent. Victims are used "for someone else's edification." And in particular, "it is the victimization of women that is tied to a psychology of redemption."[23] Suffering becomes glorified as a means of redemption for both the victims and their oppressors.

Along with their analysis of the classic atonement images, Brown and Parker assess some modern restatements of atonement. Their conclusion is that these restatements have not helped the problem. They have merely issued new versions of passive submission modeled on Jesus as the "Christian" response to abuse and oppression.[24]

---

21. Brown and Parker, "For God So Loved," pp. 8-9.
22. Brown and Parker, "For God So Loved," p. 11.
23. Brown and Parker, "For God So Loved," p. 12.
24. Brown and Parker, "For God So Loved," pp. 13-26.

In Chapter 3 we observed the way in which the abstract categories of classic Christology and atonement images accommodated and reflected the church's identification with the social order and its acceptance of the sword. These are violence-related issues. In Chapter 4, we saw James H. Cone's analysis of how the abstract categories developed by theologians who came from the ruling class accommodated and reflected the western church's accommodation and reflection of slavery and belief in white, European superiority. These are also most obviously violence-related issues. In Brown and Parker we now observe another facet of the violence implicit in traditional atonement imagery. And in their case, it is not only that violence is accommodated, although that is true. Beyond accommodation of violence, the atonement images themselves provide a model of divinely sanctioned violence and of passive submission to that violence. For people, particularly women, who live in abusive and oppressive environments, Brown and Parker believe, identifying with the Jesus pictured in this model can underscore and sustain their victimization and their sense that the Christian calling is to endure the abuse and oppression.

Brown and Parker do not articulate a comprehensive atonement formula as a foundation for Christian faith that avoids the problems of an image of abuse. In fact, they believe that atonement theology must be jettisoned. "We must do away with the atonement, this idea of a blood sin upon the whole human race which can be washed away only by the blood of the lamb."[25] However, they want to remain within the Christian fold. They provide a list of statements that should characterize Christian faith and challenge abusive imagery. Their suggestions include: focus on the heart of Christianity as "justice, radical love, and liberation"; the assertion that Jesus "did not choose the cross" and lived "in opposition to unjust, oppressive cultures"; that Jesus' death was an "unjust act, done by humans who chose to reject his way of life and sought to silence him through death," which "is not redeemed by the resurrection"; that "suffering is never redemptive, and suffering cannot be redeemed; that "fullness of life is attained in moments of decision" when one chooses to join the struggle with "those who have refused to be victims and have refused to cower under the threat of violence, suffering, and death"; that "death is overthrown when "the threat of death is refused and the choice is made for justice, radical love, and liberation." Finally, "Resurrection means that death is over-

25. Brown and Parker, "For God So Loved," p. 26.

come in those precise instances when human beings choose life, refusing the threat of death. Jesus climbed out of the grave in the Garden of Gethsemane when he refused to abandon his commitment to the truth even though enemies threatened him with death."[26]

Brown and Parker and Narrative Christus Victor

I do not agree with Brown and Parker at the point of rejecting atonement. But because their concerns are valid and their critique of classic atonement images is telling, it is important to bring their position into conversation with narrative Christus Victor.

A first point is to affirm the validity of their concern about abuse of women and of children, and their concern that Christian theology not be used to justify that abuse.

Second, it is important to understand why Brown and Parker can make the claim that atonement images have modeled abuse. As an entry to that question, recall the questions for distinguishing atonement theories from each other that were used in Chapter 2 and that were further developed in Chapter 3 to elucidate narrative Christus Victor. These questions asked about the object or target of the death of Jesus; they asked who needed and who was responsible for the death of Jesus. For satisfaction theory as Brown and Parker understand it, it is God who is offended and needs Jesus' death as a payment, and it is God who organized the plan that sent the Son so that his death could be that payment. It is because God not only needs the death of Jesus and but also sends Jesus for the purpose of providing that death that Brown and Parker can depict it with the image of divine child abuse. It is difficult to avoid the logical conclusion that the Father is the author of the death of the Son. While some consider the image controversial,[27] it does seem to follow the trajectory taken by Jesus' death when we ask who established the process and toward whom or what the death was directed. The same is true for Abelard's moral influence theory. Remember that for the moral influence theory, sinful humankind — us — is the target of the death of Jesus. God gives us the death of the Son as the

---

26. Brown and Parker, "For God So Loved," pp. 27-28.

27. Chapter 7 deals with writers who object to the label of "divine child abuse" and attempt to defend Anselm against that charge.

supreme example of God's love for us. The Father sets up the Son to die as an act of God's love toward us. Since the Father has Jesus die and directs that death toward us, it is again possible to see why Brown and Parker use the image of divine child abuse for the moral influence theory. Finally, there is Christus Victor, where Jesus' death is targeted at the devil. In Brown and Parker's view, the Father hands the Son over to death by the devil in exchange for the devil freeing the souls of sinners. The Father uses the Son's death as a ransom payment. Within that view of Christus Victor, "divine child abuse" may be a controversial image, but once again it fits the logic of the trajectory of Jesus' death, which is innocent suffering because of the Father's desire to save sinful others.

Narrative Christus Victor avoids the problems that Brown and Parker identify for classic Christus Victor, as well as the problems they find with satisfaction and moral influence atonement models. In narrative Christus Victor, Jesus' mission is certainly not about tricking the devil. Neither did the Father send him for the specific purpose of dying, nor was his mission about death, as is the case for both satisfaction and moral atonement models. Jesus' mission had a life-giving purpose — to make the reign of God visible, to display life under the rule of God. Rather than holding up an image of passive submission to suffering, this mission was a model of active resistance to the life-denying, oppressive forces of the social order. And since narrative Christus Victor emphasizes the earthly manifestation of the reign of God in Jesus, it is most certainly not a spiritualized version of the individual's interior journey to the dark night of the soul. In fact, the spiritualization of evil into primarily an interior struggle so that the social order is not challenged accompanies the so-called Constantinian shift, to which narrative Christus Victor is an explicit alternative. And since Jesus' mission was to make the reign of God visible, his death was not the will of God as it would be if it is a debt payment owed to God. In narrative Christus Victor, the death of Jesus is clearly the responsibility of the forces of evil, and it is not needed by or aimed at God.

While narrative Christus Victor avoids many of the problems described by Brown and Parker, from their perspective the most difficult aspect of narrative Christus Victor may be its handling of the suffering and death of Jesus. While narrative Christus Victor does not require death as a salvific necessity, this motif nonetheless depicts Jesus' death as the inevitable result of his mission to make manifest the reign of God in human history. While Jesus' mission was not to die, his dying was the direct result of posing an ultimate threat to the powers of evil. It seems that posing an ultimate threat to the powers of evil provokes an ultimate response, namely the effort to eliminate Jesus. Thus his death seems inevitable although not willed by God nor specifically chosen by him. He was willing to die in pursuit of his mission, even while the purpose of the mission was not death. And while Jesus' death was not the will of God, the ultimate power of the reign of God manifests itself in the resurrection of Jesus because he was killed. Then resurrection overcomes death, the last enemy. Whether this view of Jesus' death and resurrection meets Brown and Parker's criteria that "suffering is never redemptive" and that death is overthrown by a choice for "justice, radical love, and liberation" is unclear. A second, significant point of difference between narrative Christus Victor and Brown and Parker is the lack of an eschatological dimension of the depiction of resurrection. The response of narrative Christus Victor to that component appears in the discussion of Julie Hopkins to follow.

An analogy from human experience can perhaps explain how the inevitability of death differs from willing death, and differs from saying that the purpose of the mission is to die. Most of us know stories of people who risked death for the sake of a cause to which they were committed — missionaries carrying the gospel to supposedly inhospitable regions, parents taking a risk to save a child, environmental activists trying to save trees, and more. Examples abound. And some of these folks have died in the process of working for the chosen cause. But when they died, it was not because they chose to die, nor went on a suicide mission for the purpose of dying. Rather, death was the result of pursuing another goal. In a similar way, with narrative Christus Victor it is possible to understand that even though there is salvific meaning in the life, death, and resurrection of Jesus, the purpose of his mission was not to die but to bring life by making the rule of God visible.

With narrative Christus Victor I intend specifically to pose an alternative to the abusive atonement images rejected by Brown and Parker. However, it remains an open question whether narrative Christus Victor satisfies their search for an understanding of the work of Christ in which Jesus did not choose the cross and his death is not redeemed by resurrection. If it is not satisfying, however, it should be clear that narrative Christus Victor takes seriously their critique of traditional motifs.

Julie M. Hopkins

The image of abuse in satisfaction atonement that offended Brown and Parker is also offensive to Julie N. Hopkins. As Hopkins understands it in *Towards a Feminist Christology*,[28] satisfaction atonement depends on the assumption — now observed a number of times — that wrongdoing creates an imbalance that can only be righted through punishment. Justice, including divine justice, depends on punishment. Hopkins considers such a doctrine repugnant. "It is morally abhorrent to claim that God the Father demanded the self-sacrifice of his only Son to balance the scales of justice." She adds, "A god who punished through pain, despair and violent death is not a god of love but a sadist and despot."[29]

A history of harmful effects on women drives Hopkins's critique of satisfaction atonement.[30] Sin has long been linked to sex, while the Latin church has followed Augustine in believing that original sin was transmitted through sex, with women bearing the consequences of Eve's sin. Since Jesus had to die to atone for sin, women were then blamed for his death. They had two ways of making satisfaction for that guilt: "either in a spirit of passivity and obedience to bear the pain of childbearing and submit to their husbands or to transcend their sex and become like men through celibacy and ascetic practices."[31] Hopkins quotes from medieval sources to illustrate extreme lengths to which nuns and mystics went in imitating the suffering of Christ in satisfaction.

A second dimension of harmful effects on women is the vulnerability of young women to incestuous relationships in authoritarian family settings. Since satisfaction atonement holds up an image of divine submission, an authoritarian family structure that emphasizes passive submission and obedience to men makes a young woman "vulnerable to sexual abuse from her father or male relatives." "For," as Hopkins explains, "in the eyes of the child the identity of the father is confused with images of an Almighty God Father demanding obedience and threatening judgement whilst Jesus becomes the role-model for her (loving?) self-sacrifice."[32] In

---

28. Julie M. Hopkins, *Towards a Feminist Christology: Jesus of Nazareth, European Women, and the Christological Crisis* (Grand Rapids: Eerdmans, 1995).

29. Hopkins, *Towards a Feminist Christology*, p. 50.

30. Hopkins, *Towards a Feminist Christology*, p. 51.

31. Hopkins, *Towards a Feminist Christology*, p. 51.

32. Hopkins, *Towards a Feminist Christology*, p. 52.

yet another abusive application, Hopkins points out that "Not only women, but Black slaves in the West Indies and Anti-bellum America, Indians in Latin America, Africans, peoples from the Indian Subcontinent and Asiatics were 'kept in their place' by a form of Christianity which engendered passivity and an ethic of self-sacrifice."[33]

But alongside these harmful dimensions, Hopkins recognizes the complex appeal of the crucified Christ that produces what seem to be contradictory applications. On the one side, the image of Jesus on the cross "has encouraged oppressed peoples to accept their suffering under their taskmasters as in some sense redemptive." At the same time, "the suffering of Jesus gave them a sense of comfort, for God in Jesus understood their pain and grief and shared their heavy load."[34]

Hopkins deals with this twofold application by distinguishing between descriptive and prescriptive theology. "If suffering people choose to identify with Jesus on the cross and find there comfort, strength and inspiration to live, then the role of the theologian is to reflect upon these experiences of redemption." However, a theologian ought never develop a prescriptive theology of suffering, which demands "penitential self-denial" of already subjected people.[35]

Thus Hopkins suggests a redefined understanding of Jesus' death rather than rejection of atonement outright as did Brown and Parker. In place of atonement that renders suffering salvific, Hopkins suggests a radical restructuring of understandings of God and of the suffering of Jesus that she calls "the scandal of the vulnerable God."[36] In Hopkins's interpretation, the suffering and death of Jesus show that God clearly identifies with and understands the plight of oppressed and suffering people. God was present in the death of Jesus, not because suffering was necessary but because God chose to be in solidarity with suffering humanity. Jesus did not proclaim the necessity of suffering. To the contrary, "his ministry was life-affirming; he sought to eradicate pain and social distress and preach Good News to the poor and heavy hearted." Thus his death was not willed by God. It was a "tragedy and a prophetic exposure of the nihilistic tendencies of those who idolize power."[37] Whether or not Jesus intended that

33. Hopkins, *Towards a Feminist Christology*, p. 52.
34. Hopkins, *Towards a Feminist Christology*, p. 53.
35. Hopkins, *Towards a Feminist Christology*, p. 54.
36. Hopkins, *Towards a Feminist Christology*, p. 55.
37. Hopkins, *Towards a Feminist Christology*, p. 56.

his action to confront "the Roman political and Jewish sacerdotal powers" precipitate an apocalyptic crisis, the followers of Jesus came to the "revolutionary religious insight" that "God was present at the crucifixion, not as an impassive transcendental observer, but as actively sharing with the victim in a solidarity of suffering and grief."[38]

In Hopkins's view, by emphasizing the compassion of God for the sick and unhappy, Jesus had prepared the way for the disciples to understand God's identification with the oppressed. This new insight had a revolutionary impact on the first Christians, and inspired them to be a social movement that lifted up the oppressed. This "conception of God's power stood absolutely in contrast to Roman emperor worship."[39] The revolution was short-lived, however. Very soon the process began of reinterpreting Jesus in terms of "mainstream Greco-Roman philosophical categories." The results were the "paradoxical dogmas of the councils of Chalcedon and Nicea," which fit Jesus into the prevailing philosophy rather than showing that in the cross of Jesus, "God is present and in loving solidarity with those who suffer at the hands of corrupt and violent people."[40] Thus Hopkins rejects the Greek concept of God, articulated in Chalcedon, which allows a transcendent God to be unaffected by the suffering of Jesus while at the same time allowing Jesus to die. In Hopkins's view, the identifying of God with suffering humanity through the death of Jesus must mean that "God has chosen to abdicate divine power where human freedom is concerned." Why God chose to abdicate in this way is a "mystery."[41]

At this point, Hopkins is dealing with theodicy. She rejects the traditional answers. "In my opinion," she says, "it is impossible to logically justify the Goodness of God in the light of human suffering and evil."[42] As she perceives the problem, one is confronted with a choice about the nature of God. One option is "the classical Neo-Platonist/Christian conception of a wholly Other transcendent God," who is "impassive and uninvolved." The option chosen by Hopkins is a conception of God that "is personally present in the mode of loving solidarity, vulnerability and suffering within our

38. Hopkins, *Towards a Feminist Christology*, p. 56.
39. Hopkins, *Towards a Feminist Christology*, p. 56.
40 Hopkins, *Towards a Feminist Christology*, pp. 57, 58; see also p. 70.
41. Hopkins, *Towards a Feminist Christology*, p. 59.
42. Hopkins, *Towards a Feminist Christology*, p. 62.

human and planetary history."[43] This is the God whom Hopkins described as having abdicated power where it concerns human freedom.

> This God did not rise up in sublime justice and take Jesus down from the cross or strike his oppressors with thunderbolts from heaven. But this God felt the pain of Jesus and the grief of forsakenness.[44]

As was true for Brown and Parker, in Hopkins's construction of Christology, resurrection lacks an eschatological dimension. It is primarily a challenge to believing people to make a compassionate commitment to life. Since modern science can neither prove nor disprove resurrection, Hopkins believes that the resurrection was probable, and that it is worth the risk of faith where knowledge falls short.[45] For a feminist theology shaped by experience of women, resurrection then inspires one to live as though the justice of God made present in Jesus still lives. We should "try to believe that God acts in history with dynamic efficacy to justify the victims of oppression, torture and execution, that the message, goodness and presence of a prophet such as Jesus of Nazareth cannot be obliterated by human evil." This kind of belief in the resurrection "challenges us to a passionate commitment to Life."[46]

Julia N. Hopkins and Narrative Christus Victor

Hopkins underscores the harmful dimensions of satisfaction atonement images and its underlying assumption of retributive violence, which demonstrates the need for rethinking the Christian theology of atonement. The effort of narrative Christus Victor to articulate an understanding of the death and resurrection of Jesus that does not redeem suffering and that avoids a model of God as the author or agent of the death of Jesus thus finds resonance in Hopkins's work.

Further, Hopkins's description of the change of the first Christians from the social revolutionary stance provoked by Jesus' life-giving mission

---

43. Hopkins, *Towards a Feminist Christology*, p. 62.
44. Hopkins, *Towards a Feminist Christology*, p. 62.
45. Hopkins, *Towards a Feminist Christology*, p. 68.
46. Hopkins, *Towards a Feminist Christology*, p. 71.

to an understanding of Jesus that was compatible with mainstream Greco-Roman philosophy is parallel to the description in Chapter 3 of the series of evolutionary changes symbolized by Constantine. Christian faith and the church evolved from a stance that challenged the social order to a stance that supported and expressed itself through the institutions and thought forms of the social order.

Narrative Christus Victor has a more profound view of resurrection that does Hopkins or Brown and Parker. The eschatological dimension of resurrection in narrative Christus Victor means that Christian life now, in history, is more than a mere commitment to life. It is the beginning of the actualization of the reign of God. It is the inbreaking of a new age. At the same time, narrative Christus Victor demonstrates that one need not abandon a high Christology in order to counter the abusive images of satisfaction atonement. Even when it does not depend on Nicene-Chalcedonian terminology, in narrative Christus Victor God is fully present in the life, death, and resurrection of Jesus. Resurrection is not simply inspiration to continue to challenge oppression. Resurrection is the ultimate victory of the reign of God that was made present in Jesus.

While Hopkins believes that Jesus' death is caused by "the nihilistic tendencies of those who idolize power," she also believes that his death did demonstrate God's identification with and compassion for the sick and unhappy. This is a divine act "aimed" at sinful humankind. Further, the function of this act was to inspire the disciples to take up a social movement that lifted up the oppressed.[47] Both these impulses concerning the death of Jesus are aimed at sinful humankind, which is the case for moral influence atonement. At the same time, this depiction by Hopkins of the death of Jesus lacks the eschatological dimension that is intrinsic to narrative Christus Victor. It seems, therefore, that Hopkins's supposed radical restructuring of understandings of God and the suffering of Jesus is not really very radical. It is actually a reformulation of the moral influence motif, with an emphasis on God's identification with the oppressed.

47. Hopkins, *Towards a Feminist Christology*, p. 56.

Rita Nakashima Brock

Rita Nakashima Brock's reformulation of Christology and atonement in *Journeys by Heart*[48] emerges specifically from her critique of the patriarchal and hierarchal character of mainstream Christendom theology. As an alternative, Brock constructs a Christology of relation or what she calls "erotic power."

Brock follows Brown and Parker and Hopkins in suggesting that traditional satisfaction atonement poses a model of child abuse. Brock objects to an understanding of Jesus' work in which his death is claimed to reveal the loving nature of the Father. When Jesus is said to suffer in our place, she believes, then the primary element is that we feel the relief for having escaped punishment, and we are absolved from any need to suffer the consequences of our sin. And of course, she believes, if Jesus' suffering is interpreted as a loving act of the Father, that is an image analogous to the abuse of children.[49] When Jesus suffers (is punished) in our place, Brock contends, what is missing "is interdependence and mutuality. We are not called to embrace our own suffering." Nor are we called "to discover the gifts of grace in our connectedness to ourselves and others."[50]

In contrast to the oppressive character of patriarchy, Brock poses the concepts of "heart" and "erotic power" as orienting characteristics of her alternative construction. As Brock uses the term "heart," it is a metaphor for the human self and its capacity for intimacy. Heart "involves the union of body, spirit, reason and passion." What we know "by heart" comes from the "center of all vital functions," and "is the seat of self, of energy, of loving, of compassion, of conscience, of tenderness, and of courage." Brock uses heart as a name for human being as a being capable of mutual interaction and mutual relationship, in contrast to patriarchy, which damages relationships of mutuality.[51]

Brock uses the name "erotic power" for the feminist, liberating power that restores and nurtures relationships of the heart, in contrast to the power of hierarchy that is characterized "by dominance, by status, by au-

48. Rita Nakashima Brock, *Journeys by Heart: A Christology of Erotic Power* (New York: Crossroad, 1988).

49. Brock, *Journeys by Heart*, pp. 56-57.

50. Brock, *Journeys by Heart*, p. 56.

51. Brock, *Journeys by Heart*, pp. xiv-xv.

thority, and by control over people, nature, and things."[52] Feminist eros differs markedly from eros as "lust or sexuality" as male-dominated society understands it. "Feminist Eros is grounded in the relational lives of women and in a critical, self-aware consciousness that unites the psychological and political spheres of life, binding love with power." "As it creates and connects hearts," Brock writes, erotic power "involves the whole person in relationships of self-awareness, vulnerability, openness, and caring." The usual understanding of power is "dominance and the ability to have one's way." Erotic power is more inclusive. It is "an ontic category," that is, "a fundamentally ultimate reality in human existence" that provides an "understanding of the dynamics of power within which dominance and willful assertion can be explained." Thus "all other forms of power emerge from the reality of erotic power."[53]

Erotic power "produces creative synthesis, and is enhanced by the relationships that emerge from creative synthesis. It produces not fusion and control, but connectedness." Thus erotic power "integrates all aspects of the self, making us whole."[54] All forms of power emerge from this integrative whole of erotic power, either in destructive or life-giving forms. As the basis of being itself, "all existence comes to be by virtue of connectedness . . . . Erotic power is the fundamental power of existence-as-a-relational-process."[55] This understanding of erotic power is the basis for Brock's critique of patriarchy as well as traditional Christology and atonement.

The problem with patriarchal ideologies, then, is that they "split off parts of ourselves." As a result, a "self-righteous split divides self and world so that psychological self-examination and personal responsibility are set against the political realities of institutionalized oppression."[56] While Brock acknowledges that God as father has been "a powerful and complex metaphor"[57] and that it need not be entirely banned from use, it is clear that this metaphor poses significant problems in a patriarchal society. With the virtual absence of "a nurturing, intimate father" in a patriarchal society, a child can be pushed towards "identification with the powerful

---

52. Brock, *Journeys by Heart*, p. 25.
53. Brock, *Journeys by Heart*, p. 26.
54. Brock, *Journeys by Heart*, p. 39.
55. Brock, *Journeys by Heart*, p. 41.
56. Brock, *Journeys by Heart*, p. 42.
57. Brock, *Journeys by Heart*, p. 53.

[but distant] father as a move toward self-protection." Such a process "leaves the needs of children unmet," and reinforces patriarchal submission. In its best form, the patriarchal father can "produce a kind of community solidarity," but then women remain "outside the ecumenical brotherhood."[58]

The father-son analogies pose particular problems for many atonement images. Whatever their form (Brock notes four categories[59]), they assume a notion of original sin for which the remedy is "punishment of one perfect child" by "the perfect father." In other words, Brock points out, satisfaction atonement is based on the assumption that making right or doing justice is to punish. This punishment then enables the father to "forgive the rest of his children and love them."[60] An image of a divine, abusive father seems inescapable. Brock notes that the trinitarian formulas are used in an attempt to absolve God as father from this "punitive aspect by asserting that the consequences for human sin are actually taken into the divine existence, such that divine suffering takes away human suffering." With suffering thus attributed to the loving nature of God rather than to the son's work, the transaction is claimed to reveal the loving nature of the Father, who would sacrifice "his most beloved and only son" for sinful humanity. As a result, the faithful escape punishment, and they "are absolved of the need to suffer the consequences of sin." Human beings are encouraged to believe that "our own suffering has been taken away by someone else's suffering and by a cosmic transaction within the divine life."[61]

What is missing from this scheme, according to Brock, "is interdependence and mutuality. We are not called to embrace our own suffering . . . . And to discover the gifts of grace in our connectedness to ourselves and others. Instead we are enjoined to look to a suffering and power outside us, both greater than ours."[62] From these atonement images, then, one gains a

58. Brock, *Journeys by Heart*, pp. 53-54.

59. Following J. F. Bethune-Baker in *An Introduction to the Early History of Christian Doctrine*, Brock lists the following four categories: "(1) through Jesus' death the enemies of God are reconciled to each other; (2) humanity is under bondage to sin, requiring Jesus' death as ransom; (3) sin causes humanity to be at a deficit so Jesus' death pays the debt; or (4) Jesus Christ is a propitiation, a pure sacrifice, who cleanses humanity of sin" (Brock, *Journeys by Heart*, p. 55).

60. Brock, *Journeys by Heart*, p. 55.

61. Brock, *Journeys by Heart*, pp. 55-56.

62. Brock, *Journeys by Heart*, p. 56.

"sense of relief from escaping punishment." To experience God's grace means to avoid the punishment one deserves. At the same time, there is nothing in the experience of grace that sets a new direction for the one spared punishment. The grace of the Father allows "a select group" to occupy a favored position with the father, while the "overall destructiveness of the oppressive systems of the patriarchal family" remain intact.[63] In terminology used in Chapters 3 and 4, Brock believes that satisfaction atonement separates salvation from ethics — the sinner is saved, that is, has his or her penalty paid, but this legal transaction says nothing about the consequent saved life.

Such images of atonement and salvation, Brock believes, are analogous to images of the neglect and abuse of children. Such abuse becomes acceptable because it reflects "divine behavior — cosmic abuse, as it were. The father allows, or even inflicts, the death of his only perfect son." While all atonement images emphasize the father's grace and forgiveness as though they are available to sinners apart from their being "good and free of sin," the availability of grace and forgiveness is in fact "contingent upon the suffering of the one perfect child."[64] Although the atonement image does not name the conclusion specifically, again it appears that the logic of the formula makes God the author of the death of Jesus.

Brock notes that the traditional atonement images, which proclaim forgiveness on the basis of a previous act of divine grace, perhaps have some beneficial aspects. They can, for example, "lead to a self-acceptance and forgiveness of others." At the same time, these doctrines clearly have problems. Brock agrees with analysis from Chapters 3 and 4, which said that the "abstractness"[65] of traditional atonement motifs means that they contain little or nothing that challenges the unjust status quo. In particular, they contain nothing that challenges assumptions of patriarchy and hierarchy. These atonement doctrines "do nothing to transform dualistic and punitive patriarchal family structures," and they "remain focused on the dependent relation of individual believers to a transcendent father." This relationship is outside of history and thus does nothing to challenge the injustices that occur in history. "There is little in the traditional doc-

---

63. Brock, *Journeys by Heart*, p. 56.
64. Brock, *Journeys by Heart*, p. 56.
65. Brock, *Journeys by Heart*, p. 57.

trines to lead us to concrete analysis of the social dimensions of sin or to a social sense of incarnation."[66]

Brock builds on but also goes beyond Rosemary Radford Ruether's previously noted critique of patriarchy in classic Christology. Brock accepts Ruether's conclusion that Jesus transcended patriarchy and that Jesus thus serves as evidence for a feminist Christology. He challenges social structures, "which is essential to any feminist understanding of Christianity."[67] But Brock also points out that in Ruether's picture of Jesus, he is a "hero and liberator."[68] This picture of Jesus has him challenge the entrenched power structures on behalf of those on the underside, which means that "the relationship of liberator to oppressed is unilateral." Jesus speaks for victims but the "brokenhearted do not speak *to* the strong."[69] Thus beyond an understanding of Jesus who confronts oppressive structures on behalf of the oppressed, Brock argues that the challenge to the powers of oppression must "be accompanied by a move toward self-awareness and self-affirmation" by the oppressed. Without the formation of new relationships, merely shattering the powers results in further "fragmentation of the self."[70] For Brock, those whom Jesus liberates must also have an impact on him. Brock believes that missing from Ruether's feminist, prophetic Jesus "is the presence of members of Jesus' community as embodying God/dess and having a transforming impact on him."[71]

Brock's concept of interactive erotic power leads her to construct an understanding of Jesus that avoids "a heroic Jesus who alone is able to achieve an empowering self-consciousness through a solitary, private relationship with God/dess."[72] Brock develops "Christa/Community" as the christological concept that includes Jesus but is only complete when seen in relation to the community around Jesus that makes manifest the interactive and relational dimensions of erotic power. Brock is

> developing a christology not centered in Jesus, but in relationship and community as the whole-making, healing center of Christianity. In that

66. Brock, *Journeys by Heart*, p. 57.
67. Brock, *Journeys by Heart*, pp. 64, 65.
68. Brock, *Journeys by Heart*, p. 65.
69. Brock, *Journeys by Heart*, p. 65. Emphasis Brock's.
70. Brock, *Journeys by Heart*, p. 66.
71. Brock, *Journeys by Heart*, p. 66.
72. Brock, *Journeys by Heart*, p. 66.

sense, Christ is what I am calling Christa/Community. Jesus participates centrally in this Christa/Community, but he neither brings erotic power into being nor controls it. He is brought into being through it and participates in the cocreation of it. Christa/Community is a lived reality expressed in relational images.[73]

It is this community, rather than the individual person of Jesus, which serves as the locus of authority for Christians.

In Brock's illustration of Christa/Community from the Gospel of Mark, the stories of Jesus' acts of healing and exorcism play a central role. Brock draws on several New Testament scholars to argue that the miracle stories of Jesus are not instances of merely returning a system gone awry to the status quo. Rather Jesus' healings are instances of divine inbreaking to challenge and overcome an oppressive status quo and to establish a new order in its place. Such healings "convey the meaning of wholeness and of Christa/Community as a relational event."[74] "Actions to heal brokenheartedness shatter old orientations to self and power and open fissures that birth erotic power."[75] The exorcisms described by Jesus have a parallel interpretation. As Brock understands Mark's narrative, "exorcism stories use demons to depict the loss of self-possession," and a story such as the Gerasene Demoniac "represents the emergence of a different power, the only power capable of restoring heart instead of imposing a new form of external control."[76]

In her reading of Mark, Brock emphasizes that Jesus' death was neither inevitable nor made necessary by a divine plan of salvation.[77] God did not will the death of Jesus. Like Brown and Parker and Hopkins, Brock rejects all soteriologies that would glorify death or make Jesus' death salvific; she rejects understandings in which Jesus' death is "asserted to be the ultimate sign of self-sacrifice and divine self-giving, and a symbol of the willingness of true believers to sacrifice themselves out of devotion to higher authority or will," or interpretations that see Jesus taking others' burdens and dying "in their stead."[78] These rejected descriptions, of course, come from Anselmian, satisfaction atonement.

73. Brock, *Journeys by Heart*, p. 52.
74. Brock, *Journeys by Heart*, p. 72.
75. Brock, *Journeys by Heart*, p. 74.
76. Brock, *Journeys by Heart*, pp. 76, 79.
77. Brock, *Journeys by Heart*, p. 93.
78. Brock, *Journeys by Heart*, p. 90.

Brock also rejects Christus Victor as it came to be understood in the official church. Although Jesus' death was interpreted as a conquering of the powers of sin and death, his resurrection did not appear to result in "the downfall of power of political oppression." Consequently, "the official church made the meaning of his death spiritual and other-worldly." And hope became hope in "personal salvation" through a divinely appointed savior. Quite obviously this salvation did not appear in a meaningful way in the real world in which people lived. Hope resided in a future life, "granted only by God through Jesus," but humanity remained virtually helpless within this life.[79]

Instead of understanding Jesus' death as necessary, Brock argues that the important point is that the community responded to it "by maintaining connections within its community, connections from which emerged both a stronger need for power as control and a creative response to tragedy." Jesus' death was "not an event necessary to reveal erotic power or save humankind." Instead, the brokenheartedness that was revealed by Jesus' death was created by the "political systems of patriarchal society."

Jesus' death does reveal that it takes courage to confront the powers of oppression, "but the point of the risk is not to invite death. The risk is a profound affirmation of the possibility of life beyond oppression." Brock understands Jesus' risk as "a commitment to solidarity with those crushed by oppressive powers and to the expectation that justice must prevail." Jesus' action of cleansing the temple is an example of civil disobedience, which shows the danger of defying authority.[80]

For Brock, the resurrection of Jesus took on meaning when the community around Jesus refused to allow death to defeat them. When they "remembered his presence and affirmed divine power among them," they were continuing the life of Jesus on earth. "The community of faithful disciples restores erotic power and the hope of wholeness for their community by not letting go of their relationships to each other and not letting Jesus' death be the end of their community."[81]

79. Brock, *Journeys by Heart*, p. 91.
80. Brock, *Journeys by Heart*, p. 94.
81. Brock, *Journeys by Heart*, p. 100.

Rita Nakashima Brock and Narrative Christus Victor

Alongside the construction of narrative Christus Victor in Chapter 2, and black theology in Chapter 4, Rita Nakashima Brock's *Journeys by Heart* is another in a series of efforts to construct a comprehensive theology that is not beholden to the inherited, violence-accommodating theology of Christendom. If narrative Christus Victor developed from an effort to avoid the accommodation of the sword, and if black theology arose to avoid the accommodation of racism in the inherited European theology of Christendom, then Brock writes to free women of the patriarchal and hierarchal dimensions of that same theology. Further agreements include the argument that Jesus' death was not willed by God nor required by a divine plan of salvation.

A number of emphases from Brock find resonance in narrative Christus Victor. These include the observation that satisfaction atonement depends on the principle of retributive justice or compensatory violence; that the abstract formula of satisfaction supports the status quo, including patriarchal structures; and that satisfaction atonement separates salvation from ethics — the transaction of punishing Jesus in place of punishing sinners says nothing about the ethical direction of the saved ones (those spared punishment). In the presentation of narrative Christus Victor, it was emphasized that not God but the powers of evil killed Jesus. Thus narrative Christus Victor is fully in accord with Brock in identifying forces of evil rather than God as the ultimate agency behind the death of Jesus, and it obviously avoids transformation into the spiritualized form of Christus Victor to which Brock objects.

Further, Brock's analysis underscores elements of patriarchy and hierarchy in traditional theology, with a particular focus on why these emphases are harmful to women when they exist within a theology that promises salvation because the perfect father has willed the death of his perfect son. In agreement with Joanne Carlson Brown, Rebecca Parker, and Julie N. Hopkins, Brock makes clear that satisfaction atonement in particular as well as other traditional atonement images picture father and son — God the Father and his Son Jesus — in an abusive relationship. The father wills the death of an innocent son for the benefit of the rest of the father's children. Narrative Christus Victor agrees with this assessment of classic atonement motifs. These motifs are predicated on the father's willing the death of the son, against a backdrop in which doing justice means to inflict punishment. The assumption behind traditional atonement images, in particular satisfaction atonement, is that of divine retribution; the fundamental activity of God in salvation is to insure sin is balanced by punishment. Sinful human beings are saved because God inflicted the punishment on Jesus rather than on the sinners.

While narrative Christus Victor supports Brock's analysis of the classic atonement images, differences appear when we consider Brock's construction of an alternative. I indicate three differences. The first concerns the lack of an objective character to the work of Christ in Brock's understanding of the community around Jesus that features restored relationships of mutuality. The community around Jesus emerges when relationships are restored, but there is nothing about the death and resurrection of Jesus that changes the nature of reality in an objective way. In Christa/Community the death and resurrection of Jesus have not fundamentally reordered the forces of the world under the reign of God. Salvation happens only when people perceive Jesus and join the interactive relationships of the community. In contrast, in narrative Christus Victor the fundamental orientation of power in the universe has been altered for those who perceive the resurrection of Jesus. Those who perceive and believe the resurrection understand that the reign of God has been made visible in history. And the reign of God is thus established whether or not any of us choose to submit to it. That idea of a fundamental change in perceptions of the order of the universe is missing in Brock's view of Jesus and community. This missing element is similar to the absence of a profound view of resurrection in Julia Hopkins, and also applies to the list of components that Brown and Parker provide to characterize a nonabusive Christian theology. Brown and Parker, Hopkins, and Brock may not agree that their atonement theologies are remakes of Abelard. But in their lack of an objective accomplishment for resurrection apart from the transformed sinner's own response, their views are similar to Abelard's.

A second difference between Brock and narrative Christus Victor concerns Christa/Community as the locus of Christian identity. Brock posed Christa/Community as the full-orbed feminist Christology that avoids the patriarchal, hierarchal, and abusive dimensions of the received Christology. In Christa/Community Jesus is one but not the sole representative of erotic power, the basis of the new, nonhierarchal community of healing and hope. In contrast, with narrative Christus Victor it was stressed that the fullness of the reign of God was present in Jesus. The victory of the rule of God over the powers of evil would be incomplete were Jesus not the bearer of the fullness of the reign of God. Thus on this particular point, narrative Christus Victor is closer to Rosemary Radford Ruether's approach than to Brock's. It needs also to be said that this difference with Brock is more theoretical than practical. In terms of the working out in history of the victory of the rule of God, narrative Christus Victor agrees with Brock that the communal, interactive dimensions of the reign of God in Jesus are visible only in the interactions of Jesus with the people around him. It is in those interactions that one sees Jesus' rejection of the sword and his many actions that challenge patriarchal structures and the subservient role of women. And similar to Christa/Community, narrative Christus Victor also believes that the believing community continues the mission of Jesus to make present the reign of God in the world. Thus narrative Christus Victor retains a theological insistence on Jesus as the full revelation of God but supports Christa/Community as the lived manifestation of the rule of God.

The third point of disagreement with Brock concerns her view of Christa/Community based on erotic power as a comprehensive answer to the sins of patriarchy, hierarchy, and abuse. Brock's view is heavily influenced by process thought, which attempts to understand all processes as part of a metaprocess that is moving all of reality in the direction of the reign of God. Brock's construction of erotic power as the basis of all power means that ultimately all sins become sins of domination and the problem of the world is fragmentation. Patriarchal ideologies split off parts of ourselves, which leads to polarizations and makes differences into oppositions. Brock's answer is to posit erotic power as the power from which all power emerges and which pulls things back together. Recognizing and recovering erotic power as the basis of relationships then means bringing these separations and polarizations together again in an integrated and mutually interactive community.

The problem with this approach to an integrated community of healing is that it assumes all broken relationships reflect the same kind of fundamental problem or fundamental need. But this approach does not adequately acknowledge different kinds of participation and responsibility in broken relationships; and it does not adequately acknowledge that those differing kinds of responsibility then require different kinds of healing. For example, two sisters who become estranged from each other in a fight about how to divide equally the property inherited from their father may be said to participate in the same way in the brokenness of their relationship, and they need the same kind of healing. That is not the case for a wife who is trapped in an abusive relationship. She participates in brokenness and fragmentation differently than does her husband and she needs a different kind of healing than does her abusive husband. Or consider the situation that comes from the racist history of United States society, in which white women have participated in the oppression of black women. Given that history, one way of becoming free of patriarchy, hierarchy, and abuse does not apply to white and black women in the same way, and what is liberating for white women does not necessarily speak for black women. Of course, Brock is aware of the problem created by these unequal relationships.[82] But her discussion of the healing of broken relationships on the basis of erotic power is a kind of one-size-fits-all solution. It works for the broken relationship of the estranged sisters who fought as equals about an inheritance but does not adequately consider the different kinds of healing required for those on opposite sides of an unequal or oppressive relationship. How narrative Christus Victor treats the different kinds of participation in oppression is discussed in Chapter 6 in conversation with womanist theology.

Carter Heyward

Carter Heyward's *Saving Jesus From Those Who Are Right*[83] provides one more feminist answer to the problems that a number of feminist theologians have discovered in the traditional forms of Christology and atonement. To understand Heyward's critique and challenge to traditional atonement, it is necessary to survey her perception of human existence, and the problems that patriarchy and authoritarian power pose.

Heyward understands the essence of being human as existing in mutuality. Mutuality does not mean merely that human beings form relationships, and it is much more than the relationships among people. "Mutuality is the *creative basis* of our lives, the world, and God." It means that human beings exist in "relation," where relation is "the radical connectedness of all

---

82. Brock, *Journeys by Heart*, pp. xiv-xv, 110 n. 4.

83. Carter Heyward, *Saving Jesus From Those Who Are Right: Rethinking What It Means to Be Christian* (Minneapolis: Fortress Press, 1999).

reality, in which all parts of the whole are mutually interactive."[84] It is in the interconnectedness of all of reality that we find God and experience the power of God.

> So then we find our sacred power neither 'in' Jesus nor 'in' ourselves but between and among us. God is in the dynamic, sparking movement among and between us, within and beyond us, beneath and above us. . . . The Spirit brooding over creation, the One who casts down the mighty from their thrones, this God is the movement that connects us all, the whole creation, through all that has been and all that will be, now and forever![85]

If creation exists in mutuality, evil consists of the breaking or betraying of the relationships of mutuality. It is "rooted in non-mutual, authoritarian relational dynamics that, in the real world, are usually patriarchal."[86] Heyward ascribes three characteristics to authoritarian power. It is "wielded over others," it "remains in the hands of the dominant party," and it shapes the subordinate characters "according to the judgment and will of the dominant." Such top-down power in the hands of the few betrays mutuality and is inherently evil.[87]

When faced with questions of good and evil, as Heyward understands authoritarian religion, it has a simple answer — "*obedience* to the Father." A primary image of Jesus in this authoritarian religion is that of "Obedient Son of His Father."[88] In the human arena, this authoritarian, patriarchal structure makes all people subject to the divine Father as his children, while also establishing some humans with authority over others, with a right, "like God," "to demand and reward obedience and to punish disobedience." In the patriarchal context of authoritarian religion, this dynamic breeds an unhealthy "ethic of obedience." Those on the obedience side of the relationship can develop "masochistic emotions," in which they desire to be loved by God as the source of being while simultaneously desiring punishment for having offended the Father. Those on the authority side of the relationship, in "an identification with the Father God," can develop a

84. Heyward, *Saving Jesus*, p. 62.
85. Heyward, *Saving Jesus*, p. 61. Emphasis Heyward's.
86. Heyward, *Saving Jesus*, p. 77.
87. Heyward, *Saving Jesus*, pp. 58-59.
88. Heyward, *Saving Jesus*, p. 79.

"sadistic experience" in which they try to feel like God through "exercise of male (or surrogate male) headship, parental discipline, and an embodied sense of erotic fulfillment through disciplinary rituals."[89]

Heyward objects to the idea of "obedience" as the primary concept to describe our relationship to God. Obedience as mere submission to authority does not teach children to develop "the capacities for the inner-discernment and moral-reasoning that accompany mature life in the Spirit."[90] Obedience "suggests that God is a power *over* us more than a Spirit *with* us. Instead of obedience, Heyward suggests "mutuality" as the basis of life in the Spirit. She suggests that God "needs us as loving partners, needs us to be spirited participants in a movement for justice-love in the world" rather than obedient children. And in this context then, Jesus is understood as a "healing presence."[91]

This understanding of human existence in mutuality and of the evil of authoritarian power is the basis for Heyward's critique and rejection of traditional Anselmian atonement doctrine. Atonement, Heyward says, is the doctrine that "has been the primary theological vehicle" through which the church has attempted to understand these patterns of father-right and paternal responsibility, "specifically of how the father 'rights' the relationship between Himself and His disobedient children."[92]

If God is the patriarchal Father to whom obedience is owed by the Son, Heyward says, then the charges previously heard from Brown and Parker, Hopkins, and Brock, namely that God is a divine child abuser, are indeed true.[93] Heyward calls the image of a God who would offer his son to die for others "a construct in the minds of ruling-class men who are frightened of their own and others' embodied passion, sensuality, and yearnings for mutuality." In contrast to this patriarchal God, Heyward argues that the God who was embodied in Jesus and with whom Jesus was living in relationship "was yearning for mutuality" and would not then cause the death of the loved one.[94]

Further and most profoundly, Heyward argues that traditional substitutionary and sacrificial atonement "drives a huge and misleading

89. Heyward, *Saving Jesus*, p. 80.
90. Heyward, *Saving Jesus*, p. 81.
91. Heyward, *Saving Jesus*, pp. 80-82.
92. Heyward, *Saving Jesus*, p. 80.
93. Heyward, *Saving Jesus*, p. 151.
94. Heyward, *Saving Jesus*, p. 151.

wedge between how we experience God's love and suffering and how we experience *our own* love and suffering." Most Christians, Heyward says, believe that their actions to bring healing and liberation are only human experiences and differ from God's actions.[95] In the traditional view, God demonstrates love and restores justice by a "willingness to punish and be punished (for remember that Jesus is God in this story, both Father and Son)." The early church fathers wanted a God who was more than human, who as God "offered Himself as a blood sacrifice 'for the sins of the world.'" And of course it is true, Heyward says, that God suffers because of the sins of the world. However, in rejecting the traditional view, Heyward notes that a friend does not punish by humiliating and destroying the loved ones. When we live in a relationship of mutuality with God, and of Jesus with us and with God, it is clear that God does not demonstrate love for humanity by destroying the Son. "We need to say no," Heyward concludes, "to a tradition of violent punishment and to a God who would crucify us — much less an innocent brother in our place — rather than hang with us, struggle with us, wait with us, and grieve with us."[96]

Heyward's alternative to the God who demonstrates love by using the violence of blood sacrifice is a God who suffers with humankind. This is incarnation and atonement of presence, where incarnation and atonement become the same divine action toward and with humanity. Those who live a justice-seeking life cannot avoid suffering with those who experience injustice. Atonement, "making right relation with God," occurs then in the context of wrongdoing. Atonement is occurring "whenever God is incarnate (made flesh) in any context of violence." In this light, the image of Jesus shedding blood "for us" is not the result of "a deity who, in the image of a father, would hand his son over to be crucified," but rather the image of Jesus' love and solidarity with us. "For Christians, the cross can be an image of Jesus' love and solidarity, of what it cost him and what it costs all who suffer because they love." Such participation in incarnation and atonement as an act of solidarity is more than a spiritual event. "It is also a political, social, ecological and pastoral movement of liberation from larger and small forces that are cruel, violent, apathetic, or ignorant of what humans and other creatures need in order to live and thrive."[97] Iden-

95. Heyward, *Saving Jesus*, p. 171. Emphasis Heyward's.
96. Heyward, *Saving Jesus*, pp. 171-75.
97. Heyward, *Saving Jesus*, pp. 121-22.

tifying with humanity in this way, as an act of making justice-love present, means that Jesus' mission was not to die but to live.[98]

Heyward's atonement image builds from a picture of God as one with us. God "is devastated that Her human friends have betrayed her," and she calls repeatedly for us to return. When we turn away and continue to deny our participation in evils such as white privilege, God offers herself "as friend." She reaches toward us as a friend, who longs for us to reciprocate. This reaching out is an offer of grief and forgiveness that continues eternally, in spite of our continual wrongdoing. It is not thinkable that such a God would or could engage in the act of punishing and killing the loved one or loved ones. This act of atonement involves two movements. In the first, God reaches toward us. In the second, we are "moved through solidarity, community, friendship, prayer and other resources to God, to live willingly in the Spirit." Such movement "involves our repentance, our commitment to turn from the wrong we have done and live differently by turning to God and one another in the struggle for mutuality." This movement of incarnation and atonement is what the story of Jesus was and is about "insofar as we embody it in our lives," and thereby also "become agents of atonement."[99]

When we apply the question about the object of the death of Jesus used to distinguish atonement images to Heyward's atonement theology, it is clear that the atoning work of Jesus — his life and his death — are aimed at rebellious humankind. As Carter says, "The cross can be an image of Jesus' love and solidarity, of what it cost him and what it costs all who suffer because they love."[100] Making sinful humankind the object of Jesus' life and death clearly locates Heyward's incarnation and atonement of presence and identity with humankind in the family of moral influence atonement images. As Heyward herself tells us, her perspective "radicalizes the Abelardian tradition."[101]

98. Heyward, *Saving Jesus*, p. 138.
99. Heyward, *Saving Jesus*, pp. 165-66.
100. Heyward, *Saving Jesus*, p. 122.
101. Heyward, *Saving Jesus*, p. 241 n. 19.

Carter Heyward and Narrative Christus Victor

Narrative Christus Victor finds a number of points of resonance with Heyward's assessment of traditional Anselmian, substitutionary atonement. The two agree in rejecting an atonement image predicated on the assumption that God restores a just relationship with humanity through divinely initiated and divinely sanctioned violence. And as has been emphasized more than once, in narrative Christus Victor, as in Heyward's reconstruction, the mission of Jesus was to live rather than to die; we participate or share in Jesus' mission to confront evil and injustice by making the rule of God visible; and the impetus for the evil that killed Jesus came from the rebellious powers and not from God.

Narrative Christus Victor differs from Heyward at several important points, which stem from her orientation within an Abelardian motif. First, Heyward's model does not entirely escape the image of divine child abuse. Heyward rejects the penal substitutionary view of God who punished and instead emphasizes that God suffered with Jesus on the cross, which was an act of solidarity and love with humankind whose result was to move sinners to God. But when one recalls the distinguishing question about the object of the death of Jesus, however, it is obvious that the death of Jesus is aimed at sinful humankind and that it had to be intended by God if God's love is to be revealed in Jesus' death. Thus identifying incarnation and atonement as the same activity, as Heyward does, camouflages but does not eliminate the fact that God needs the death of Jesus as an act of love in Abelardian atonement. And hidden under the incarnation is still an image of the Father who causes the Son to suffer for the sake of the Father's other children. The point that appeal to incarnation or stressing the suffering of God with Jesus (rather than understanding God as punishing sin in Jesus) does not eliminate the abusive image will be discussed further in Chapter 7, when the same argument is used by those who attempt to defend Anselm against feminist charges of divine child abuse.

A different element of disagreement with Heyward appears in conjunction with the observation that her restructuring of the Jesus story omits almost completely the resurrection of Jesus. That omission contrasts sharply with narrative Christus Victor. The resurrection gives narrative Christus Victor objective and eschatological dimensions not present in Abelardian atonement. In Abelardian atonement, atonement happens — that is, actual change in the relationship between God and sinful humanity

— when human beings perceive Jesus' identity with them and make a choice to cease their denial of sin. Until that happens, relationships in the world do not change and human beings are not changed. In contrast, for narrative Christus Victor the resurrection signifies that the order of the cosmos has been determined, that the reign of God has been revealed as ultimately established whether or not rebellious human beings recognize it. And for those who do, the resurrection is a revelation of the true power of the cosmos. And it is the future culmination of that order of God which provides the eschatological dimension of our life within history and thus makes clear why it is indeed worthwhile to suffer with the oppressed in the name of the reign of God.

Throughout *Saving Jesus* Heyward makes an impassioned plea for nonviolence based on the mutuality of all of creation. That is a welcome plea. "We cannot undo evil with evil, violence with violence, cruelty with cruelty, fear with fear."[102] At the same time she makes an exception for "revolutionary situations" in which people believe that only violence can stop evil that is working against them.[103] She also calls nonviolence "a collective public force" that is "seldom a practical or very real option for individuals." Debating those particular points is beyond the scope of the book in hand.[104] Here I will only point out that if Jesus' way does make God present with us, that way is true whether or not the evil powers recognize it, and that on occasion "suffering with" really means just that.

A last point of difference grows out of Heyward's vision of restored mutuality as the basis of godly existence. As was the case for Brock's Christa/Community based on erotic power, Heyward's mutuality makes oppressors and oppressed guilty of the same sin, namely betrayal of mutuality. Observing Jesus "with us" and the consequent move to restore mutuality does not address explicitly the different ways that oppressors and oppressed have participated in the rupture of mutuality and does not

---

102. Heyward, *Saving Jesus*, p. 113.

103. Heyward, *Saving Jesus*, pp. 138-39.

104. For arguments that nonviolence is indeed a real option for individuals, see John H. Yoder, *What Would You Do?: A Serious Answer to a Standard Question* (Scottdale, Pa.: Herald Press, 1983); Richard L. Deats, ed., *The Theory of Nonviolence*, Active Nonviolence: A Way of Life, a Strategy for Change, vol. 1 (Nyak, N.Y.: The Fellowship of Reconciliation, 1991); and Shelley Douglass and Melinda Moore, eds., *The Practice of Nonviolence*, Active Nonviolence: A Way of Life, a Strategy for Change, vol. 2 (Nyak, N.Y.: The Fellowship of Reconciliation, 1991).

adequately express that very different movements should be expected from oppressors and oppressed in order to achieve reconciliation. How narrative Christus Victor addresses the different modes of participation in oppression and the different movements involved in reconciliation will be addressed in conversation with womanist theology in Chapter 6.

Conclusion

Feminist writers on atonement and Christology have observed additional elements of violence in traditional atonement imagery, beyond that pointed out in earlier chapters. While feminists offer differing alternatives, this survey has revealed significant agreement on problems posed by traditional atonement imagery: because salvation of sinners depends on the Son's willing submission to violence willed or needed by the Father, it poses an image of divine child abuse. The logic of what is required for satisfaction points to the will of God behind the death of Jesus. Such an image is particularly harmful for women and for others in oppressed situations. Further, to the accommodation of the sword, slavery, and racism by the ahistorical, abstract formulas of traditional atonement that was pointed out in earlier chapters, feminists add that these formulas accommodate patriarchy and male supremacy. Conversation between feminist writers and narrative Christus Victor indicates that narrative Christus Victor avoids the problems for traditional atonement indicated by feminists while also posing its own challenges to the several feminist voices.

The following chapter puts narrative Christus Victor in conversation with womanist theology. The result is yet more additions to the violence problems associated with traditional atonement.

6 *Womanist Theology on Atonement*

Introduction

Alongside black and feminist theology, the growing body of theological writing by womanists[1] also poses sharp challenges to traditional atonement

---

1. Womanist theology takes its name and guidelines from the following, oft-quoted definition of "womanist" that Alice Walker provides in her *In Search of Our Mother's Garden:*

> 1. From *womanish*. (Opp. of "girlish," i.e., frivolous, irresponsible, not serious.) A black feminist or feminist of color. From the black folk expression of mothers to female children, "You acting womanish," i.e., like a woman. Usually referring to outrageous, audacious, courageous or *willful* behavior. Wanting to know more and in greater depth than is considered "good" for one. Interested in grown-up doings. Acting grown up. Being grown up. Interchangeable with another black folk expression: "You trying to be grown." Responsible. In charge. *Serious.* 2. Also: A woman who loves other women, sexually and/or nonsexually. Appreciates and prefers women's culture, women's emotional flexibility (values tears as natural counter-balance of laughter) and women's strength. Sometimes loves individual men, sexually and/or nonsexually. Committed to survival and wholeness of entire people, male *and* female. Not a separatist, except periodically, for health. Traditionally universalist, as in: "Mamma, why are we brown, pink, and yellow, and our cousins are white, beige, and black?" Ans.: "Well, you know the colored race is just like a flower garden, with ever color flower represented." Traditionally capable, as in: "Mamma, I'm walking to Canada and I'm taking you and a bunch of other slaves with me." Reply: "It wouldn't be the first time." 3. Loves music. Loves dance. Loves the moon. *Loves* the Spirit. Loves love and food and roundness. Loves

doctrines. While womanist theology shares some elements with black and feminist theologies, it is also clearly distinguished from both.[2] The womanist critique reflects the particular perspective that black women bring to the discussion. Womanist thought includes the threefold focus on racism, sexism, and poverty, as well as other kinds of oppression. Stated succinctly, womanist theology emerged as a challenge to white feminists, whose presumption to speak for all women ignored the different experiences of black and white women, and as a challenge to the male dominance of early black theology, all the while making poverty (and other kinds of domination) an integral part of the theological agenda. Though womanists write for black women and for the black church, theirs is a comprehensive theology with an agenda that addresses white North Americans as well as African Americans. As Kelly Brown Douglas said, "dialogue with black women's history is also imperative for students who are not black and female. It gives them a chance to discover their relationship to black women's history."[3]

Womanist Particularity[4]

Katie Cannon

As was true for black theology and to a lesser extent for feminist theology, womanist writers make a specific point of speaking from a perspective that

---

struggle. *Loves* the Folk. Loves herself. *Regardless*. 4. Womanist is to feminist as purple to lavender.

Alice Walker, *In Search of Our Mother's Garden* (San Diego: Harcourt Brace Jovanovich, 1983), pp. xi-xii.

2. Dwight N. Hopkins, *Introducing Black Theology of Liberation* (Maryknoll, N.Y.: Orbis Books, 1999), pp. 88-90, 125-56.

3. Kelly Brown Douglas, "Teaching Womanist Theology," in *Living the Intersection: Womanism and Afrocentrism in Theology,* ed. Cheryl J. Sanders (Minneapolis: Fortress Press, 1995), p. 150. Garth Kasimu Baker-Fletcher similarly notes that his theology "is written in a Black voice to Black folks, but ought to be seen also as part of the transgressive naughtiness that challenges all persons to partake of its particularity as a way of looking at their own cultural, religious, and racial particularities" (Garth Kasimu Baker-Fletcher, *Xodus: An African American Male Journey* [Minneapolis: Fortress Press, 1996], p. xiv).

4. Some material on womanist particularity and on Christology in this chapter appeared in a different context in J. Denny Weaver, "Nicaea, Womanist Theology, and Anabaptist Particularity," in *Anabaptists and Postmodernity,* ed. Susan Biesecker-Mast and Gerald

is different from the dominant view that is shown to be both white and male. In her *Black Womanist Ethics*,[5] one of the earliest books from womanist perspective, Katie Cannon spoke of the difference between ethics for the dominant class and ethics for the dominated class. Already as a young child she had wondered how to relate her grandmother's Christian teaching that "God's universal parenthood" embraced "the equal humanity of all people" with the oppression and exploitation of black people by white people who called themselves Christians. "How could Christians who were white, flatly and openly, refuse to treat as fellow human beings Christians who had African ancestry?"[6]

Cannon eventually realized that the ethical systems of the dominant and the dominated could not be reconciled. The dominant system was "predicated on the existence of freedom," and stressed such virtues as "self-reliance, frugality and industry." Practicing these qualities enabled one to develop positive self-image and to move upward in society. But when this same society withheld economic and political power from blacks because of their supposed inferiority, the values of self-reliance, frugality, and industry were ineffectual for African Americans.[7] The dominant system assumed that the moral agent possessed "self-determining power," but withheld that freedom from blacks. Language about accepting suffering and making sacrifices for a principle sound very different when one is in a position to choose to suffer, as opposed to "the masses of Black people," for whom "suffering is the normal state of affairs."[8] In contrast to the dominant ethic, "Black faith and liberation ethics" discuss "defying oppressive rules or standards of 'law and order' which unjustly degrade Blacks in the society," purge blacks of self-hate, and promote their "human validity." Such ethical values from the black community "are not identical with the body of obligations and duties that Anglo-Protestant American society requires of its members."[9] Cannon's *Black Womanist Ethics* draws on the par-

---

Biesecker-Mast, The C. Henry Smith Series, vol. 1 (Telford, Pa.: Pandora Press U.S.; co-published with Herald Press, 2000), pp. 251-80.

5. Katie G. Cannon, *Black Womanist Ethics* (Atlanta: Scholars Press, 1988).

6. Cannon, *Black Womanist Ethics*, p. 1. See also Katie Geneva Cannon, "Moral Wisdom in the Black Women's Literary Tradition," in *Katie's Canon: Womanism and the Black Soul of the Community* (New York: Continuum, 1995), p. 57.

7. Cannon, *Black Womanist Ethics*, p. 2. See also Cannon, "Moral Wisdom," p. 58.

8. Cannon, *Black Womanist Ethics*, p. 3. See also Cannon, "Moral Wisdom," pp. 58-59.

9. Cannon, *Black Womanist Ethics*, p. 3. See also Cannon, "Moral Wisdom," p. 59.

ticular experiences of African-American women to develop a liberation ethic that empowers African Americans and confronts the racist, male-dominated and classist elements of our society.

Emilie Townes

As her way of asserting the particularity of womanist theology, Emilie Townes pointedly called womanist writing "biased." That is, womanist writing very specifically reflects the particularity of the threefold oppressions, racism, sexism, and poverty, that impact many African-American women. Womanist writing thus features a "critical perspective" on the "legacy of ignoring race and class issues" in feminist thought and early black theology's disregard for "gender and class." The womanist witnesses thus work for "love and justice in the midst of oppression and fallenness." Their "bias" shows that "all forms of theological discourse are open for reconsideration and critique."[10] This critique applies, of course, to "Eurocentric discourse." The particularity of the womanist critique makes plain the particularity of the inherited Eurocentric theology of Christendom.[11]

Such assertions show the particular perspective of womanist writers. Their impulse to construct theology that does not pass through the violence-accommodating theology of Christendom finds resonance in narrative Christus Victor as a theology of atonement and is a complement to black theology's expression of theology from an African-American perspective. Emilie Townes points out that black theology has accepted the critique and challenge from womanists, as is evident in the writings of James Cone and Garth Kasimu Baker-Fletcher, who were featured in Chapter 4.[12] While Susan Brooks Thistlethwaite's *Sex, Race*

10. Emilie M. Townes, ed., *A Troubling in My Soul: Womanist Perspectives on Evil and Suffering,* Bishop Henry McNeal Turner Series, vol. 8 (Maryknoll, N.Y.: Orbis Books, 1993), p. 2.

11. Townes, *Troubling,* p. 2.

12. See Townes, *Troubling,* p. 2; Hopkins, *Introducing Black Theology,* pp. 10, 88-90, 125-56; James H. Cone, *For My People: Black Theology and the Black Church* (Maryknoll, N.Y.: Orbis Books, 1984), pp. 122-39; James H. Cone, *My Soul Looks Back* (Maryknoll, N.Y.: Orbis Books, 1986), pp. 115-23; James H. Cone, *A Black Theology of Liberation: Twentieth Anniversary Edition* (Maryknoll, N.Y.: Orbis Books, 1990), pp. xv-xvi; James Cone, *Black Theology and Black Power* (Maryknoll, N.Y.: Orbis Books, 1997), pp. x-xi; and comments throughout Baker-Fletcher, *Xodus,* and Karen Baker-Fletcher and Garth Kasimu Baker-Fletcher, *My Sister, My Brother: Womanist and XODUS God-Talk,* Bishop Henry McNeal

and God[13] remains the only thorough treatment of racism by a white feminist, recent feminist writers, illustrated by Brock and Heyward in Chapter 5, also acknowledge the validity of the womanist challenge. Womanist theology thus continues to develop as a comprehensive theology written from the perspective of African-American women.

Delores Williams

Delores Williams's *Sisters in the Wilderness*[14] presents the most comprehensive constructive of theology from a womanist perspective. Williams holds up Hagar, servant of Abraham's wife Sarah, as the biblical figure with whom black women identified. As understood by black women, Hagar's story is that of the female slave, the woman whose destiny is and has been "shaped by the problems and desires of her owners."[15] For Sarah, motherhood is a privilege that will grant her status in the world. For Hagar, motherhood is a coerced experience, forced upon her by Sarah, her mistress. As a slave, Hagar is forced to submit to the sexual advances of Abraham, and functions as Sarah's surrogate. In other words, Hagar is exploited by another woman as well as by a man. After the birth of Ishmael, Hagar took her son and escaped into the wilderness, making herself "the first female in the Bible to liberate herself from oppressive power structures."[16] In the wilderness, Hagar and Ishmael were facing death when God came to them. On one occasion, as a matter of survival, God told Hagar to return with Ishmael to the tent of Abraham and Sarah, which was the place of bondage. The second time, God provided Hagar with new vision so that she could use her own resources to survive.[17]

Hagar's story of survival in the tent of Abraham and Sarah or in the wilderness becomes the paradigm of the female-centered tradition of Afri-

---

Turner/Sojourner Truth Series in Black Religion, vol. 12 (Maryknoll, N.Y.: Orbis Books, 1997).

13. Susan Brooks Thistlethwaite, *Sex, Race and God: Christian Feminism in Black and White* (New York: Crossroad, 1991).

14. Delores S. Williams, *Sisters in the Wilderness: The Challenge of Womanist God-Talk* (Maryknoll, N.Y.: Orbis Books, 1993).

15. Williams, *Sisters in the Wilderness*, p. 15.

16. Williams, *Sisters in the Wilderness*, p. 19.

17. Williams, *Sisters in the Wilderness*, p. 5.

can-American biblical appropriation. Williams calls this the "survival/quality-of-life tradition of African-American biblical appropriation,"[18] and it is the basis of her critique of early black and feminist theologies, and of the inherited theological tradition of European Christendom. This narrative of Hagar embodies the elements of the lives of many African-American women — pregnancy and motherhood as a coerced experience, struggle for survival with only God as a support, various kinds of surrogacy, and economic realities related to homelessness.[19] Williams concludes,

> African-American Christians need doctrine in their churches. But they need *doctrine that emerges from African-American people's experience with God,* not doctrine 'inherited' from oppressive Eurocentric forms of Christianity, not female-exclusive doctrine formulated centuries ago by male potentates. . . . It is God's continuing work in the African-American community's ever-present struggle for economic justice, for physical and emotional survival and for positive quality of life that forms 'the stuff' of black Christians' doctrines of resistance.[20]

The fact that Hagar was not fully liberated provides the basis for Williams's womanist critique of the early black liberation theology of James Cone. Rather than liberating, sometimes God provides the means to survive within the exploitative situation, as when God counseled Hagar and Ishmael to return to the household of Sarah and Abraham rather than to die in the wilderness. Thus womanist theologians may question Cone's claim that God's activity is always that of liberation, and they may question his use of exodus as the biblical paradigm for all African Americans. With Hagar as model, Williams argues, sometimes God supports survival rather than liberation.[21] Further, Williams points out that the liberating experience depicted by Cone was essentially male dominated and used male models. Thus womanist use of the Hagar story critiques the male-dominant characteristic of the African-American religious community. Williams suggests that black theology needs to give attention to another kind of history, namely "women's re/production history." Through this

---

18. Williams, *Sisters in the Wilderness,* p. 6.
19. Williams, *Sisters in the Wilderness,* summary ch. 1, developed chs. 2-5.
20. Williams, *Sisters in the Wilderness,* pp. 217-18.
21. Williams, *Sisters in the Wilderness,* pp. 144-53.

lens, Williams says, we would see not just a male-dominated struggle for black liberation, but

> the entire saga of the race. We see the survival intelligence of the race creating modes of resistance, sustenance and resurrection from despair. We see the exploitation of the community's spiritual, material and intellectual resources by extra-community forces met by the uncanny, redemptive response of the religion black women created in the African-American denominational churches.[22]

And as an alternative to "black experience," Williams suggests that "wilderness experience" is a better and broader term to describe African-American existence in North America today. The latter term encompasses both male and female experience, as well as both horizontal (human to human) relations and vertical (God to human) relationships.[23]

Alongside this critique of black theology, Sarah's exploitation of Hagar provides the point of entry for womanist critique of feminist theology. Hagar's treatment by Sarah foreshadows how white women have participated in the oppression of black women. The experience of African-American women has frequently been that of surrogates. When white women were elevated to a sexless ideal in the nineteenth century, black women became their surrogates as the coerced sexual partners of white men. When black men had their masculinity or maleness taken away by the white power structure after the Civil War, it was black women who did physical work in the fields and became the real rulers as well as wage earners of families, both functions in which they were surrogates for men.[24] White women have hired black women as surrogate mothers — "mammies" — for their white children — paying low wages and simultaneously forcing the black women into neglecting their own children in order to care for the children of white women. Feminist theologians have assumed that the experience of white women is normative for all women. In consequence, womanist theologians such as Williams charge that feminist theology has ignored the difference between the experiences of black and white women,

22. Williams, *Sisters in the Wilderness*, p. 158.
23. Williams, *Sisters in the Wilderness*, pp. 159-61.
24. See the discussion of surrogacy in several chapters, as well as specific discussion of feminist-womanist dialogue, Williams, *Sisters in the Wilderness*, pp. 178-99.

and the extent to which white women have assisted in the exploitation and oppression of blacks. Examples of this white women's oppression include the racist attitudes of such renowned nineteenth-century feminists as Susan B. Anthony and Elizabeth Cady Stanton, who helped to prevent African Americans from gaining the vote in the aftermath of the Civil War.[25] Williams's *Sisters in the Wilderness* draws on a great deal of such historical material in developing a womanist perspective on the experience of black women.

Womanists on Atonement

Delores Williams

Examining the role of Hagar as surrogate provides Delores Williams with a fundamental critique of Anselmian atonement theology. In the version of European Christendom exemplified by what Williams called "mainline Protestant churches,"[26] sinful humankind was redeemed because Jesus died on the cross as a substitute for humans, taking their sin and punishment upon himself. Viewed from Williams's womanist perspective, this means that in substitutionary atonement "Jesus represents the ultimate surrogate figure." When attached to Jesus, surrogacy "takes on an aura of the sacred." Given the exploited experience of black woman as surrogates in both white and black contexts, womanist theologians do not want to endorse any understanding of Jesus' work that models surrogacy. "If black women accept this idea of redemption," Williams asked, "can they not also passively accept the exploitation that surrogacy brings?"[27] In this critique of substitutionary atonement, Williams finds common cause with feminist writers such as Brown and Parker, who question salvation built on an image of the father willing the death of his son.[28] Williams suggests an understanding of Jesus' work in which his death is not willed by God and in which salvation is assured by his life of resistance and by survival strategies to help people overcome the death of identity. Womanist theologians

---

25. Delores S. Williams, "The Color of Feminism: Or Speaking the Black Woman's Tongue," *The Journal of Religious Thought* 43, no. 1 (Spring-Summer 1986): 42-58.

26. Williams, *Sisters in the Wilderness*, p. 161.

27. Williams, *Sisters in the Wilderness*, p. 162.

28. Williams, *Sisters in the Wilderness*, pp. 199-201.

"must show that redemption of humans can have nothing to do with any kind of surrogate or substitute role Jesus was reputed to have played in a bloody act that supposedly gained victory over sin and/or evil. . . . Rather it seems more intelligent and more scriptural to understand that redemption had to do with God, through Jesus, giving humankind new vision to see the resources for positive, abundant relational life."[29] This means that in the vision of Jesus, the reign of God "is not something that one has to die to reach. Rather, the kingdom of God is a metaphor of hope God gives those attempting to right the relationship between self and self, between self and others, between self and God as prescribed in the sermon on the mount, in the golden rule and in the commandment to show love above all else."[30]

In Williams's construction, the image of Jesus on the cross "is the image of human sin," an "image of defilement, a gross manifestation of collective human sin." Clearly, it was the human representatives of evil, not God, who were responsible for the death of Jesus. And Jesus did "not conquer sin through death on the cross." In the wilderness (Matt. 4:1-11), he conquered sin "by resistance," by resisting the temptations posed. Thus Jesus conquered sin, Williams says, "in life, not in death." And as God did not intend the death of Jesus, womanist theologians can then show black women that "God did not intend the surrogacy roles they have been forced to perform."[31] Rather, in Jesus, God has provided a vision of how to live rather than how to die.

> Jesus showed humankind a vision of righting relations between body, mind and spirit *through an ethical ministry of words* (such as the beatitudes, the parables, the moral directions and reprimands); *through a healing ministry of touch and being touched* (for example, healing the leper through touch; being touched by the woman with an issue of blood); *through a militant ministry of expelling evil forces* (such as exorcising the demoniacs, whipping the moneychangers out of the temple); *through a ministry grounded in the power of faith* (in the work of healing); *through a ministry of prayer* (he often withdrew from the crowd to pray); *through a ministry of compassion and love.*

29. Williams, *Sisters in the Wilderness*, pp. 164-65, quote p. 165.
30. Williams, *Sisters in the Wilderness*, pp. 165-66.
31. Williams, *Sisters in the Wilderness*, p. 166.

Humankind is, then, redeemed through Jesus' *ministerial* vision of life and not through his death. There is nothing divine in the blood of the cross. God does not intend black women's surrogacy experience. Neither can Christian faith affirm such an idea. Jesus did not come to be a surrogate. Jesus came for life, to show humans a perfect vision of ministerial relation that humans had very little knowledge of. As Christians, black women cannot forget the cross, but neither can they glorify it. To do so is to glorify suffering and to render their exploitation sacred. To do so is to glorify the sin of defilement.[32]

Missing from this view of Jesus' ministerial vision that saves through life rather than through death is the emphasis on resurrection that appears in narrative Christus Victor. Womanist Karen Baker-Fletcher fills that lacuna. In *My Sister, My Brother*, Karen Baker-Fletcher appropriates Delores Williams's challenges to traditional Anselmian atonement theology. But Baker-Fletcher adds the important reminder that while "atonement theory is problematic, we are still left with the historical reality of the cross."[33] She suggests that an emphasis on the resurrected Jesus refocuses the interpretation of Jesus' death as well. We need to rethink "*how* we preach Christ crucified,"[34] so that preaching glorifies God. Glorifying the cross as though Jesus came to die actually glorifies the "human capacity to oppress others."[35] In contrast, emphasizing the resurrection shifts the focus to the power of God to overcome oppression. And it then becomes clear that persecution and violence suffered by those who resist evil and injustice is not salvific suffering nor a cross to bear like Jesus bore the cross. Rather, this suffering is the result of an "ethic of risk," which is the result of "actively struggling for social justice."[36] This ethic of risk is an "alternative to the ethic of sacrifice" that has glorified suffering.[37] A very important implication of this ethic of risk is that it makes clear that Jesus' death is not a divinely willed sacrifice but the product of human evil.

---

32. Williams, *Sisters in the Wilderness*, p. 167.
33. Baker-Fletcher and Baker-Fletcher, *My Sister, My Brother*, p. 77.
34. Baker-Fletcher and Baker-Fletcher, *My Sister, My Brother*, p. 79.
35. Baker-Fletcher and Baker-Fletcher, *My Sister, My Brother*, p. 79.
36. Baker-Fletcher and Baker-Fletcher, *My Sister, My Brother*, p. 79.
37. Baker-Fletcher and Baker-Fletcher, *My Sister, My Brother*, p. 80.

JoAnne Marie Terrell

Since it deals with black theology as well as womanist theology, JoAnne Marie Terrell's analysis of the cross in *Power in the Blood? The Cross in African American Experience*[38] might be called a second-generation womanist writing. Terrell's comprehensive treatment deals with the history of blood atonement based on the surrogacy of Jesus and its appropriation in the theological justification of slavery and oppression of African Americans as well as of women generally. Terrell also deals with the restructuring of this doctrine in recent black and womanist theology, including authors treated in this book, James H. Cone, Jacquelyn Grant, Kelly Brown Douglas, and Delores Williams.

Terrell's history of atonement doctrine in womanist perspective notes the shift of church from countercultural witness to that of entrenched power and authority that has occurred since Constantine. Included was Anselm's use of a feudal model for divine-human relationships, as well as other circumstances down to current times in which a "hermeneutics of sacrifice" was used to enforce surrogacy and sacrifice on subjugated peoples. Thus Terrell supports the arguments of Delores Williams that atonement theories with Jesus as "surrogate/scapegoat" have supported violence and Rita Nakashima Brock's contention that these atonement images constitute divine child abuse.[39] "Contrary to efforts of many people in the black church to harmonize and thus retain all atonement theories, Terrell notes that womanist theologians have emphasized a "Christology 'from below'" that stresses "the deeds of the historical Jesus and not the idealized Christ, in keeping with the liberative traditions of the religious community."[40]

In her conclusions, Terrell states that it is important to assert, with Delores Williams, "that God did not condone the violence of the cross or black women's surrogacy" and that, rather than seeing Jesus as sent by God to die, the scripture testifies "that God indeed sent Christ, but for more honorable purposes."[41] This analysis builds on Terrell's assessment of the

---

38. JoAnne Marie Terrell, *Power in the Blood? The Cross in African American Experience,* The Bishop Henry McNeal Turner/Sojourner Truth Series in Black Religion, no. 15 (Maryknoll, N.Y.: Orbis Books, 1998).

39. Terrell, *Power in the Blood?* p. 107.

40. Terrell, *Power in the Blood?* p. 108.

41. Terrell, *Power in the Blood?* p. 121.

love of God expressed through Israel, in which "Yahweh reveres and does not require blood." Thus in Israel there developed an alternative to the violence in the cultures around Israel, and a rejection of any understanding of sacrifice that features injury to "someone or something for the sake of someone or something else." Thus while there is "*something* of God in the blood of the cross," it is not an act of divinely sanctioned violence. Rather it "highlights the egregious nature of every historical crime against humanity and the Divinity," which means that "the cross is about God's love for humankind in a profound sense."[42] At the same time, Terrell is more inclined than Williams to affirm the positive ways that Jesus' suffering has been appropriated in the black church tradition. Terrell would retain and use the empty cross as a "sign of our own resurrection" whereas Williams considers it a symbol of "innocent suffering and violence" that teaches that "something good can result from violence."[43] Williams would use as primary Christian symbols images such as "the dove, the mustard seed, the fish and the loaves, [and] lighted candles," which represent what Jesus lived for ("mercy, justice, healing, and spiritual transformation of humankind") rather than what he died for.[44] Terrell will keep the empty cross, saying that it signifies God's continuous empowerment, and the continuous intercession of the spirit of Jesus Christ with God's people. Thus Terrell concludes, "Not the resurrection but Christ's intercession signals the end of the gospel story and the beginning of Christ's significance for us, 'on our behalf.'"[45]

Womanists on Theodicy

Womanist answers to the problem of theodicy shine additional light on the atonement question about who needed or was responsible for the death of Jesus. Their discussion also constitutes a further example of the significance for interpretation of social location or the difference between dominant and dominated perspectives.

The assumptions behind the traditional way of posing the question of theodicy, womanists point out, is that an omnipotent God could choose to

42. Terrell, *Power in the Blood?* pp. 123-24.

43. Terrell, *Power in the Blood?* p. 125. Terrell quotes Delores S. Williams, "A Crucifixion Double Cross?" in *The Other Side,* September-October 1993, p. 26.

44. Williams, "A Crucifixion Double Cross?" p. 26.

45. Terrell, *Power in the Blood?* p. 125.

prevent evil.[46] Thus to ask how evil can exist when there is an omnipotent God is a question that raises doubts about either the existence of God or the omnipotence of God. The assumptions of the question, womanists point out, reflect the concerns and the worldview of those in a position of dominance or control. Those who identify with the dominant and ruling forces of the social order presume that God reflects their dominance and controls all. It is this linking that leads some thinkers to abandon the idea of the omnipotence of God, or even to reject the idea of God's existence outright. In Chapter 5, for example, we observed that Julie Hopkins formulated the problem of theodicy in this way. Her solution, it will be remembered, was to abandon the omnipotence of God. Womanists take a quite different direction.

In the slave narratives, womanists point out, slaves and other oppressed African Americans posed the question of theodicy differently than did those from the dominant perspective. Even though slaves lacked control over their lives and experienced overwhelming evil, they never doubted that God existed, and they believed that God's presence sustained them in their bondage. For them, the fact that they felt God's presence in the midst of their oppression and survived was itself a demonstration of the existence of God. Katie Cannon illustrates this perspective on theodicy through analysis of the sermon, "The Wounds of Jesus," from a Zora Neal Hurston novel. This sermon emphasized a story of redemption for African Americans that began with Jesus' wounds suffered for them on Calvary. One image in the sermon is that of the "damnation train" pulling out of the Garden of Eden "loaded with cargo going to hell" as it plows through the story of biblical Israel on the way to Calvary. To save us from that train, "Jesus stood out on the train track like a rough-backed mountain and shed

46. For womanist discussions of theodicy, see Clarice J. Martin, "Biblical Theodicy and Black Women's Spiritual Autobiography: 'The Miry Bog, the Desolate Pit, a New Song in My Mouth'," in *A Troubling in My Soul: Womanist Perspectives on Evil and Suffering,* ed. Emilie M. Townes, Bishop Henry McNeal Turner Series, vol. 8 (Maryknoll, N.Y.: Orbis Books, 1993), pp. 13-36; Cheryl A. Kirk-Duggan, "African-American Spirituals: Confronting and Exorcising Evil Through Song," in *A Troubling in My Soul: Womanist Perspectives on Evil and Suffering,* ed. Emilie M. Townes, Bishop Henry McNeal Turner Series, vol. 8 (Maryknoll, N.Y.: Orbis Books, 1993), pp. 150-71; Katie Geneva Cannon, "'The Wounds of Jesus': Justification of Goodness in the Face of Manifold Evil," in *A Troubling in My Soul: Womanist Perspectives on Evil and Suffering,* ed. Emilie M. Townes, Bishop Henry McNeal Turner Series, vol. 8 (Maryknoll, N.Y.: Orbis Books, 1993), pp. 219-31; Terrell, *Power in the Blood?* pp. 142-44.

his blood in order to derail the train of damnation."[47] In their context, slaves knew that evil and suffering did not originate with God but with human beings — first in the Garden of Eden and then continuing in the white folks who maintained evil institutions such as slavery. Thus Cannon concludes that a womanist approach does not ask whether God exists and how to justify God's goodness in the face of evil. "Rather, womanist protagonists contend that God's sustaining presence is known in the resistance to evil."[48] JoAnne Terrell expresses the same point in terms of human evil. "As a child of six or seven, having very little to go on doctrinally but having had devastating experiences of physical emotional abuse on which to reflect, I reformulated the classical theodical statement in this God-affirming way: *Since* God is so good, why are people so evil?"[49] Parallel to Katie Cannon, Clarice J. Martin uses the spiritual autobiography of Maria W. Stewart to argue that God is on the side of the oppressed and that one obeys God by resisting oppression.[50] Cheryl A. Kirk-Duggan makes similar points using African-American spirituals as sources.[51]

Womanists on Christology

Given the critique of traditional atonement imagery, it will not surprise that womanists also find problems with traditional Christology.

Kelly Brown Douglas

Kelly Brown Douglas's *The Black Christ*[52] develops a womanist perspective on Christology in conversation with the African-American tradition. Douglas notes that a theology that focused on belief in the incarnation, with little attention to what Jesus did on earth, enabled slaveowners to be Christian while also justifying slavery. "What Jesus did on earth has little if

47. Katie Geneva Cannon, "Wounds of Jesus," pp. 225-26.
48. Cannon, "Wounds of Jesus," p. 229.
49. Terrell, *Power in the Blood?* p. 143.
50. Martin, "Biblical Theodicy," pp. 13-36.
51. Kirk-Duggan, "African-American Spirituals," pp. 150-71.
52. Kelly Brown Douglas, *The Black Christ*, The Bishop Henry McNeal Turner Studies in North American Black Religion, no. 9 (Maryknoll, N.Y.: Orbis Books, 1994).

anything to do with what it means for him to be Christ. His ministry to the poor and oppressed is virtually inconsequential to this interpretation of Christianity."[53] The implications were that (i) little was required for salvation. One had merely to accept the belief that God had become human in Jesus. Thus "white people could be slaveholders *and* Christian without guilt or fear about the state of their souls," and blacks could be Christians without challenge to their status as slaves; and (ii) slavery actually served a good purpose since it "provided the opportunity for Africans to attain this salvific knowledge" about the incarnation.[54]

Douglas describes her own womanist pilgrimage with classic Nicene-Chalcedonian Christology. Womanist understandings emerge, she says, from the black tradition in which men and women "confessed Jesus as Christ because of what he did during his time as well as in their own lives. They did not make this confession because of his metaphysical make-up." Those in the slave community "were most likely unaware of the Nicene/Chalcedonian tradition," as are many African-American Christians today. Although Douglas grew up in the Episcopalian tradition and could recite the Nicene creed and accepted it as part of the wider Christian tradition, she says, the creed did not explain for her how Jesus was the Christ. "Reflective of my upbringing in the wider Black religious community, I believed that Jesus was Christ because of what he did for others, particularly the poor and oppressed." The Nicene-Chalcedonian tradition is not integral to that confession, Douglas notes, and many black Christians "tend not to consider it relevant to their own beliefs about Jesus."[55]

Along with the fact that Nicene-Chalcedonian tradition does not seem relevant for many black Christians, Douglas noted several aspects of the Nicene-Chalcedonian formulation that appear inconsistent with her reading of Jesus as presented in the Gospels. For one, by focusing on incarnation, "it diminishes the significance of Jesus' actions on earth. His ministry is virtually ignored." Further, the confession "moves directly from the act of incarnation to the crucifixion and resurrection," which implies that "what took place between Jesus' birth and resurrection — the bulk of the Gospels' reports of Jesus — is unrelated to what it means for Jesus to be the Christ." And finally, emphasizing the uniqueness of Jesus' metaphysical nature "makes

53. Douglas, *Black Christ*, p. 13.
54. Douglas, *Black Christ*, pp. 13-14. Emphasis Douglas'.
55. Douglas, *Black Christ*, pp. 111-12.

what it means to be Christ inaccessible to ordinary Christians. There becomes little reason to strive to be an example of Christ in the world, because to be Christ requires a divine incarnation, which happened only in Jesus. . . . He is seen as someone to be worshipped, believed in, but not followed or imitated." Douglas concluded, "A womanist understanding of the Black Christ avoids these shortcomings." Nonetheless, this womanist understanding does not remove Nicene-Chalcedonian speculation from the picture. Rather "This formulation is seen as a part of a continuing tradition in which those who confess Jesus as Christ attempt to discern the meaning of that confession. It does not, however, have any normative significance as womanist theologians attempt to articulate Christ's meaning for the Black community."[56] That is, womanist particularity points to the particularity of Nicea-Chalcedon. Rather than allowing Nicea-Chalcedon to float in an authoritative and normative status that transcends particularity, this womanist critique makes it one conversation partner among several.

Jacquelyn Grant

Jacquelyn Grant's *White Women's Christ and Black Women's Jesus*[57] pursues the difference between white and black perspectives in an analysis of feminist Christology. Like other womanists, Grant points out the ways that both nineteenth- and twentieth-century feminist thought has treated with neglect or worse the experience of black women. In an essay concerned with a revisioning of the idea of servanthood, Grant asks

> Which women's experience is the source of theology? Further, one could ask, how do these experiences impact the direction taken in one's theological perspective? Is it the experience of the daughters of slaveholders or the experience of the daughters of slaves? These two experiences are irreconcilable as they stand.[58]

56. Douglas, *Black Christ,* pp. 112-13.

57. Jacquelyn Grant, *White Women's Christ and Black Women's Jesus: Feminist Christology and Womanist Response,* American Academy of Religion Series, no. 64 (Atlanta: Scholars Press, 1989).

58. Jacquelyn Grant, "The Sin of Servanthood: And the Deliverance of Discipleship," in *A Troubling in My Soul: Womanist Perspectives on Evil and Suffering,* ed. Emilie M. Townes, Bishop Henry McNeal Turner Series, vol. 8 (Maryknoll, N.Y.: Orbis Books, 1993), pp. 208-09.

Like other womanists, Grant asserts that "Black women must do theology out of their tri-dimensional experience of racism/sexism/classism. To ignore any aspect of this experience is to deny the holistic and integrated reality of Black womanhood. When Black women say that God is on the side of the oppressed, we mean that God is in solidarity with the struggles of those on the underside of humanity."[59] Although Grant does not distance herself as far from the classic tradition of Christology as does Brown Douglas, it is clear that for Grant a womanist Christology must first of all reflect womanist rather than inherited European concerns.

While Delores Williams's *Sisters in the Wilderness* deals with classic atonement doctrine, she also notes the implications of a womanist critique of Nicene-Chalcedonian Christology. Her concern is that the discussion of Christology should be more than an abstract issue debated by the academicians. Williams's comments echo Cone's critique that the abstract categories of Nicea and Chalcedon lend themselves to claiming Jesus while justifying acts of oppression in the name of Christ. Thus Williams says

> Black women's question about Jesus Christ is not about the relation of his humanity to his divinity or about the relation of the historical Jesus to the Christ of faith. Black women's stories . . . [and] an Afro-centric biblical tradition . . . attest to black women's belief in Jesus/Christ/God involved in their daily affairs and supporting them. Jesus is their mother, their father, their sister and their brother. Jesus is whoever Jesus has to be to function in a supportive way in the struggle. Whether we talk about Jesus in relation to atonement theory or christology, we womanists must be guided more by black Christian women's voices, faith and experiences than by anything that was decided centuries ago at Chalcedon.[60]

Narrative Christus Victor and Womanist Theology

A number of issues give narrative Christus Victor a great deal of affinity for womanist discussions of atonement, Christology, and theodicy. Parallel points include the intent to construct theology that is not limited by

59. Grant, *White . . . Black*, p. 209.
60. Williams, *Sisters*, p. 203.

the inherited European tradition, the critique of atonement based on divinely modeled violence, an active mission for Jesus in opposition to oppression, and the idea that God is not the author of evil and that God did not arrange the death of the Son. Also clear for womanist thought and for narrative Christus Victor is that questions about atonement have their counterparts in analysis of Nicene-Chalcedonian Christology, so that the focus on the life of Jesus presents a narrative-based alternative to classic Christology.

Of primary importance for womanists is the issue of surrogacy and surrogate suffering. Out of the historical experience of being submitted to multiple injustices in which they were forced to bear suffering and oppression from white men and women and from black men, womanists reject any understanding of the death of Jesus that would base salvation on innocent suffering on behalf of another. The classic understandings of atonement, in particular Anselmian satisfaction atonement, do posit salvation on the basis of Jesus as innocent victim who submits obediently the will of the Father. In womanist analysis, this atonement view holds high for black women an image that glorifies innocent suffering, which is precisely the image womanists reject. Womanist constructions of atonement focus on the life rather than the death of Jesus, and see salvation happening when Jesus confronts evil, heals, engages in exorcisms, and in other ways makes the reign of God present in the face of evil and oppression.

In womanist understanding, Jesus does not passively submit to unjust suffering. On the contrary, he actively confronts it in a life-affirming and life-giving ministry. This activist rather than passive mode is very significant. Victims are passive. Victims can only submit. To resist evil and oppression is to cease being a passive victim, even if suffering results. That suffering is not salvific, although it is the price of beginning to resist. Resisting is the beginning of accepting responsibility rather than merely accepting passively. This suffering is the price of what Karen Baker-Fletcher calls an "ethic of risk."[61]

Narrative Christus Victor is an atonement motif that turns passive victims into responsible actors in the history of salvation. Narrative Christus Victor makes a point of opposing evil rather than passively submitting to it. Identifying with or following the Jesus of narrative Christus Victor may indeed be costly; it may indeed entail suffering and even death.

---

61. Baker-Fletcher, *My Sister, My Brother*, p. 79.

But that suffering is no longer suffering that is salvific in and of itself, and it is not suffering whose origin or object is God, or that happens because in some way God needs it without compelling it. This is suffering that is the result of opposing evil, as Jesus' suffering and death were the result of opposing evil. This suffering is an ethic of risk.

Further, womanist thought provides the insight that enables narrative Christus Victor to respond well to different kinds of participation in sins involving oppression and unequal power relationships. It is virtually self-evident that those in the dominant categories — men over women, whites over blacks, wealthy over the poor, and so on — have shared in oppression. While oppressed persons are also sinful and sinners, their participation in those oppressive and sinful systems differs from that of their oppressors. Delores Williams writes of participation either "in society's systems that devalue Black women's womanhood (humanity) through a process of invisibilization" or by failing to "challenge the patriarchal and demon-archal systems in society."[62] In other words, oppressed persons who acquiesce in their oppression, or who accept the inferior identity foisted on them by dominators, are actually complicitous in that oppression. They cease participating in their oppression, not when they actually achieve liberation, but when they take up resistance to it.

While it is both possible and necessary to spell out the ways that oppressors and oppressed have complicity in sin much farther, the important point at this juncture is that Williams points toward a model for dealing with the different ways that oppressed and oppressors are implicated as sinners. The image of "changing sides" in narrative Christus Victor incorporates these two ways of participating in sin. Although they were in the opposition to the reign of God in very different ways, both oppressed and oppressors switch sides and submit to the rule of God. The oppressed ceased acquiescing to oppression and join the rule of God; oppressors cease their oppression and submit to the rule of God. Coming from different directions, both oppressed and oppressors have their existence transformed by the rule of God, and together they join in making visible the opposition to oppression by the reign of God. Narrative Christus Victor is a model that accounts for different kinds of participation in the sinful social

---

62. Delores S. Williams, "A Womanist Perspective on Sin," in *A Troubling in My Soul: Womanist Perspectives on Evil and Suffering*, ed. Emilie M. Townes, Bishop Henry McNeal Turner Series, vol. 8 (Maryknoll, N.Y.: Orbis Books, 1993), p. 146.

order and in contexts of oppression, and for subsequent mutual struggle of Christians against oppression.

A final point of convergence between womanist thought and narrative Christus Victor is the idea that it is not God but the forces of evil in the world that are responsible for the death of Jesus. This discussion involves theodicy, and contributes directly to the discussion of atonement. Recall the questions from Chapter 3 about who was responsible for the death of Jesus or who needed the death of Jesus. In narrative Christus Victor it is the human representatives of evil in the world who conspire to kill Jesus, while in satisfaction and moral influence models God is the agency behind the death of Jesus. When those are the two options, it is self-evident that the womanist discussion of theodicy is also an answer to the question about the agency of Jesus' death. The God who frees Israelite slaves is a God who opposes oppression, not the God who orchestrates the death of the Son. And in their worship and in their resistance, the African-American slaves experienced freedom in the resurrected Christ and lived in hope of future physical freedom as well. As Cheryl Kirk-Duggan says, in language reminiscent of narrative Christus Victor,

> Spirituals affirmed that Christ, the King, enabled African-Americans to transcend the limitations of slavery. . . . Spirituals profess a Christ who defeated death at the cross and assures the faithful of eternal life in states of goodness. Death never conquers life. Life in Christ conquers death. Death is swallowed up in victory. Life is a pilgrimage, a mysterious given. A constructive theodicy accepts the defeat of death on the cross, the gift of life through the resurrection and celebrates the invitation to the victim and victimizer for reconciliation toward healing presented at the Eucharist.[63]

Walter Wink advances an argument similar to womanists on theodicy. Wink enters the discussion from the context of prayer. Since prayers are not always answered, Wink says, the usual assumption is that the prayer was incorrect, or the faith of the one praying was weak, or that on the basis of superior wisdom, God chose not to answer. Wink objects to making these the only three options.

Actually prayer involves three parties: God, we who pray, and the pow-

---

63. Kirk-Duggan, "African-American Spirituals," p. 163.

ers of evil. While God is sovereign over history and while the powers of evil have been defeated by the resurrection of Jesus, the powers nonetheless still rule in the interval before the culmination (the return of Jesus). These powers can and do come between us and God. All healing is of God.

> But if the Powers flush PCBs and dioxin into the water we drink, or release radioactive gas into the atmosphere or insist on spraying our fruit with known carcinogens, God's healing power is sharply reduced. . . .
>
> But when one race enslaves another to labor in its fields, or to dig its mines, or when children's lives are stunted by sexual abuse or physical brutality, or when whole nations are forced to submit to the exploitation of other states more powerful, then what is God to do? We may pray for justice and liberation, as indeed we must, and *God hears us on the very first day.* But God's ability to intervene against the freedom of these rebellious creatures is sometimes tragically restricted in ways we cannot pretend to understand. It takes considerable spiritual maturity to live in the tension between these two facts: God has heard our prayer, and the Powers are blocking God's response.[64]

But we must remember that while the powers of evil "can thwart God" in the interim, in eschatological perspective the reign of God has already triumphed in the resurrection of Jesus. Thus "delay of the Kingdom was not fatal to Christian belief."[65] The weakness of the powers of evil is exposed.

> Many innocent people may die, while the Powers appear to gain in invincibility with every death, but that is only an illusion. Their very brutality and desperation is evidence that their legitimacy is fast eroding. Their appeal to force is itself an admission that they can no longer command voluntary consent. When sufficient numbers of people withdraw their consent, the Powers inevitably fall.[66]

In the interim until that fall — the consummation of the reign of God — God is with us in the midst of evil. "On a practical level, then, the problem

---

64. Walter Wink, *Engaging the Powers: Discernment and Resistance in a World of Domination,* The Powers, vol. 3 (Minneapolis: Fortress Press, 1992), p. 311.

65. Wink, *Engaging the Powers,* p. 313.

66. Wink, *Engaging the Powers,* p. 313.

of evil is dealt with through prayer and action, in the everyday attempt to bend evil back toward the purposes of God." And the actions of believing people to make present the reign of God is prayer to God that acknowledges the powers; and their prayers "are a form of social action."[67]

These arguments about theodicy reflect narrative Christus Victor's understanding of the death of Jesus. The death of Jesus is not carried out within the will of God in order to satisfy a divine requirement for justice. Rather, the death of Jesus displays the character of the powers of evil that oppose the reign of God.

Following on the heels of the feminist arguments in Chapter 5, this chapter has displayed womanists' further development of the discussion about images of abuse. In addition, we have observed womanist objections to the absence of ethical dimensions in classic christological formulas, as well as a proposal for a different understanding of theodicy. Narrative Christus Victor resonates with these arguments, and in particular accepts the feminist and womanist argument that satisfaction atonement lends itself to the image of divine child abuse and to the logical conclusion that God the Father is the agent or the cause behind the death of the Son.

It is obvious, however, that not everyone agrees with this analysis of the image of satisfaction atonement. There are a number of writers who acknowledge that the issues concerning abusive imagery raised by feminists and womanists are valid, but who nonetheless specifically reject the validity of the charge that satisfaction atonement is an image of divine child abuse, and who seek to defend Anselmian satisfaction atonement. Chapter 7 turns to these defenses of Anselmian atonement.

---

67. Wink, *Engaging the Powers*, p. 317.

7 Conversation with Anselm
and His Defenders

Introduction

A number of writers attempt to defend satisfaction, sacrificial atonement in the face of the critique brought by feminists and womanists. This chapter engages these defenders.

At the outset, it is important to emphasize that the efforts at defense and rehabilitation of satisfaction atonement all acknowledge the importance and validity of the challenges raised by feminists and womanists. The defenses then attempt to speak to the issues raised rather than merely asserting the truth of satisfaction atonement.

Responses to the feminist and womanist challenges have followed variations of three broadly defined and related strategies. One move is to rehabilitate the ideas of punishment and vicarious suffering. A second tack is to shift emphasis away from punishment by recovering additional themes and emphases within satisfaction that have been covered over by too much stress on punishment. As a variant of the second strategy, the third tactic acknowledges the validity of the critique of punishment by blaming the excesses on Protestant reformers such as John Calvin and appealing to an earlier, different emphasis in Anselm's *Cur Deus Homo.* Many though by no means all these defense strategies are exercised by writers who reflect the Reformed tradition.

The Defenders of Anselm

Redefinitions, Reemphases, and Rehabilitation

William Placher seeks to reinterpret punishment and vicarious suffering in a positive light. He cited 2 Corinthians 5:21 ("For our sake he made him to be sin who knew no sin, so that in him we might become the righteousness of God") as the text that demonstrates why vicarious punishment and vicarious suffering are biblical but also "captures as vividly as anything in scripture much of what many contemporary Christians find so repugnant about traditional doctrines of the atonement." In this light, Placher attempted to reinterpret substitutionary suffering so that it avoids the "standard objections," namely that it "fosters human suffering," poses an image of a "vindictive God," and "assumes an idea of vicarious punishment that makes no moral sense."[1]

In agreement with comments voiced throughout this book, Placher notes that the judicial system of the United States is based on the idea of retribution and punishment. In this system, the first question is whether the individual actually committed the crime. If the answer is "yes," then justice is done when punishment is handed out. The assumption is virtually universal that to do justice means to inflict punishment on the perpetrator of a crime. Punishment is a quid pro quo arrangement, an act of vengeance, in which pain is inflicted on the perpetrator in compensation for the pain he or she inflicted.

According to Placher, this model of criminal justice is the model on which substitutionary atonement is based. Sin must be punished. God punished Jesus in our place, and we are saved because we have avoided punishment. Placher believes, however, that North American society has not drawn the appropriate lesson from Jesus' atoning death. In Placher's view, since Jesus has already borne the ultimate punishment, the criminal justice system need not and should not focus on punishment as the means to remove guilt. In fact, since Christ has taken on their guilt, "they now stand innocent" and the need for human beings to seek retribution has come to an end. Because Jesus was ultimately punished, "we should stop

---

1. William C. Placher, "Christ Takes Our Place: Rethinking Atonement," *Interpretation* 53, no. 1 (January 1999): 6-7.

punishing the guilty." Christian political activity should focus on rehabilitation rather than retribution.[2]

Placher believes that this interpretation of Jesus' vicarious death responds to the three standard objections that he outlined. First, this interpretation does not foster abuse or glorify suffering, Placher argues, because Jesus suffered voluntarily for a good cause. "Christ is not a scapegoat, dragged to the Temple for sacrifice, but a volunteer in the battle against evil." Thus feminists are correct to challenge an interpretation of Jesus' suffering that would encourage victims of injustice to endure, an interpretation that Placher claims is not found in substitutionary atonement when properly understood. But in light of Jesus' suffering, comfortable Christians who have benefited from injustice should be encouraged to submit to accept "suffering in the service of justice, peace, and liberation." "We may have to take some risks for our faith."[3]

Second, on the question of a vindictive God, Placher notes that the New Testament emphasis is not on God's need to be reconciled to us but on "[our] need to be reconciled to God." Placher argues that inner trinitarian relations mean that God bore the suffering with Christ rather than standing apart as an angry God who needed to be placated. God's act is one of love for us sinners in bearing with Christ on the cross the suffering

2. Placher, "Christ Takes Our Place," pp. 12-15, quote p. 15

Applying the assertion in the book of Hebrews that the death of Christ is the end of all sacrifice, John H. Yoder makes the same application of satisfaction atonement as does Placher (H. Wayne House and John Howard Yoder, *The Death Penalty Debate: Two Opposing Views of Capital Punishment* [Dallas: Word, 1991], pp. 158-60). However, Yoder does not thereby validate satisfaction atonement. In fact, he stated that he shared discomfort with the retributive assumptions of satisfaction atonement. But Yoder then argued that the psychic desire for punishment is so pervasive that in seeking to reduce the violence that comes with exercise of the death penalty, we would do better to accept the assumption of retribution and then argue that the death of Jesus ended the need for retribution rather than to challenge the assumption with alternative theology (John Howard Yoder, *The Case for Punishment* [John Howard Yoder's Home Page, 1995, ch. 5 and n. 9, accessed 1 July 2000, http://www.nd.edu/~theo/jhy/writings/home/welcome.htm]. This argument is parallel to Yoder's use of justifiable war theory. While he disagreed with the presupposition of justifiable war theory, he also supported careful application of the criteria as a way to reduce violence in the world (John Howard Yoder, *When War Is Unjust: Being Honest in Just-War Thinking*, 2nd ed. [Maryknoll, N.Y.: Orbis Books, 1996]). While my theological orientation is strongly influenced by Yoder, as acknowledged in the Preface and Introduction, this book shows that I have chosen to engage in the theological task he eschewed.

3. Placher, "Christ Takes Our Place," p. 16.

that pays for sin. "The pain that God endures on the cross is the price love pays for taking sin seriously but refusing to stop loving."[4] Thus Placher shifts emphasis away from the role of God in punishing sin and toward what God has done for sinners.

The discussion of God sharing the pain with Jesus leads to the point of whether it is "just for one to bear what is due another?" This is the third of what Placher called the standard objections to satisfaction atonement. To show that it is in fact just, Placher used some contemporary analogies in which it might be accepted that one person bears another's pain. For example, one of his analogies involved a popular couple who would choose voluntarily to sit in detention at school and share the punishment with "the bad kids, the troublemakers" and then "somehow detention center becomes the best place to be in school."[5]

By recovering ideas that have fallen from view, David Wheeler would reposition the images of blood and vicarious sacrifice for the modern world. Rather than seeing sacrificial atonement as a form of divine punishment, he suggests recovering: sacrifice as an expression of gratitude; sacrifice as an event that demonstrates the costliness of restoring relationships; and the idea that sacrifice absorbs evil and leads to expiation. These three emphases should be "enfolded into" the concept of a "compassionate God" in contrast to the seemingly harsh and judgmental God who orchestrates Jesus' vicarious and bloody sacrifice. In essence, Wheeler is redefining sacrifice to be "fundamentally *relational* in nature and only analogically juridical or liturgical."[6] He suggests a twofold purpose for these redefinitions and changed emphases — staying connected to the past and speaking to the future.

> If we reposition the cross and the blood of Christ for an age of ecological challenges and depth psychology, and if we interpret these images in terms of the costliness and interconnectedness of life, then perhaps we can tap into the richness of Christian tradition within the church *and* speak meaningfully to the cross's cultured despisers.[7]

4. Placher, "Christ Takes Our Place," pp. 16-17.

5. Placher, "Christ Takes Our Place," p. 13.

6. David Wheeler, "The Cross and the Blood: Dead or Living Images?" *Dialog* 35, no. 1 (Winter 1996): 12. Emphasis Wheeler's.

7. Wheeler, "Cross and Blood," p. 13.

Like Placher's second move, Wheeler shifts emphasis away from punishment and toward emphasis on God's compassion for sinners.

Thelma Megill-Cobbler acknowledges that feminists rightly challenge "any view of the cross which depicts Jesus as a passive and innocent victim put to death by the will of a God who fits the definition of an abusive father or an unjust tyrant."[8] What feminists reject "is the idea that the death of Jesus fulfills the requirements of God's justice in order that sin be forgiven."[9]

As a counterproposal to the feminist argument, Megill-Cobbler suggests that the God depicted as abusive does not represent the entire atonement tradition. "I propose that there is today in the wider tradition an ongoing conversation over reinterpretation of penal imagery for atonement, a conversation which speaks against the hegemony of the image of a punishing God."[10] Megill-Cobbler's answer is to shift emphasis from the image of a punishing God and penal substitution, which is particularly strong in Calvinist and Reformed traditions, to the image of a God who identifies with victims. Christ bears punishment with us rather than instead of us, and it was humankind rather than God who demanded that Jesus be put to death. Abelard was correct to see that it would be cruel of God to consider the death of his son agreeable.[11] Drawing on Martin Luther, Megill-Cobbler says that Christ is on our side, and in that location he is not a judge or angry tyrant. When the penal imagery is then joined to the images of struggle and victory, we see a God who chooses to be with us even at great cost, and that resurrection overturns the human verdict on Jesus and vindicates the one who acted in God's name. "Jesus has undergone and upholds the judgment of God, not in the sense of enduring retribution, but by intervening at great cost to set things right."[12]

When Megill-Cobbler shifts the emphasis from Christ's death as enduring an imposed penalty to that of "taking on the consequences of human estrangement in order to make justice," there is a change from understanding the work of Christ in passive to active voice. "Making justice involves struggle as well as endurance."[13] In Megill-Cobbler's view, under-

8. Thelma Megill-Cobbler, "A Feminist Rethinking of Punishment Imagery in Atonement," *Dialog* 35, no. 1 (Winter 1996): 14.

9. Megill-Cobbler, "A Feminist Rethinking," p. 16.

10. Megill-Cobbler, "A Feminist Rethinking," p. 16.

11. Megill-Cobbler, "A Feminist Rethinking," pp. 17-18.

12. Megill-Cobbler, "A Feminist Rethinking," p. 19.

13. Megill-Cobbler, "A Feminist Rethinking," pp. 19-20.

standing that "at the cross God identifies with the victims of suffering and bears the consequences of human sin" provides an activist, justice orientation toward atonement rather than the image rejected by feminists of a "bloodthirsty God" who punishes a passive Jesus.[14]

Leanne Van Dyk suggests a different set of emphases to defend traditional atonement doctrine against the misuse that has happened, "many times," in abusive ways. She notes that misuse in abusive fashion does not make Christianity an abusive theology per se, as she believes Joan Carlson Brown has charged. More importantly, similar to William Placher, Van Dyk suggests that paying closer attention to the doctrine of the Trinity will correct the "multiple caricatures and misreadings" of a radical critique of atonement. The claim of "divine child abuse," Van Dyk says, "implies that the relationship between the Father and the Son is one of domination, control, and punitive anger." In contrast, correct atonement theology presupposes or emphasizes "the inner trinitarian cooperation and gracious initiative of the Triune God. No coercion was exercised in the Godhead, no sadistic pleasure taken in suffering, no punishment meted out to satisfy an abstract divine justice."[15] The mutuality of the Trinity "renders incomprehensible the charge of divine child abuse," and shows that the inner trinitarian relations are characterized by "mutual cooperation and purpose." Furthermore, the mutual cooperation and purpose of the Trinity emphasize that Christ's death and resurrection are "for us and our salvation," rather than aimed at satisfying God.[16] Van Dyk's final argument is to proclaim atonement a "mystery," whose ultimate meaning and expression we cannot fathom. All atonement theories "express in limited, analogical language the reality of God's decisive act on behalf of a broken world." None of the atonement theories really explains how it works, although each expresses some aspect of God's act. Thus rather than fully explaining, they "focus our attention, illuminate the truth and point beyond themselves to God."[17] It is

14. Megill-Cobbler, "A Feminist Rethinking," p. 20.

15. Leanne Van Dyk, "Do Theories of Atonement Foster Abuse?" *Dialog* 35, no. 1 (Winter 1996): 24. Margo Houts also appeals to the Trinity in this fashion to defend traditional atonement doctrine (Margo G. Houts, "Atonement and Abuse: An Alternative View," *Daughters of Sarah* 18, no. 3 [1992 Summer 1992]: 30).

16. Van Dyk, "Do Theories?" p. 24.

17. Van Dyk, "Do Theories?" p. 25. Another version of the mystery argument is Rachel Reesor, "Atonement: Mystery and Metaphorical Language," *Mennonite Quarterly Review* 68, no. 2 (April 1994): 209-18.

on the basis of such reemphases and qualifications that Van Dyk believes that satisfaction atonement can be shorn of the excesses pointed out by feminists and saved for modern believers.

Nancy Duff appropriates the offices of Christ in the Reformed tradition to defend satisfaction atonement doctrine. She acknowledges the legitimate critique of atonement doctrines by feminists and womanists, and notes that they remind the reformed tradition of something that it had known but forgotten, namely that the divine action begins with "the least favored," and that "the very nature of the gospel demands that the voices of those who suffer be heard."[18]

After pointing out seeming inadequacies in Gustaf Aulén's typologies and distortions in the way feminists and womanists interpret traditional atonement imagery, Duff suggests that the traditional Reformed understanding of the threefold office of Christ can point a way around these inadequacies. She sees this approach as a correction of the Reformed tradition, in which Calvin did make "indiscriminate connection between Christ's suffering and ours, [which] coincides with the counsel sometimes given to abused women that they should accept their abuse as 'the cross they have to bear.'"[19] Duff's proposal focuses on the prophetic office, which has traditionally been interpreted in terms of Jesus' teaching and example. Duff suggests that if the prophetic office is properly understood "as the apocalypse (revelation) of God's act of reconciliation," it can answer the problems raised by recent critiques of atonement doctrine as well as set the stage for understanding the priestly and kingly offices.[20]

Duff notes that in his quotation from Isaiah 61 in the synagogue at Nazareth, Jesus emphasized the immediate ("today" [Luke 4:21]) "apocalyptic inauguration of the New Age," and the universal, cannot-be-earned character of God's love. This prophetic mission has implications for atonement when it is understood in light of incarnation and the two natures of Christ. When these doctrines are held together, Duff argues, the cross "cannot rightly be interpreted as something God *required of* or *did to* Jesus, but something God *did for* us." Further, as the fully human and fully divine Messiah, Jesus' death "has a uniqueness and a finality that cannot be repeated." Thus we do not become

---

18. Nancy J. Duff, "Atonement and the Christian Life: Reformed Doctrine from a Feminist Perspective," *Interpretation* 53, no. 1 (January 1999): 22.

19. Duff, "Atonement and Christian Life," p. 24.

20. Duff, "Atonement and Christian Life," p. 26.

victims like Christ, and Jesus cannot be presented as an example to abused women, urging them to submit to further violence. "The abused wife does not 'represent Christ' through exemplary self-sacrificial love." Rather, Christ represents us and represents the abused woman. "Christ makes known to her and the world that her suffering represents *the opposite* of God's will."[21]

For Duff, the prophetic office emphasizes the "'cannot-earn' and universal character of God's love" in atonement. However, it is important to realize, she continues, that God's way of being with us is "both dynamic and contextual." God's presence takes one form "if we are perpetrators of sin," and another form "if we are the victims of someone else's sin." In a very important statement, Duff concludes

> That God is our ally against a common enemy does not allow us to take up our cross in the form of a holy crusade or assume that God tolerates any action we choose to inflict on our enemies. Nor does God's unconditional love of our enemies mean that God tolerates their sins against us as "the cross we must bear."

Thus in atonement doctrine, Duff continues, we hold together forgiveness from guilt and freedom from the power of sin. "Humanity not only needs to be *forgiven* for guilt incurred through sin, but *freed* from the power of sin which holds the human will captive and causes some people to be victimized at the hands of others."[22]

Margo Houts freely acknowledges that atonement theology "does frequently operate with an abusive edge," but attributes the excesses to which Joanne Carlson Brown objects to "nonbiblical distortions and theoretical accretions which need to be excised."[23] Like the previous defenses noted, Houts also appeals to doctrines of the Trinity and the deity of Christ to emphasize divine cooperation in atonement, notes multiple biblical images none of which can carry the entire meaning of atonement, charges the Reformers with the overemphasis on punishment, differentiates between redemptive and masochistic forms of suffering, and proclaims atonement doctrine a mystery that can never be fully fathomed.[24]

---

21. Duff, "Atonement and Christian Life," p. 27. Emphasis Duff's.
22. Duff, "Atonement and Christian Life," pp. 29-30. Emphasis Duff's.
23. Houts, "Atonement and Abuse," p. 29.
24. Houts, "Atonement and Abuse," p. 29.

But beyond supporting the emphases previously noted in the defenses of satisfaction atonement, Houts adds an additional element, namely some explicit critique of Anselm's theory. She notes that Anselm focused on Christ's death, "rather than viewing Jesus' life and ministry, death and resurrection as a whole." His view is also "excessively individualistic, overlooking the corporate and systemic dimensions of evil, while failing to address the creation of a new covenant community." Finally, Houts adds, Anselm is more concerned with "remission from the penalty of sin (justification) than with release from the power of sin (sanctification)." This emphasis means that "guilt can be removed while the reality of sin remains existentially unchanged."[25] In light of these problems with Anselmian atonement, to refurbish satisfaction atonement Houts would emphasize an array of biblical images rather than focusing only on satisfaction, and would also stress biblical understandings of "the Godhead and incarnation" as part of atonement doctrine.[26]

Catherine Pickstock blames the excesses of a judicial and penal view of satisfaction atonement on developments from Luther and Calvin. Anselm's atonement, Pickstock says, depended on the idea "that Christ was one of our kin and could take our debt upon Himself," with atonement regarded as "achieving reconciliation with God, our ultimate parent." Thus Pickstock asserts that Anselm's view of atonement did not feature reparations to an offended God. "There is no real sense that God Himself requires any compensation, or even that God has been insulted by sin, since God is perfect and replete." It is not God but "divine justice" that has been insulted and "the bond between man and God" that has been broken. Sinful humankind cannot restore this justice or the ruptured bond.

> Only God is able to restore this bond since man has rendered himself powerless through sin, and the compensation for sin which consists in the gratuitous act of a sinless man offering His own death flows back from God towards man since God Himself, being replete, does not need to receive this gift. Hence, for the Middle Ages, it was Christ's divinized humanity which was offered as a gift to humankind.[27]

---

25. Houts, "Atonement and Abuse," p. 30.

26. Houts, "Atonement and Abuse," pp. 30, 31.

27. Catherine Pickstock, *After Writing on the Liturgical Consummation of Philosophy* (Oxford: Blackwell, 1998), p. 156.

Pickstock points out that it was the idea of restoring the bonds of kinship that was abrogated by Luther and Calvin and replaced by atonement framed in judicial terms. In this Protestant form it was now "God's unknowable sovereign will" that was offended, and which required "punishment of humanity in compensation." Divine decree then required the "punishment by death of a perfect man, absolutely obedient to the divine will; such a man can only be a divine man." This change in atonement image altered the character of atonement itself. As Pickstock described it, "The relationship of the believer to the Atonement is no longer one of being incorporated into the Son and thereby achieving an affective state of reconciliation with the Father, but rather one of simply accepting a transaction carried out by God on our behalf." Pickstock clearly favors the Anselmian rather than the Luther-Calvin version as the former includes roles for the Son and the Holy Spirit, which can be understood as "swept into the reciprocal exchanges which take place within the Trinity."[28]

Although Pickstock does not mention feminist or womanist challenges to satisfaction atonement, her dismissal of the Luther-Calvin version addresses some of the supposed worst attributes of satisfaction identified by feminists and womanists. As Pickstock compares the versions of Anselm and the Protestant reformers, it is clearly the Luther-Calvin view that lends itself most readily to the image of "divine child abuse" and to the image of passive innocent suffering and surrogacy that were so offensive to feminists and womanists.

Anselm and Cur Deus Homo

The most thorough, recent reading of Anselm and *Cur Deus Homo* appears in R. W. Southern's fine biography of Anselm.[29] While my initial analysis of *Cur Deus Homo* follows Southern, the final results draw out implications of Anselm's atonement doctrine that Southern did not envision.

Anselm developed satisfaction atonement to replace the prevailing view that Christ's death was a ransom payment that God owed to the devil. As Southern described this view, Adam and Eve had made themselves sub-

---

28. Pickstock, *After Writing*, pp. 156-57.
29. R. W. Southern, *Saint Anselm: A Portrait in a Landscape* (Cambridge: Cambridge University Press, 1990).

ject to the devil in perpetuity. "Their sin created a new social contract of the universe: so long as the Devil kept within the bounds of his jurisdiction the arrangement freely entered into by the ancestors of the human race could not justly be overturned." However, by trying to extend his dominion to the sinless Christ, "the condition on which he held a just dominion over the human race was broken." As a result, the one who had been unjustly condemned to die by the Devil "inherited the Devil's jurisdiction, and under whatever conditions He wished, He could restore mankind to the end for which the human race had been created." This process also revealed God as the "master strategist of the universe," who "had outmaneuvered the enemy on a cosmic scale."[30]

In Section I.vii of *Cur Deus Homo*, Anselm allowed Boso to provide the argument against this view. Since all things, including "the devil and man belong to God alone, and neither one stands outside God's power," it is not possible for the devil to have rights that God is bound to honor. Even though sinners deserve to be tormented by the devil, it is nonetheless "unjust for the devil to torment" them. Even though "man deserved to be punished," "the devil had earned no right to punish him." The devil acted not by God's orders, "but only with the permission of God's incomprehensible wisdom, which orders even evil things for good."[31] As Southern emphasizes, Anselm's response was to deny any rights of the devil and to remove him from the equation, and to make sinful humankind responsible directly to God.[32] We will return presently to examine the full ramifications for the contemporary debate of Anselm's move to eliminate the devil from the equation. For the moment, it is sufficient to note how much the image of victory over the devil differs from narrative Christus Victor developed in Chapter 2. The elements rejected by Anselm are not part of narrative Christus Victor.

Southern provides the following outline of the answer Anselm developed to replace the inherited theory of conquering the devil.

1. The Problem
  i. Man was created by God for eternal blessedness.

---

30. Southern, *Saint Anselm*, pp. 207-8.
31. Anselm, "Why God Became Man," in *A Scholastic Miscellany: Anselm to Ockham*, ed. and trans. Eugene R. Fairweather, The Library of Christian Classics (Philadelphia: Westminster, 1956), p. 108 (I.vii).
32. Southern, *Saint Anselm*, p. 209.

    ii. This blessedness requires the perfect and voluntary submission of Man's will to God. (Freedom is to love the limitations appropriate to one's being.)

    iii. But the whole human race has refused to make this submission (and has thus lost its freedom).

    iv. No member of the human race can restore the lost blessedness, because even perfect obedience cannot now make up for lack of obedience in the past.

    v. Therefore the created universe is deprived of its due harmony, and in the absence of external aid, the whole human race has irretrievably forfeited the blessedness for which it was created.

2. **The Necessity of Salvation**

    i. God's purpose in the creation of Man and the universe has been frustrated.

    ii. But it is impossible that the purpose of an omnipotent Being should be frustrated.

    iii. Therefore a means of redemption must exist.

3. **The Solution**

    i. To restore the lost harmony and blessedness, an offering of obedience must be made equal to or greater than all that has been lacking in the past.

    ii. Only Man, as the offender, *ought* to make this offering; but no man can do this, because he already owes to God all and more than all he has to offer.

    iii. Only God *can* make an offering which transcends the whole unpaid debt of past offenses; but God ought not to make it, because the debt is Man's.

    iv. Since only Man ought to, and only God can, make this offering, it must be made by one who is both Man and God.

    v. Therefore a God-Man is necessary for the Redemption of the whole Creation.[33]

One point relevant for the contemporary debate concerns the attitude of Jesus toward his role in atonement. Anselm argued that Jesus was not

---

33. Southern, *Saint Anselm*, p. 206.

compelled or coerced by God. Even though the death of an innocent man was required in order to satisfy the honor of God, God "did not force him to die or allow him to be slain against his will; on the contrary, he himself readily endured death in order to save men."[34] While it can be said that it was God's will for Jesus to die since sinners could be saved in no other way, that willing is not coercion. Because of his perfect obedience, Jesus willed what God willed, and Jesus' death for sinners was thus voluntarily and freely offered. "Christ himself freely underwent death, not by yielding up his life as an act of obedience, but on account of his obedience in maintaining justice, because he so steadfastly persevered in it that he brought death on himself."[35] This argument appears not to allay the suspicion of the modern feminist and womanist critiques, which charge that satisfaction atonement holds up an unhealthy image for abused women. But for those who accept Anselm's logic, it does allow the defenders of satisfaction atonement to claim that it portrays Jesus not as a helpless victim but as an active participant in opposition to evil.

Related to the issue of Jesus' voluntary submission to death is the question of God's agency in Jesus' death. In light of the modern charge that satisfaction atonement makes God the author of Jesus' death and is thus a model of divine child abuse, how does Anselm understand the role of God in Jesus' atoning death? Anselm does not speak to the question in this particular form. Since responding to the question involves more than citing Anselm's answer, my analysis of this particular form of the question is deferred to the following section, which responds to the defenders of satisfaction atonement.

A third important point concerns the place of punishment in Anselm's theory. What humankind and every "rational creature" owes to God is that "every inclination . . . be subject to the will of God." The slightest deviation from God's will, even the glance of an eye,[36] is sin. This obedience is the "sole and entire honor which we owe to God, and God requires from us." Withholding obedience is to steal what belongs to God, namely God's honor. This stealing or withholding obedience thus incurs a debt owed to God. As long as the stolen debt is not repaid, the sinner "re-

34. Anselm, "Why God Became Man," p. 111 (I.viii).
35. Anselm, "Why God Became Man," p. 113 (I.ix).
36. Anselm, "Why God Became Man," pp. 138, 139 (I.xxi).

mains at fault." To redeem sinners then requires that the debt owed to God
— to God's honor — must be repaid.[37]

It is following this definition of sin and the need for repayment of the
debt to God's honor that Anselm mentions the necessity of punishment.
The lead in to his comment about punishment is a statement that it is "not
fitting" for God to remit sin "by mercy alone, without any payment for the
honor taken away from him." It then follows that "to remit sin in this way
is the same thing as not to punish it." This means that satisfying sin is
equated with punishing it. "And since to deal rightly with sin without satisfaction is the same thing as to punish it, if it is not punished it is remitted
irregularly."[38]

While Anselm thus considered the punishment of sin necessary, it is
far from his primary focus. In the just cited comments about punishment,
he does not say that Christ's death is punishment. Above all there is no in-
dication at all that in the death of Jesus, God is exercising on Jesus the punishment that sinners deserve, or that God is punishing Jesus in place of
punishing sinners. The defenders of satisfaction atonement such as
Catherine Pickstock, whose strategy is to blame the worst excesses of penal
substitution on the Protestant Reformers, particularly John Calvin, and to
discover a different emphasis in Anselm are thus quite correct. Anselm did
not have a penal substitutionary understanding of vicarious suffering.
Using a different image, he explained how Jesus' death paid the debt that
sinful humankind owed to the honor of God.

I follow R. W. Southern's interpretation of Anselm's view of debt payment in the medieval feudal context. Southern accepts the conclusion that
Anselm's thesis could stand on its own with every trace of feudal imagery
removed, but contends that Anselm's arguments were nonetheless clearly
colored by the social arrangements that surrounded him.[39] "The *Cur Deus
Homo*," Southern says, "was the product of a feudal and monastic world on
the eve of a great transformation."[40]

The social order known to Anselm consisted of the lord and his vas-

---

37. Anselm, "Why God Became Man," p. 119 (I.xi).

38. Anselm, "Why God Became Man," p. 120 (I.xii).

39. Southern, *Saint Anselm*, pp. 221-22. A similar argument, in part dependent on
Southern, is Timothy Gorringe, *God's Just Vengeance: Crime, Violence and the Rhetoric of Salvation*, Cambridge Studies in Ideology and Religion, no. 9 (Cambridge: Cambridge University Press, 1996), pp. 85-103.

40. Southern, *Saint Anselm*, p. 222.

sals. While those below the lord had varying kinds of status in the hierarchy (knights, freemen, serfs), the emphasis always fell on their submission to the will of the lord at the top of the hierarchy.[41]

This hierarchical social order described the state of humankind as Anselm understood it. He pictured the relationship of God to humanity in terms of the feudal lord and the vassals who owed him service. At the beginning of history, human beings had renounced the service due to the divine lord, and Adam's descendants were condemned to lose their inheritance. However, the lord then provided a way for humankind to be restored to service. "At a great cost, the lord had paid the default in full," and also "made it possible for future deficiencies to be paid," if the stipulated conditions were met. The conditions were "faith, submission, and repentance." As Anselm understood them, these conditions were rigorous, and few met them. Most were not prepared to submit the flesh to the law of God; thus few would be saved. In this regard, monks were superior to "other men in their more complete submission. The laity had all kept something back."[42]

Anselm knew that feudal lords were often "brutal, licentious, and violent." But he "accepted the oppressive social framework of his day because it was the only social order that he knew," Southern said. For Anselm, the feudal hierarchy "represented order." In spite of the oppressive conditions, "it gave pictorial vividness to his central idea of service due from Man to God, on which mankind had defaulted, and which could be made good only by God's doing it himself on behalf of his tenant."[43]

The language Anselm used in *Cur Deus Homo* to examine God's honor reflects this feudal setting. Sin is withholding obedience due to God, and humankind thus incurs a debt owed to God. Once withheld, it can be repaid, the debt satisfied. "Justice requires the preservation of God's honour." Southern comments that "the language could scarcely be more feudal, and the thought it expresses is only intelligible if the language is understood in a strictly contemporary sense."[44]

In this feudal context, Southern explains, "honour" was different from

41. Southern, *Saint Anselm*, p. 222.
42. Southern, *Saint Anselm*, p. 222.
43. Southern, *Saint Anselm*, p. 224.
44. Southern, *Saint Anselm*, p. 225.

and more than a general sense of reverence. It encompassed the man's *"es-tate."* That estate began with his "landed property," but also included

> his due place in the hierarchy of authority, his family background, and his personal honour. The fundamental crime against anyone was to attempt to diminish this complex of rights and status. The seriousness of the crime was quite independent of the rebel's immediate intentions or power to give effect to his intentions: it was his disloyalty, the loosening of the social bond, which made the outlaw. Conversely, it was the maintenance of the king's "honour" which preserved his kingdom, of the baron's "honour" which preserved his barony, and so on down the scale. "Honour" was essentially a social bond which held all ranks of society in their due place.[45]

Southern poses this feudal conception of honor as the backdrop for Anselm's understanding of God's honor.

> God's honour is the complex of service and worship which the whole Creation, animate and inanimate, in Heaven and earth, owes to the Creator, and which preserves everything in its due place. Regarded in this way, God's honour is simply another word for the ordering of the universe in its due relationship to God. In withholding his service a man is guilty of attempting to put himself in the place of the Creator. He fails; but in making this attempt, he excludes himself from, and to the extent of his power destroys, the order and beauty of the universe. His rebellion requires a counter assertion of God's real possession of his honour, not to erase an injury to God, but to erase a blot on the universal order. To do this, God as Man makes good the damage; and God as Lord takes seisin of his honour once more. And so the whole *servitium debitum* of the universe is reestablished, and God's "honour" in its full extent is displayed in the restored order and beauty of the whole.[46]

Stated very briefly, for Anselm, the atoning death of Jesus repaid the debt that humankind had incurred to God's honor, and order was restored in the universe. With reference to the recent challenges to images of punish-

45. Southern, *Saint Anselm*, pp. 225-26.
46. Southern, *Saint Anselm*, p. 226.

ment and penal substitution in atonement, it is obvious that the particular images most objectionable to feminists and womanists are not Anselm's images. When Jesus' death is the payment owed to God's honor, then Jesus is not being punished by an offended God. This description of the atonement transaction pictures God as a feudal lord to whom honor and service is due, but it does not picture God directly as the one who abuses the son.

Responding to the Defenses of Satisfaction

Although the defenders of satisfaction atonement followed some strategies in common, their defenses also exhibited significant variations in approach. Some strategies seem almost mutually exclusive. It is difficult, for example, to hold Placher's rehabilitation of punishment together with the efforts of Wheeler, Megill-Cobbler, Van Dyk, and Houts to downplay punishment while emphasizing God's suffering with Christ. Placher's rehabilitation of punishment seems mutually exclusive with the efforts of Pickstock to purge punishment from atonement by blaming it on Protestant reformers and appealing to Anselm. As a very general first point, it is possible to say that there is no consensus on how to preserve satisfaction atonement. And further, the diverse and mutually contradictory strategies might indicate that the preeminent concern of these writers is more to defend satisfaction by any means available than to ask whether satisfaction atonement truly reflects biblical understandings of the life and work of Christ. In this regard, Margo Houts's response to the feminist critique of satisfaction went the farthest in acknowledging the possibility of other biblical atonement motifs and in recognizing nonbiblical and problematic dimensions of satisfaction atonement in Anselm himself as well as in later Calvinist versions.

More important for present purposes than the fact of differing strategies among satisfaction's defenders, however, is the fact that none of the defenses of satisfaction atonement did more than blunt or camouflage the element most offensive to the radical critics of traditional satisfaction atonement, namely its modeling of divinely sanctioned violence. And except for Placher, who reaffirmed it, none of these defenses dealt with the fundamental assumption of satisfaction atonement, namely that justice or making right depends on punishment, the balancing of sin/evil on one side with violence/punishment on the other. The defense strategies leave us with the problematic dimensions of satisfaction atonement intact, but now obfuscated by being surrounded with other motifs and emphases. Pointing out that Anselm pictured God as a feudal lord to whom honor and obedience are due rather than as a vengeful God that inflicts punishment covers over but does not change the fact that paying the debt owed the feudal lord requires death to balance prior sin. A version of satisfaction atonement with punishment redefined or with a renewed emphasis on God's suffering with Jesus is still an image in which salvation depends on the necessary death of Jesus as a debt payment; it is still an image in which justice depends on the violence of punishment. It is still salvation based on voluntary, passive submission to necessary suffering. Stressing the voluntary nature of Jesus' act, rather than the Father's requirement of it, does nothing for the problem such an image upholds for those who have born the brunt of direct abuse — for slaves or those whose ancestors have been slaves; for women and children who have found themselves living on the receiving end of abusive relationships. This is still an image that makes submission to abusive authority a virtue. No amount of blunting the edges by hiding it behind other motifs or refraining from following all the implications of Anselm's argument can get around the fact that his atonement image is still one of passive, innocent suffering that is owed to God.

I agree with feminists and womanists and black theologians that such an atonement image is unhealthy for human beings, in particular those who have experienced oppression directly or have had it mediated by their immediate history. Further, in a point that is also very significant, such blunting of the edges of Anselm's motif does not speak to the ahistorical character of the motif that focuses on death and says virtually nothing about the resurrection of Jesus, and that is irrelevant for ethical reflection other than to encourage passive suffering. Anselm does not mention the life and the actions of Jesus, other than to indicate that in addition to the satisfaction atonement, he had other reasons for becoming the God-man.[47] I believe that defending satisfaction on the basis of such multiple correctives, additions, reemphases, and prunings is analogous to defending a hierarchical view of male-female relationships by explaining that if the man truly loves and cherishes his wife, then hierarchy and male leadership is not a dominating relationship. I find these defenses of Anselm no more satisfying than such a defense of male dominance.

47. Anselm, "Why God Became Man," p. 161 (II.xi).

To understand most specifically why none of these defense strategies does more than camouflage the violence problem, let us return one more time to the questions concerning the object or goal of the death of Jesus (who or what it is aimed at), who or what needs the death of Jesus, and who or what is the cause or agent of Jesus' death. For Anselm, the death was aimed at the honor of God. And the honor of God remains the object whether the Father wills or needs the death of the Son or the Son of his own volition chooses to offer it. In the penal substitutionary form of satisfaction atonement, as developed by Protestant reformers, the object of the death is God's law; in some way the death satisfies requirements of the law that sin be punished. And again, the death is aimed at the law whether God the Father wills that Jesus fulfill the law's requirement or Jesus voluntarily offers to satisfy the law. For the moral theory associated with Abelard, the object of the death of Jesus is sinful humankind. For Christus Victor in its classic form, the object of Jesus' death is the devil. As will become more clear presently, the question of the object of the death of Jesus does not fit within the framework of narrative Christus Victor.

Similar answers appear when one poses the question in terms of who or what needed the death of Jesus. For Anselm, it is God's honor that needed the death. For penal substitution the death was needed by divine law. In the moral theory, sinners can be said to need the death in order to see God's love made visible. Finally, in classic Christus Victor, the devil might be said to need the death in fulfillment of the contract. For narrative Christus Victor, the death is not needed by any divine manifestation, nor can sinners in bondage to sin be said to need the death of Jesus. In fact, being in the service of the powers of evil and causing the death puts them in opposition to the reign of God.

The most controversial question is to ask who was responsible for killing Jesus or for having him killed. In classic Christus Victor, it is obvious that the devil was responsible for the death of Jesus. However, when Anselm deleted the devil from the picture for satisfaction and moral theories, the picture changed markedly. Since the divine order needs the death to satisfy the debt owed to God, and since humankind obviously cannot arrange any plan to rescue itself or to pay its debt, only God remains as the one for whom God arranged the plan by which the Son could pay the debt. And since only God can arrange the plan, the logic of the satisfaction motif itself makes God the author of the death of Jesus in Anselm's model. And one is face to face with the contradiction noted by Raymund

Schwager that Jesus, who resists and confronts evil nonviolently, and the evil powers that use violence to kill Jesus, must both be acting according to the will of God. The same scenario applies to the penal substitutionary version that emerged from the Protestant reformers — God arranged the scenario that would produce Jesus' death as the punishment demanded by God's law. Why it is important to visualize the controversial claim that the logic of satisfaction atonement makes God the author of the death of Jesus will become clear shortly.

As one example of how the defenses of satisfaction only blunt the edges and do not deal with the divinely sanctioned violence that is intrinsic to it, let us briefly consider Pickstock's appeal to Anselm. In Anselm as correctly depicted by Pickstock, it is not God who is offended but rather "divine justice and the bond between man and God." But notice the answers that appear when Pickstock's formulation is tested by the foregoing questions. Divine justice — God's justice — is what Jesus' death is aimed at. It is divine justice — God's justice — that needs the death of Jesus. Without the death, divine justice would not be restored. And most tellingly, God is the agent who arranged the scenario whereby Jesus could be killed so that his death would satisfy divine justice. Thus whether it is God directly offended, as for the Luther-Calvin scenario, or God indirectly, as in Anselm's scenario of divine justice, the death of Jesus is still ultimately directed Godward. And it is God who established the process that produced that Godward-directed death. As Pickstock said, God is the only one who can restore the divine justice and the bond between humans and God.[48] Thus when divine justice needs the death of a sinless man in order for divine justice to be restored, it is in fact God, in this image, who is the agent behind the death of Jesus. The fact that the death is called satisfaction of "divine justice" rather than punishment of an innocent man in place of punishing sinful humanity does not alter the fact that God is the agent behind the death. The conclusion is that Pickstock's description of Anselm does not respond to the charges against satisfaction atonement made by feminists and womanists. Pickstock has only supplied less blatantly offensive images and language for a motif that still contains the intrinsic dimensions that offend feminists and womanists.

That the offensive elements are only blunted or camouflaged becomes particularly evident in the assessment of *Cur Deus Homo* itself, and South-

48. Pickstock, *After Writing*, pp. 156-57.

ern's own analysis points toward that camouflage in a way that he did not suspect. As was previously noted, in *Cur Deus Homo* Anselm rejected the idea that the death of Jesus was a victory over the devil. Stated differently, rejecting that motif meant, as Southern observed, that Anselm's contribution to the atonement discussion was to remove the devil from the equation and to make sinful humankind directly responsible to God alone.[49]

A paramount problem for Anselm in *Cur Deus Homo* was to show the necessity of the incarnation, namely that the God-man was the only possible way that God could have saved sinners, but to pose that argument without making it necessary or a requirement that God act in this way. The idea of requirement or obligation seems to place limits on God, which is unthinkable in light of God's omnipotence. Unbelievers, identified by Southern as Jews in London, were advancing the claim that the incarnation "entailed the humiliation of God."[50] Anselm's answer was that it was not humiliation because becoming the God-man was the only way that God could have saved sinful humankind. Thus rather than being the humiliation of God, "it showed only the lengths to which God was prepared to go for Man's salvation."[51]

The problem was that such language seemed to say that the incarnation was *necessary*, a charge that critics raised against Anselm. In response to this problem, Anselm developed the criterion of "fittingness" as a way to depict what was necessary but without placing a limitation on God. Southern identifies the "fittingness" of God's activity as the second of Anselm's original theological axioms, following the argument for the necessity of God's existence in Anselm's *Proslogion*.[52]

Anselm was faced with a problem of language. Southern notes that he lacked words to describe adequately the role of God. While using words like "cannot" and "ought not" about God appear "to suggest a limit to God's omnipotence," Southern says, at the same time Anselm wanted to say that "there are some acts — such as acts of injustice — which would be a diminishing of God's absolute Being, and therefore must be excluded from consideration, not because of any limitation in God, but because of defects inherent in the acts themselves." This leaves us with a situation

---

49. Southern, *Saint Anselm*, pp. 209-11.
50. Anselm, "Why God Became Man," p. 104 (I.iii). See also p. 201.
51. Southern, *Saint Anselm*, p. 201.
52. Southern, *Saint Anselm*, pp. 201-02.

where "the 'cannots' of human language have to be translated into the 'cans' of absolute Being, and we have no language for doing this." Any explanation is therefore "provisional."[53] Nonetheless, it left Anselm's opponents claiming that his theological program depended on "logical legerdemain."[54]

Removing the devil from the equation and making humankind responsible directly to God rendered the language problem acute about the necessity of incarnation. Sinners owed their debt to God rather than to the devil, a debt they were absolutely unable to pay. God could forgive but not without payment of the debt that only God could pay. Anselm's answer was that the God-man could and did pay the debt. Applying the category of "fitting" and "fittingness" to God's act was Anselm's solution to the problem of how to say that God redeemed humankind in the only way possible while avoiding any obligation on the part of God.

However, deleting the devil from the equation also subjected God to another problem of appearance that Anselm did not address directly and apparently did not envision. With the devil removed from the equation, only God remains as the agent behind the scenario that produces Jesus' death as the necessary debt payment to divine honor. The logic that points to God as the author of the death of Jesus comes from Anselm himself, precisely because he deleted the devil from the equation. Since the death is aimed at God as part of the equation but sinners cannot pay the debt to God's honor for themselves; and *since the devil is not paying anything to God nor obeying the will of God nor even any longer in the equation,* God is the only possible one remaining who can oversee the death of Jesus so that it pays the divine debt to justice. The logic behind Anselm's atonement image points to God as the agent behind the death of Jesus.

Although the question emerges quite specifically from the move of deleting the devil from the atonement equation, Anselm did not directly address the issue of who was the author or the agent of the death of Jesus. One can speculate that Anselm might have responded to this query as he did about the "necessity" of the incarnation, by replying that God did not really kill the Son because it was "fitting" that God arrange the death of the Son in order to satisfy divine honor.

There is however another dimension to the discussion about God's

53. Southern, *Saint Anselm*, p. 207.
54. Southern, *Saint Anselm*, p. 210.

authoring the death of the Son. Stating the point in this provocative way points to the assumption underlying the idea of satisfaction atonement in any of its versions. That assumption is that salvation, however defined, is linked to or depends on the equation of doing justice with inflicting punishment. In this case the punishment is the ultimate penalty of death. Doing justice or righting injustice depends on punishment. When sin has corrupted the order of the universe, the punishment of death pays the debt that balances sin and restores order. When the divine law has been broken, the punishment of death fulfills the legal provision required for making right. When justice demands punishment of sinners, Jesus endures that punishment — death — in their place. Any and all of the variations of satisfaction atonement assume that restoring the balance between injustice and justice depends on the ultimate punishment of death. Satisfaction atonement, in any of its variants, is atonement that assumes divinely authored and divinely sanctioned violence of the death penalty as the means to restore justice, as the basis of salvation. Satisfaction atonement is based on an intrinsically violent assumption — restoring justice means punishment. Restoring justice means balancing the evil of sin on one side with violent punishment on the other side. And in any of the versions of satisfaction, it is God who sends the God-man to pay the penalty that supplies that balance and restores divine justice.

The understanding that doing justice means inflicting punishment is an assumption that Anselm never doubted. And it is quite obvious that that assumption does not depend on a feudal backdrop. The argument is correct that Anselm's satisfaction atonement can stand with all the feudal imagery removed.[55] The assumption reigns virtually unchallenged today as the foundational principle of the North American judicial system. In the popular mind, to "do something" about crime means to punish. To get "tough on crime" means to demand harsher punishments. In the process of his effort to rehabilitate satisfaction atonement, William Placher both articulated this assumption about the judicial system and assumed it in his redefinition of penal atonement. Placher even appealed to the divinely sanctioned violence of punishment in substitutionary atonement to suggest a change in the way Christians should approach criminal justice. Because God has ultimately punished Jesus (by having him killed), Placher

55. John McIntyre, *St. Anselm and His Critics: A Re-Interpretation of the* Cur Deus Homo (Edinburgh: Oliver and Boyd, 1954). See also p. 221.

said, we are freed from having to punish criminals and should focus on their rehabilitation.

Following through the logic of the questions concerning the object of Jesus' death and the agent of Jesus' death shows that the quid pro quo violence of "doing justice means inflicting punishment" is just as true for Anselm's version as for the penal substitutionary variant that developed in the Reformed tradition. The difference concerns only variations in the object of the death required as payment and the name for what it accomplishes. Fundamental to all versions is the assumption that the good of salvation depends on the violence of punishment. And it is God who emerges as the ultimate punisher.

It is important to realize that this analysis of satisfaction atonement is not the product of a supposedly one-sided reading of Jesus' work or of the biblical material. It flows from the logic of satisfaction atonement itself. As Southern emphasized, Anselm removed the devil from the equation, making sinful humankind responsible directly to God. The resulting debt owed to God was not one that humankind could pay. Only God could pay that debt. By Anselm's own understanding, God was in charge of the process that paid the debt owed to God's honor, except that Anselm attempted to define God's enactment of the process with language that did not obligate God. But Anselm's whole effort to develop a "fitting" understanding of God's work was a result of removing the devil from the equation and leaving only God as the power responsible for or involved in Jesus' death as an act of debt payment. Further, it is to God's honor that the debt is paid. The honor of God needed the debt payment, and God paid that debt with the death of Jesus. God is in the image of the ultimate punisher. It is not being one-sided but rather starkly clear about the logic of this saving work to say that God is in charge of the process, that God pays or punishes, and that God is paid or vindicated by punishment. To then say that God the Father killed Jesus in order to pay the debt, and that the killing of Jesus is a model of divine child abuse may be a provocative image — but it flows from the logic of satisfaction atonement itself. To emphasize the Father's role in the death of the Son is no less true an image and no more one-sided than the salvage attempts, which chose to emphasize the Father's suffering with the Son on our behalf and say little about the debt paid to God's honor.[56] Em-

---

56. There is tension in satisfaction atonement between the trinitarian claim that God is like and with the Son, and the fact that the debt is also paid from the Son to the Father,

phasizing the Father's sharing of the Son's suffering obfuscates the fact that the logic of satisfaction still requires that the Son pay a debt to the Father's honor, and still assumes that doing justice means punishment. Make no mistake about it. Satisfaction atonement *in any form* depends on divinely sanctioned violence that follows from the assumption that doing justice means to punish.

For those contemplating for the first time how an assumption of Christian nonviolence impacts the Christian doctrines of Christology and atonement, the idea of divinely sanctioned violence of punishment as the basis of justice may not seem like a problem. After all, the Christian tradition has a long history of accommodating violence via the doctrine of supposedly justifiable war, and the idea that doing justice means punishment is the hallmark of United States criminal justice procedures. I submit, however, that it is very much a problem of Christian faith. The classic orthodox formulation of the Trinity emphasizes that each person of the Trinity participates in all the attributes of God. According to this doctrine, it would be heretical to develop attributes in one person of the Trinity that were different from the other persons of the Trinity. That idea is already contained in the key formula of Nicea, which said that Jesus was "one in being" [*homoousios*] with the Father. Thus in the orthodox formulations, and as was stated in several of the efforts to rehabilitate satisfaction, Jesus as the revelation of God reveals the very character and being of God. I suggest, however, that if Jesus rejected the sword and his actions portrayed

---

which of necessity views them in different rather than interpenetrating roles. Gustaf Aulén called this image of different roles a "discontinuous Divine work," in contrast to the "continuous Divine work" of classic Christus Victor, which envisioned God in or with Christ confronting the devil (Gustaf Aulén, *Christus Victor: A Historical Study of the Three Main Types of the Idea of Atonement*, trans. A. G. Herbert [New York: Macmillan, 1969], p. 5). The variants of satisfaction atonement have also emphasized continuous or interpenetrating and discontinuous or different roles of Father and Son. The image challenged most often as a model of "divine child abuse" pictures satisfaction atonement primarily in penal substitutionary terms, with the Father punishing/causing the death of the Son. In this case, Father and Son play different roles. The emphasis on the suffering of the Father with the Son in dying to pay the debt focuses on God's payment of the debt for us. Here Father and Son are playing the same role in an interpenetrating way. Alongside the "divine child abuse" image for the versions of the motif with different roles for Father and Son, emphasis on the Father's participation in the Son's suffering and death might have its own, equally controversial image, namely "divine suicide." Many centuries ago it might have had a nickname like patripassianism.

nonviolent confrontation of evil in making the reign of God visible, then it ought not be thinkable that the God who is revealed in Jesus would orchestrate the death of Jesus in a scheme that assumed that doing justice meant the violence of punishment. If Jesus truly reveals God the Father, then it would be a contradiction for Jesus to be nonviolent and for God to bring about salvation through divinely orchestrated violence, through a scheme in which justice depended on violent retribution.

A further problem of the logic of "justice equals punishment" in satisfaction atonement is the ethical model that it poses for Christians. Those most sensitive to this model are those whose history has involved abuse and suffering — women abused by spouses; children abused by adults; slaves; people whose ancestors were slaves; native peoples expelled from their ancestral lands by immigrants with technically superior weapons; persons who currently experience oppression because of race, gender, nationality, poverty, sexual orientation, and more. Earlier I noted that the various salvage efforts for satisfaction do not remove this abusive image, but rather camouflage it with additional motifs and emphases. Satisfaction poses the temptation to accept such suffering as salvific, as suffering that identifies the sufferer with Jesus. This stance entails a passivity that accepts rather than resists the existing injustice. Feminists and womanists are correct to protest the image it poses.[57]

57. D. Bentley Hart seeks to connect Anselm to the patristic tradition of salvation through divine presence and divinization and thus to produce at least a partial rehabilitation of Anselm for the Eastern Orthodox tradition. Hart locates blame for excesses and distortions of Anselm at a different door than those noted above. As Hart reports on the Eastern tradition, it has avoided Anselm because of his picturing of atonement in terms of an abstract transaction carried out almost entirely on the cross, that required nothing of believers, and that pictured an angry God exacting retribution for sin. This picture had little "salvific significance of the resurrection, or of the ontological dimension of salvation opened up in the incarnation, or of the superabundance of God's mercy (which requires no tribute of blood to evoke it)" (D. Bentley Hart, "A Gift Exceeding Every Debt: An Eastern Orthodox Appreciation of Anselm's *Cur Deus Homo*," *Pro Ecclesia* 7, no. 3 [Summer 1998]: 334.) Hart argues that these distortions and omissions reflect not Anselm himself but the negative readings of Anselm in the western tradition by critics such as Aldolph von Harnack and Gustaf Aulén. While Hart does not mention the recent challenges from feminists and womanists, what I criticize in this book has significant parallels with the views depicted by Hart as distortions, and Hart would certainly locate the discussion of this book entirely within this view of the western theological tradition, which has emphasized primarily "penal suffering and remission from debt" (p. 334).

Without assessing here whether Hart's reading of Anselm in terms of the patristic

The Case of Miroslav Volf

While Miroslav Volf does not specifically address the issue of abusive imagery raised by feminists and womanists, it is important to examine his articulation of satisfaction atonement because he situates it within an attempt to argue for nonviolence.[58] Volf's discussion responds to the question of "how to live under the rule of Caesar in the absence of the reign of truth and justice."[59] His argument begins with four ways that "the crucified Messiah challenges violence." First, by absorbing the aggression of the persecutors, the cross "breaks the cycle of violence." Second, it "lays bare the mechanism of scapegoating." Third, rather than being passive submission to violence, the cross was "part of Jesus' struggle for God's truth and justice." And fourth, "the cross is a divine embrace of the deceitful and the unjust."[60]

Volf understands this fourth challenge to violence as a statement of satisfaction atonement with emphasis on penal suffering. His argument from it is similar to that of William Placher just noted. The fact that Jesus died in order to atone for sins and restore justice in an unjust world means that we can now embrace our enemies.

> When God was made sin in Christ (2 Corinthians 5:21), the world of deceit and injustice was set aright. Sins were atoned for. The cry of the innocent blood was attended. . . . One can embrace perpetrators in forgiveness because God has embraced them through atonement.[61]

---

atonement model of "recapitulation" (p. 348) is correct, it is possible to observe that his effort also covers over rather than addressing directly the fact that satisfaction atonement depends on the logic of retribution. Whether recognizing that the ultimate sacrifice of Christ allows sinners to respond to God in humility without making reparation for particular sins (p. 340); or that Christ provides a model of obedience and assurance that one can always return to God (p. 341); or that Christ's "self-donation to the Father" constitutes "triumph over death, the devil, and sin" (p. 343); or that in trinitarian understanding the justice and mercy of God cannot be in opposition (p. 343); or that God's honor is inseparable from God's goodness (p. 346); or that "the highest law of God's inviolable justice is boundless mercy" (p. 347) — nonetheless Hart's argument still assumes that for Anselm reconciliation of sinners to God depends on a divinely initiated and God-directed death.

58. Miroslav Volf, *Exclusion and Embrace: A Theological Exploration of Identity, Otherness, and Reconciliation* (Nashville: Abingdon, 1996), pp. 275-306.

59. Volf, *Exclusion and Embrace*, p. 277.

60. Volf, *Exclusion and Embrace*, pp. 291-94.

61. Volf, *Exclusion and Embrace*, pp. 294-95.

This atoning death of Jesus is then a supreme ethical example. "The cross of Christ should teach us that the only alternative to violence is self-giving love, willingness to absorb violence in order to embrace the other in the knowledge that truth and justice have been, and will be, upheld by God."[62] Although Volf does not use the specific terms of retributive justice, his depiction of atonement clearly assumes that restoring justice or making right depends on punishment. And because the ultimate penalty was paid, we can embrace our enemies rather than seeking to punish them.

Whereas narrative Christus Victor rejects the idea of divinely sanctioned violence of satisfaction atonement, Volf embraces divine violence as the basis of justice. This embrace appears in particular in his interpretation of Revelation 19:11-19, where he juxtaposes the crucified Messiah with the rider on the white horse. Rejecting the interpretation of this text given in Chapter 2 of this volume, Volf calls it "implausible" that the rider's victory was fought not with literal weapons but by the sword in his mouth. He posits that the "violence of the divine word is no less lethal than the violence of the literal sword." In his view, the rider must exercise a "literal sword" since without this violent judgment "there can be no world of peace, truth, and of justice."[63] The God of Revelation is an angry God who restores justice by vanquishing violently those who insist on remaining beasts and false prophets.[64] "The violence of the rider on the white horse . . . is the symbolic portrayal of the final exclusion of everything that refuses to be redeemed by God's suffering love."[65]

In Volf's schema, God's patient love and God's justice are consecutive events. In the midst of our history, God waits with love and patience for humankind to cease rebelling and turn to God, who has made salvation possible through the crucified Messiah. This patience must eventually end, however, "because every day of patience in a world of violence means more violence and every postponement of vindication means letting insult accompany injury."[66] In Volf's view, this termination of patience and beginning of violent judgment does not mean that violence is the end of human history. Rather, "the judgment against the beast and the false prophet is the obverse of the salvation of those who suffer at their hands." Judg-

62. Volf, *Exclusion and Embrace*, p. 295.
63. Volf, *Exclusion and Embrace*, p. 296.
64. Volf, *Exclusion and Embrace*, p. 297.
65. Volf, *Exclusion and Embrace*, p. 299.
66. Volf, *Exclusion and Embrace*, p. 299.

ment as the restoration of justice allows for creation of the "world of justice, truth, and peace." "The end of the world is not violence, but a nonviolent embrace without end."[67]

Although this depiction of the rider with the sword on the white horse may seem to contrast with the image of the crucified Messiah, in Volf's view they form a whole. In a variant of the argument used by other defenders of Anselm, Volf reconciles the nonresistant crucified Messiah and the violence of the rider on the white horse through appeal to the Trinity. "At the *center* of the throne, holding together both the throne and the whole cosmos that is ruled by the throne, we find the sacrificed *Lamb*."[68] The cross is at the heart of God who sits on the throne. "The world to come is ruled by the one who on the cross took violence upon himself in order to conquer the enmity and embrace the enemy. The Lamb's rule is legitimized not by the 'sword' but by its 'wounds.' With the Lamb at the center of the throne, the distance between the 'throne' and the 'subjects' has collapsed in the embrace of the triune God."[69]

Since God clearly exercises the violence of vengeance, in Volf's view, the key ethical question is whether Christians imitate God's vengeance. Many advocates of both violence and nonviolence (exemplified for Volf by John H. Yoder's *Politics of Jesus*) assume that Christians do imitate God. But Volf rejects that idea because "humans are not God." Prior to the idea of imitating God "is the duty of not wanting to be God, of letting God be God and humans be humans."[70] The biblical tradition insists, Volf says, that one of the fundamental differences "between God and nonGod"[71] is that God has a "monopoly on violence."[72] However one might understand the relationship "between God's and the state's monopoly on violence" (Romans 13, Revelation 13), "Christians are not to take up their swords and gather under the banner of the Rider on the white horse, but to take up their crosses and follow the crucified Messiah." Further, nonviolence is possible now because of divine vengeance in the end. "The certainty of God's just judgment at the end of history is the presupposition for the renunciation of violence in the middle of it."[73]

---

67. Volf, *Exclusion and Embrace*, p. 300.
68. Volf, *Exclusion and Embrace*, p. 300. Emphasis Volf's.
69. Volf, *Exclusion and Embrace*, pp. 300-301.
70. Volf, *Exclusion and Embrace*, p. 301.
71. Volf, *Exclusion and Embrace*, p. 301.
72. Volf, *Exclusion and Embrace*, p. 302.
73. Volf, *Exclusion and Embrace*, p. 302.

After the assertion that Christians practice nonviolence because only God has the prerogative to use violence, Volf takes most of it back. He asserts that in a world of violence, it "may be" that consistent nonretaliation and nonviolence "will be impossible," that tyrants "may need to be taken down," that violent measures "may" have to be taken to "prevent tyrants and madmen from ascending to power in the first place." Thus it "may be" that in a violent world, the choice is not "violence versus peace" but a choice among violent options. But if what "may" happen actually happens and one makes the choice to use violence, Volf says, then "one should not seek legitimation in the religion that worships the crucified Messiah. For there, the blessing is given not to the violent but to the meek (Matthew 5:5)."[74]

Apparently Volf does not recognize that saying that violence "may be" necessary while rejecting validation for it in Christian theology is not a theology of nonviolence. Rather, he is only articulating the difference between a crusade and justifiable war theory. While a crusade claims a transcendent justification, war is always wrong in justifiable war theory. Even when it meets the criteria that establish it as the lesser of two evils, a justifiable war remains sinful and Jesus' rejection of violence is still claimed as the norm.[75]

Volf's purported advocacy of nonviolence and satisfaction atonement contains all the elements problematic for feminists and womanists. His atonement motif upholds the image of innocent suffering of the crucified Messiah, and it is the one aspect where he specifically counsels imitation of Jesus. His understanding of atonement assumes the divinely sanctioned violence of punishment as the basis for justice. By this point, it can be stated that narrative Christus Victor avoids these problems without needing to spell the argument out yet one more time.

And of course, Volf sanctions the divine violence of judgment. This sanction poses two related problems. One is that it visualizes a quite different means of conquering between the God revealed in Jesus Christ and the God of judgment at the culmination of human history. In the former, the reign of God is revealed by Jesus' nonviolent confrontation of evil; in the latter, God uses the violence rejected by Jesus. But if God must ultimately

---

74. Volf, *Exclusion and Embrace*, p. 306.
75. See the distinctions between crusade or holy war and justifiable war in Yoder, *When War Is Unjust*, pp. 11-18.

conquer violence with greater violence, then the resurrection of Jesus is not after all the ultimate establishment of the reign of God, as depicted in the writings of Paul and Revelation, and then in narrative Christus Victor.

A second problem with the divine sanction of violence becomes visible with respect to traditional trinitarian doctrine. Like the appeals to the Trinity noted earlier in defense of satisfaction atonement, Volf depicts a violent element of God that is not manifest in the crucified Messiah. In particular, the God of vengeance and justice is not revealed in the crucified Messiah. Such a division of roles among persons of the Trinity, with the role of violence reserved for God the Father but not exercised in God the crucified Son, runs counter to classic trinitarian doctrine, which holds that all attributes of God are present in each person of the Trinity and that what is true for each person of the Trinity must also be true for God as one.

From the perspective of narrative Christus Victor, a further problematic dimension of Volf's argument is the absence of resurrection from the list of four ways that the crucified Messiah challenges violence. With the focus on death rather than resurrection, as is intrinsically the case for satisfaction atonement, Volf's program misses the eschatological element of the proleptic presence of the future. This problem appears in particular in his interpretation of the rider on the white horse of Revelation 19. Here Volf understands the supposed battle and victory as a future event, and fails to recognize the significance of the fact that the rider is drenched in blood *before* the "battle." The blood-drenched rider symbolizes the resurrected Jesus, in the way the lamb standing "as if it had been slaughtered" (Rev. 5.6) is the resurrected Jesus. Thus the supposed "battle" is actually the future culmination of what has already happened, namely the victory of the reign of God over the rule of evil. The supposed battle is making fully evident the ultimate victory that was already accomplished with the resurrection of Jesus.

In spite of Volf's attempt to articulate a basis for nonviolence, the effort falters on the assumptions of divinely sanctioned, retributive violence, and leaves the door open wide to rationally justified violence, as well as posing an image of atonement that is problematic for all those who are sensitive to past uses of the image of Jesus' suffering to justify suffering and oppression.

Narrative Christus Victor: A Nonviolent Christ

In one sense, narrative Christus Victor is merely undoing Anselm's dele-
tion. Narrative Christus Victor restores to the equation the devil that
Anselm removed. However, the form taken by the "devil" or "Satan" in
narrative Christus Victor differs greatly from the devil envisioned by
Anselm. And that difference makes all the difference in the world.

I follow Walter Wink in understanding the devil or Satan as the accumulation of earthly structures that are not ruled by the reign of God. This
devil is real, but it is not a personified being who may or may not have
rights in the divine order of things.[76] Wink argued that the principalities
and powers, demons, and so on of the Bible are not independent entities
that inhabit a place. Instead, they are the "spiritual" dimension of material
structures. All powers in the world — the state, corporations, economic
structures, educational institutions, and so on — have inner and outer, or
spiritual and material dimensions. Power does not exist independent of a
material incorporation or system. The inner essence is the collective cultural ethos that surrounds a specific outer manifestation. Thus the powers
are real, although not separately existing, independent entities; and their
moral identity and character depend on whether or not they assert their
existence over against or under the lordship of Christ. None of the powers
is good in and of itself, since they all exist in a system of domination in
which they are accomplices. But as fallen powers, all are also redeemable
and thus potentially good to the extent that they submit to the lordship of
Christ. Wink's description of the powers depicts a comprehensive rule of
evil — evil that exists at all levels from the individual to the cosmic and
whose reality is expressed through institutions and the people who com-
prise institutions. Evil accumulates in institutions, and shapes adherents of
the institution in its own image, as a mob spirit leads people to commit
acts they would never contemplate alone, or as a corporation produces ex-
ecutives who conform to an unwritten and unofficial but clearly identifi-
able dress code and behavioral expectations. It was the total accumulation
of evil, the reign of Satan, that killed Jesus — and the blame for his execu-

76. See Walter Wink's powers trilogy: *Naming the Powers: The Language of Power in the
New Testament*, The Powers, vol. 1 (Philadelphia: Fortress Press, 1984); *Unmasking the
Powers: The Invisible Forces That Determine Human Existence*, The Powers, vol. 2 (Philadel-
phia: Fortress Press, 1986); *Engaging the Powers: Discernment and Resistance in a World of
Domination*, The Powers, vol. 3 (Minneapolis: Fortress Press, 1992).

tion should not be limited to specific persons or institutions. In this book, structures and people who represented this accumulation of evil in the killing of Jesus included imperial Rome, Jewish holiness code, the rabble, sleeping disciples, Judas, and Peter. But Jesus is victorious over the rule of Satan only when all dimensions of evil perceive Jesus as a threat and then collectively attempt to eliminate him. The subsequent resurrection of Jesus then reveals the reign of God as the ultimate shaper of reality, and the ultimate power in the universe. The devil or Satan is the name for the locus of all power that does not recognize the rule of God. All structures and powers that do not submit to the reign of God worship Satan or the devil defined in this way.

There is no question whether these forces and structures of the world, which serve the devil and which killed Jesus, might have rights in the reign of God — they do not. There is no question whether they act within the will of God in killing Jesus — they do not. They are not acting in such a way as to pay a debt to the honor of God. The significant contribution of narrative Christus Victor is putting the "devil" back in atonement. It provides a very different solution to the problem that Anselm tried to solve with the category of "fittingness."

In narrative Christus Victor, the cause of Jesus' death is obviously not God. Thus one need not go through the semantic nuances of Anselm to absolve God of needing the Son's death but not compelling it. There is no need to play a sleight-of-hand language game concerning whether Jesus willed himself to die or whether God willed the death of Jesus. In either case, the answer is profoundly "No." Rather, in narrative Christus Victor the Son is carrying out the Father's will by making the reign of God visible in the world — and that mission is so threatening to the world that sinful human beings and the accumulation of evil they represent conspire to kill Jesus. Jesus came not to die but to live, to witness to the reign of God in human history. While he may have known that carrying out that mission would provoke inevitably fatal opposition, his purpose was not to get himself killed. Many stories of missionaries or of parents saving their children — situations in which people faced death willingly and were killed but without willing to die — supply analogies to help us understand how Jesus' death could be inevitable but still not sought by Jesus nor willed by God.

When Jesus confronts the rule of evil, as he does in narrative Christus Victor, there is no longer the difficulty of a problematic image for victims of abuse. Jesus depicted in narrative Christus Victor is no passive victim. He is an active participant in confronting evil. Salvation happens when or because Jesus carried out his mission to make the reign of God visible. His saving life shows how the reign of God confronts evil, and is thus our model for confronting injustice. While we do not save, we participate in salvation and in Jesus' saving work when we join in the reign of God and live the way Jesus lived. That is the model appealed to in particular by black and womanist theology. Being like Jesus does not mean passive submission to suffering. It means actively confronting injustice, and in that confrontation we continue with Jesus to make the rule of God visible in a world where evil still has sway.

Above all, in narrative Christus Victor salvation and justice are no longer based on the violence of justice equated with punishment. Salvation does not depend on balancing sin by retributive violence. Making right no longer means the violence of punishment. Justice and salvation are accomplished in narrative Christus Victor by doing justice and participating in God's saving work. There is no longer any need to discuss whether those who killed Jesus were in some way carrying out the will of God even as Jesus was enacting the will of God. And most significantly, God is obviously neither the agent of Jesus' death nor the ultimate punisher.

In Chapter 3, it was demonstrated that the demise of what I have called narrative Christus Victor corresponds to the series of ecclesiological changes in the early Christian centuries symbolized by Emperor Constantine. We are now prepared to return to that argument at a more profound level. R. W. Southern depicted the feudal order assumed by Anselm. Of concern here is not the particular order of the feudal system but rather Anselm's assumption that the social order was specifically ordered under God. For Anselm, the feudal hierarchy "represented order." "It gave pictorial vividness to his central idea of service due from Man to God, on which mankind had defaulted, and which could be made good only by God's doing it himself on behalf of his tenant."[77] This is clearly a post-Constantinian view of the social order. Before the shift symbolized by Constantine, the church as the earthly manifestation of the reign of God stood in contrast to the structures of the social order not ruled by God. As we observed in Chapter 2, in Revelation the Roman empire was the earthly structure used to symbolize structures not under the rule of God. After

---

77. Southern, *Saint Anselm*, p. 224.

Constantine, the church came to identify with structures of the social order. No longer were political structures, such as the empire, seen in opposition to the church and the reign of God. Instead these structures became the means by which the church sought to extend its influence, and these structures became the means for organizing and carrying out what were assumed to be churchly and Christian missions and goals. With history, namely the structures of the social order, now assumed to be under control of the providence of God, there was no "place" left for Satan to rule within the structures of Christendom. The scope of Satan's rule was reduced to individuals and to the "pagans" beyond the political boundaries of Christendom.

Anselm's view of the social order clearly reflects the assumption that the social order reflects God's order. As Southern wrote:

> Anselm uses feudal imagery because the feudal hierarchy provided an illustration of the order which he found in the universe. The connection also works in the other direction. When we come to consider his actions in the political field, it must not be forgotten that he found feudal obligations of homage and service an acceptable image of rational order. We may judge from this that he is not likely to find any difficulty in accommodating his ideal of ecclesiastical order to the existence of complicated feudal relationships.[78]

With this sense that God's providence rules the structures of the social order, there are few if any structures left for Satan to rule within Christendom. It appears that Anselm's dismissal of the devil from the atonement equation can reflect that outlook.

Our situation on the cusp of the twenty-first century is quite different. We have become aware of the disintegration of Christendom, of the rapid demise of the assumption that the western world constituted the Christian social order. A broad spectrum of Christians who disagree profoundly about both the causes of the demise and the appropriate response to it would all agree about the decline of Christianity and its fading imprint on the world. We are once again entering a setting analogous to the status of the church in the pre-Constantinian Roman empire, in which structures of the social order are assumed not to be evidence of God's providential con-

---

78. Southern, *Saint Anselm*, p. 227.

trol; and the church is increasingly called to witness to the social order rather than to work through its structures. It becomes possible for us to visualize the rule of Satan in a way not possible for Anselm. Narrative Christus Victor is that reading of God's saving act in history with the devil reinserted in the equation.

One element of putting the devil back into the equation with narrative Christus Victor is to reintroduce a notion of the sinfulness of institutions and structures. Within the post-Constantinian synthesis of Christendom that Anselm inherited, he could assume that structures of the social order represented God's ordering of the universe. Problems with structures, i.e., sin, were due to sinful humanity, but the structures of the social order — feudal structures in the case of Anselm — could be accepted as extensions of God's ordering of the universe. Bringing the "devil" back into the equation removes the structures of the social order from God's ordering and makes them human creations. As human creations they can be aligned either with the reign of God or the rule of evil. Fallen, sinful structures are those not submitted to the rule of God. The important point is that structures that are assumed to be extensions of God's ordering of creation cannot be fallen, whereas structures that are human creations are both fallen and redeemable under the rule of God, just as human beings are fallen but redeemable under the rule of God. When "the devil" is understood as the locus of authority for earthly structures that do not acknowledge the rule of God, then the structures of the social order no longer reflect God's order, as Anselm assumed. Narrative Christus Victor understands structures as fallen but redeemable, as human beings are fallen but redeemable.

Reintroducing the devil into the equation is not the same as turning the world over to evil. Narrative Christus Victor assumes the victory of the rule of God in the resurrection of Jesus. Until the eschaton, evil is present but its rule is also limited. The heavenly hosts cheered the victory over the dragon but the voice of the angel warned that the defeated dragon could still do damage.[79] Far from turning the world over to the devil, the eschatological element of narrative Christus Victor is an evangelical call to believe that Jesus represents the rule of God and to believe in the resurrection strongly enough to live in the presence of the reign of God *now*. When Christians live by the rule of God now, the "devil" is being defeated.

Paradigm shifts do not happen overnight. Drawing out the theological

79. See Revelation 12:10-12 and the discussion in Chapter 2.

implications of a new atonement paradigm takes time. The argument of this book developed from some twenty-five years of reflection on the christological and soteriological implications of the new ecclesiology and the history of persecution from my churchly origins in sixteenth-century Anabaptism. In about that same time span, African-American men and women have developed theological programs with significant parallels to this one by following theological implications learned from a different underside of history, that of slavery and racism. In the last few decades, when white women concluded that male-dominated theology did not reflect their experiences, they have articulated alternative analyses of the presumed general theology of Christendom. Even though these expressions — from peace church, feminist, black, and womanist perspectives — are far from unanimous and contain many disagreements among themselves, without major cross-fertilization they nonetheless developed a number of parallel theological expressions that agree on the need to restructure atonement away from its dependence on the divinely sanctioned violence of punishment and oriented toward the justice-making expressions of God's saving act in Jesus.

Abandoning the idea in atonement that making right depends on punishment may appear to open the door to easy forgiveness and salvation that does not deal with guilt. But those fears are ungrounded.

Narrative Christus Victor does envision forgiveness, a forgiveness that is difficult and costly when visualized either from God's side or the side of sinful humanity. The loving and merciful God continues to love us in spite of our sin against the rule of God. The loving and merciful God sent the Son to make visible the reign of God and invite sinners to it even while we were and still are sinners and still are resisting the rule of God. We have all participated in rebelling against the reign of God. By virtue of what society is and of human beings' participation in society, we are all guilty of the killing of Jesus. In a sense, we are the "devil." God maintains the divine love and mercy even as we are part of the structures that kill Jesus. God's offer of forgiveness is always open, whether or not we accept. When we finally come to a realization of our part in the sin against Jesus and against the reign of God, we have to repent and confess our complicity in it and then join the loving embrace of God, who is still there loving us and showing mercy. When we repent, God loves and accepts us in spite of what we have done. That is God's grace, and it is costly. Showing God's love cost God the life of the Son. And making the reign of God visible was costly to Jesus — it cost him his life.

But being accepted in God's embrace under the rule of God, experiencing God's grace, receiving God's forgiveness is also costly for us. We must "pay a price" in order to experience forgiveness. Genuine repentance manifests itself in a transformed life. Repentance means giving up one life and beginning a new one. The new life may mean suffering, loss of earthly treasure, and even loss of physical life on earth. We have to leave the rule of evil and join the reign of God in resisting evil and making the rule of God visible. That change in allegiance and activity is dear; it costs us our lives, which we give to God for the rest of our time on earth.

The reconciliation to God and to fellow human beings envisioned in narrative Christus Victor is in no way the reconciliation based on tolerance and mutual acceptance of old-style Christian liberalism. In narrative Christus Victor, without transformation of life, without a cessation of oppressive activity and a beginning of confrontation of oppression, there is no reconciliation.

This transformation of life that is a manifestation of true repentance can never be fully achieved this side of the eschaton. As long as evil is still present — and it will be present until the culmination of the reign of God in the full manifestation of the resurrected Jesus — complete transformation is beyond our grasp. This statement about a transformed life can never be accused of perfectionism.

Grace and forgiveness are experienced when God invites us out of rebellion and we choose to begin transforming our lives under the reign of God. This scenario fits the paradox of predestining grace versus free will and human responsibility. God invites and chooses. It is impossible to escape the power of sin on human initiative and human effort alone. Martin Luther was correct to say that the fact that he believed was proof of his election by God. We are in bondage to sin, and only God can save. God does not forgive because we repent. Rather, repentance is a response to God's offer of unmerited forgiveness while we were still sinners. But on the other hand, we do make a choice to respond. We confess our complicity with the powers that killed Jesus, we choose to take responsibility for our life, and we choose to join the resistance to evil. We choose to change our allegiance from the reign of evil to the reign of God. In fact, it is not possible not to choose. The default position is to remain in bondage to evil. To "not choose" is to make the choice to stay under the rule of evil. A choice is unavoidable. One can only choose whether to choose actively or by default. Nonetheless, the reality of evil is such that one can only chose under the power of God. This scenario in narrative Christus Victor truly depicts Paul's words: "But by the grace of God I am what I am, and his grace toward me has not been in vain. On the contrary, I worked harder than any of them — though it was not I, but the grace of God that is with me" (1 Cor. 15:10).

An analogy may elucidate how a new allegiance, made with a firm commitment, is never fully achieved, and is a matter of both predestining grace and human responsibility. I have a friend who was once a professional hockey player, on a career track that might well have carried him to the National Hockey League. After a couple of years, however, he abandoned hockey when he realized what kind of person he was becoming. He characterized the fighting in hockey as something theoretically unnecessary for the actual play of the game, but long accepted as a part of the game's culture and impacting the way it is played. "I realized that in order to play well," he said, "I was becoming mean. And that is when I decided to leave the game." This one-time mean, professional hockey player is now a pacifist, Mennonite minister.

Imagine my friend switching from hockey to baseball. The hockey reflexes do not disappear overnight, even when he has made a firm commitment to leave one sport and learn another. And the skills of the new sport will never be perfected, and he will never play the new sport without making errors and mistakes. It would nonetheless become evident that he was becoming a baseball player, learning new skills and reflexes, even though that learning will never reach perfection and will continue as long as he plays. And the possibility of relapse into hockey-like responses and actions will always be present as well. The transformation from hockey to baseball will never be total.

This example of switching sports illustrates the paradox of grace and free will. My friend obviously engaged his own will and took responsibility for himself in deciding to retire from hockey. However, he cannot really become a baseball player and play baseball until a coach invites him and allows him to play on a team. And the coach then decides his fate as a player. The coach can continue to put my friend in the games in spite of countless errors. And when that happens, my friend has not earned his way onto the field, he is not "paying the price" for errors; he is there by grace, by the election of the coach.

This transformation from baseball to hockey is not an extreme example. My friend related to me that when he left hockey, for several years he refrained from playing any sport. His instinct to compete very intensely was just too strong. When he later had children, he began to learn to play recreationally, for fun. And as a pastor, he has focused on learning to play in a relaxed fashion in recreational settings with the youth in his congregation. But it has been necessary for him to work at learning to play recreationally, for fun. For him, playing recreationally is a learned activity, and the mean, competitive hockey instinct never disappears entirely.

Switching from hockey to baseball and learning to play recreationally after being an intensely competitive hockey player can illuminate the change in direction of the sinner who leaves bondage to evil and accepts God's open invitation to live in the reign of God. The transformation will never be finished and never perfected, but the new comment is real and ongoing and poses a visible contrast to a life not submitted to the reign of God.

Southern pointed out that in his own time, Anselm's elimination of the devil from the atonement equation was not accepted. In fact, Abelard's school was the only one that joined in accepting the refutation of rights for the devil. However, the Abelardians drew a conclusion opposite from Anselm. If humanity could make no payment to God, and "God need make no payment to the Devil, then the purpose of incarnation could not be that of making any payment at all." Rather than a debt payment, Abelard pictured the death of Jesus as God's act of supreme love, whose purpose was to "revive Man's love for God."[80] As is well known, because of its impact on the mind or psyche of sinful humanity, this view became known as the moral influence theory of atonement.

Critics of the moral influence theory have pointed out that it has no objective character. As an act of God's love, the death of Jesus accomplishes nothing until a sinner responds to it. For Abelard, nothing changes until the individual changes in response to the love of God, and then what changes is only the individual. In contrast, Anselm's satisfaction motif had a clear objective character. Jesus' death paid the debt that restored the order of the universe quite apart from whether individual sinners availed themselves of the opportunity of salvation thus provided.

While narrative Christus Victor shares Abelard's rejection of the idea that Jesus' death is a debt payment, these two atonement motifs differ in a profound way. While the death and resurrection of Jesus clearly impact the

---

80. Southern, *Saint Anselm*, pp. 210-11.

mind of the sinner, narrative Christus Victor envisions a change in the universe quite apart from any person's perception of it. With the death and resurrection of Jesus, the power structure of the universe is revealed to be different than it appears. The resurrection of Jesus is the definitive victory of the reign of God over the reign of evil, whether or not any individual sinner perceives the resurrection. When an individual does perceive the saving work of Christ and begins a transformed life under the rule of God, that individual is joining a reality already established by the resurrection of Jesus.

We are complicitous in different ways in sin against Jesus and the reign of God, according to our station in life. Those in the dominant categories — men over women, white over blacks, wealthy over the poor, and so on, have clearly shared in oppression. Oppressed persons participate in another way, namely when they participate in the systems that oppress. For example, Delores Williams writes of participation either "in society's systems that devalue Black women's womanhood (humanity) through a process of invisibilization" or by failing to "challenge the patriarchal and demonarchal systems in society."[81] In other words, oppressed persons who accept their oppression, who accept the inferior identity foisted on them by dominators, are complicitous in that oppression. While it is both possible and necessary to spell out these two ways of being complicitous in sin much farther, the important point at this juncture is to see that both oppressed and oppressors are implicated in the evil that Jesus confronted.

These different kinds of participation in oppression have troubled both the critics of satisfaction atonement and those who have sought to rehabilitate it. As we have noted, for the radical critics Jesus' submission to death as a required penalty payment poses a model of submission to oppression that has been used to encourage oppressed people to submit to their oppression. That model has also been troublesome to the defenders of satisfaction atonement, who seek to deflect it.

One dimension of Nancy Duff's defense of satisfaction was to deny Jesus' action as a model. His satisfying death cannot be a model for abused women, Duff writes. When the doctrines of incarnation and the two natures of Christ are held properly together, it is clear that the cross is some-

---

81. Delores S. Williams, "A Womanist Perspective on Sin," in *A Troubling in My Soul: Womanist Perspectives on Evil and Suffering,* ed. Emilie M. Townes, Bishop Henry McNeal Turner Series, vol. 8 (Maryknoll, N.Y.: Orbis Books, 1993), p. 146.

thing that "God *did for* us," and as the fully human and fully divine Messiah, Jesus' death "has a uniqueness and a finality that cannot be repeated." Thus we do not become victims like Christ, and Jesus cannot be presented as an example urging victims to submit to further violence.[82] The problem with Duff's answer is that it forces a pick-and-choose approach to Jesus' life and teaching. Defenders of satisfaction still want to understand Jesus as a source of liberation for oppressed peoples. Denying his confrontation of evil as a model puts one in the paradoxical position of claiming that Jesus both is and is not a model for oppressed peoples.

William Placher's rehabilitation of the idea of punishment in penal substitutionary atonement offered a different solution to the problem of how atonement addresses oppressors and the oppressed. Placher noted that many comfortable North American Christians have benefited from the injustices that the wealthy economies foist on poor people and poor nations. In light of Jesus' suffering, Placher says, it would be good for these comfortable Christians to accept some "suffering in the service of justice, peace, and liberation."[83] In other words, Placher makes the suffering of Jesus a model that comfortable Christians in the oppressor category should imitate.

While I agree with Placher that comfortable Christians ought to take risks for their faith, his suggestion has important flaws for atonement theology. Stated generally, this approach allows the social context to define theology of atonement, rather than asking how the narrative of Jesus should shape our supposedly Christian view of the world. Stated in terms of specifics, Placher's suggestion provides a theology of atonement that addresses only oppressors. How does atonement theology and Jesus' role in atonement apply to the oppressed? How does advocating that the oppressors imitate Jesus' suffering apply to the victims of oppression? Or are there different atonement theologies, one for the oppressors and another for the oppressed? Is a poor person who rises to a middle class or even wealthy lifestyle required to change atonement theologies? Can a wealthy person maintain his wealth as long as he suffers for it? In response to such questions, I suggest that a viable theology of atonement should address all people as sinners and speak to the varying conditions in which they find themselves.

82. Duff, "Atonement and Christian Life," p. 27.
83. Placher, "Christ Takes Our Place," p. 16.

Narrative Christus Victor acknowledges the sin of all people from all stations of life. It envisions a salvation that speaks to and for both the oppressed and the oppressors. The location of the oppressors is quite clear in narrative Christus Victor. They participate in any of the structures that reflect the rule of evil and oppose the reign of God. In the New Testament narrative, these are represented by the ultimate political authorities of Rome, the complicitous Jewish religious leadership, the rabble that howled for Jesus' death, the disciples who slept through his ordeal, Peter who denied knowing him, and Judas who betrayed him. Recognizing our complicity with these forces requires confession and repentance, and a change in sides, joining Jesus as a part of the host of witnesses that make visible the reign of God in contrast to the world. That transformation of life has already been discussed. The oppressors recognize their complicity in oppression and start working to undo that oppression.

Sin in the narrative Christus Victor motif can also include the way in which feminist and in particular womanist writers have depicted how oppressed people can participate in their own oppression. This participation in oppression is also sinful. It is a participation in oppression to allow the oppressive structures to define one's reality, whether African Americans accepting white, racist society's definition of their inferiority, or women allowing sexist society to define the occupations they may hold, which "looks" they should aspire to, or when to submit to abuse from a violent husband.

Victims of oppression can recognize the extent to which they have been complicitous in accepting the oppression foisted on them, and start to engage in resistance. At this level, former oppressed and former oppressors are now on the same side, together, identified with the reign of God. With each of them having undergone a transformation of life, together they confront the oppressive conditions that have enslaved them in different ways. And God's grace is obvious — God let's us join the side of Jesus, even after we have been guilty of participating in his death. This scenario also entails punishment for sin. Violence begets violence, in unending cycle. To remain on the side of the evil that confronts the reign of God is to remain on the side of God's punishment, however one would define divine punishment, and to remain a part of the ongoing cycle of violence and sin that produces more violence and sin.

In this depiction of narrative Christus Victor, Jesus is in no way the passive sufferer of satisfaction atonement. The Jesus of this imagery is an assertive activist who opposed sin, injustice, and oppression. Consider the many stories of Jesus' confronting evil people and institutions — defying prejudice against Samaritans, confronting greed, defending women against their accusers, healing on the Sabbath, cleansing the temple, and much more. This is not a model of innocent, passive submission to abuse; there is no sense here that suffering is salvific in and of itself. The Savior in this model engaged in an energetic confrontation of sin and oppression.[84] Narrative Christus Victor presents a scenario of resisting evil that upholds a message of liberation for both oppressed and oppressors. It challenges these of us who look like the dominant forces to confront the inherited and systemic evils that have bound us, and challenges victims of oppression to follow Jesus in resisting that which binds them. Narrative Christus Victor turns passive victims into active resisters.

Identifying with, following, or imitating this Jesus may indeed be costly; it may indeed entail suffering and even death. But that suffering is not suffering that is salvific in and of itself, and it is not suffering whose origin or object is God, nor happens because in some way God needs it without compelling it. This is suffering that is the by-product of opposing evil, as Jesus' suffering and death were the result of opposing evil. Karen Baker-Fletcher called this an "ethic of risk."[85]

Note has been made of the absence of the life and the deeds of Jesus in satisfaction atonement, apart from the issue of his supposed passive sub-

84. "So the womanist theologian uses the sociopolitical thought and action of the African-American woman's world to show black women their salvation does not depend upon any form of surrogacy made sacred by traditional and orthodox understandings of Jesus' life and death. Rather their salvation is assured by Jesus' life of resistance and by the survival strategies he used to help people survive the death of identity caused by their exchange of inherited cultural meanings for a new identity shaped by the gospel ethics and world view" (Delores S. Williams, *Sisters in the Wilderness: The Challenge of Womanist God-Talk* [Maryknoll, N.Y.: Orbis Books, 1993], p. 164). For additional womanist discussions of resistance, see Clarice J. Martin, "Biblical Theodicy and Black Women's Spiritual Autobiography: 'The Miry Bog, the Desolate Pit, a New Song in My Mouth,'" in *A Troubling in My Soul: Womanist Perspectives on Evil and Suffering,* ed. Emilie M. Townes, Bishop Henry McNeal Turner Series, vol. 8 (Maryknoll, N.Y.: Orbis Books, 1993), p. 22; Emilie M. Townes, "Living in the New Jerusalem," in *A Troubling in My Soul,* pp. 85-86; Cheryl A. Kirk-Duggan, "African-American Spirituals: Confronting and Exorcising Evil Through Song," in *A Troubling in My Soul,* pp. 150-71.

85. Karen Baker-Fletcher and Garth Kasimu Baker-Fletcher, *My Sister, My Brother: Womanist and XODUS God-Talk,* Bishop Henry McNeal Turner/Sojourner Truth Series in Black Religion, vol. 12 (Maryknoll, N.Y.: Orbis Books, 1997), p. 79.

mission to abuse. In contrast, the life and deeds of Jesus are intrinsic to narrative Christus Victor. They become an integral part of the picture precisely because it is through them that one knows what the rule of God looks like and how it challenges the world. Jesus' life and teaching are the benchmark for those who would identify with Jesus in giving witness to the reign of God. Stated differently, this sketch of narrative Christus Victor makes attention to ethical concerns an intrinsic dimension of salvation, of being Christian. In fact, not to participate in making the reign of God visible is not to participate "in Christ." And this discussion then reveals even more starkly the extent to which Anselmian atonement (as well as Nicene-Chalcedonian Christology) constitutes an ahistorical motif that is devoid of ethical content. Dealing with the *guilt* of sin, à la Anselm, is a way to understand salvation that is entirely outside the arena of ethics and a saved life. As James Cone, Kelly Brown-Douglas, and others have observed, this is clearly an understanding that slaveowners could accept without challenging their status as slaveowners, and that they could offer to slaves without threat to their status as slaves.

Discovering the impetus for narrative Christus Victor in Revelation and the status of the early church is not an attempt to return to or recover an earlier epoch. It is the description of a motif, a way of understanding the relationship of Christians and the church to the social order that was true for the first century and is still true in the twenty-first century. It is a description that challenges the contemporary church, contemporary Christians, to take seriously the fact that the reign of God is truly different from and a witness to the social order.[86]

---

86. While Timothy Gorringe provided a book-length critique of satisfaction atonement's foundation in the violence of retribution, he does not offer an alternative understanding of atonement other than to suggest that Abelard opens the door to a new way (Gorringe, *God's Just Vengeance*, p. 266). Citing another author, Gorringe wrote that "The crucifixion of Jesus . . . constitutes 'a permanent and effective protest against those structures which continually bring about separation at the centre and the margin'. It is this protest, I contend, rather than an endorsement of expiatory sacrifice, which is the heart of the New Testament writers" (Gorringe, *God's Just Vengeance*, p. 82). In his conclusion, which argues that the church is the community that models forgiveness and redemption, Gorringe referred to a General Synod statement that "Christian experience shows that God's response to human misdeeds does not require suffering or pain as a condition for acceptance, or demand retaliation or condemn or exclude the offender. It does not primarily aim to express divine wrath. Instead 'God accepts the offender without condoning the offence; requires the offender to face up to the reality of that offence; invites the offender into a community of

reconciliation; encourages the offender to lead life with a new attitude; declares the offender to be free from the offence; invites the person to fall in in service as a "disciple""" (Gorringe, *God's Just Vengeance,* p. 268; Gorringe's direct quotation is from C. Wood, *The End of Punishment*). I submit that rather than turning to a redoing of Abelard, narrative Christus Victor is the atonement image that fits this description of God's saving work in Christ, and that avoids the problem of satisfaction atonement, namely "that the sub-text of the doctrine [of satisfaction] is a subtle rhetoric of violence, a violence which has underwritten both state sadism and individual masochism" (Gorringe, *God's Just Vengeance,* p. 270).

Conclusion

The conclusion is inescapable that satisfaction atonement is based on divinely sanctioned, retributive violence. The various arguments that add additional biblical images, redefine punishment, point to other emphases, appeal to the Trinity, or emphasize that the Father bears the suffering with the Son serve to mitigate or camouflage but do not alter the underlying presupposition that satisfaction depends on a divinely sanctioned death as that which is necessary to satisfy the offended divine entity, whether God or God's law or God's honor. Satisfaction atonement depends on the assumption that doing justice means to punish, that a wrong deed is balanced by violence. The attempts to refurbish Anselm blunt the edges of the offending violence but do not eliminate it. Anyone uncomfortable with the idea of a God who sanctions violence, a God who sends the Son so that his death can satisfy a divine requirement, should abandon satisfaction and Anselmian atonement forthwith. I offer narrative Christus Victor as a nonviolent alternative.

It may seem audacious to challenge a centuries-long acceptance of Anselm and satisfaction atonement. And for some readers, it may feel like a challenge to salvation itself. But it has not challenged the fact of Jesus as savior. What the book has exposed is the centuries-long use of Christian theology to accommodate violence both systemic and direct.

Abandoning Anselm is not to challenge Jesus as savior, nor to abandon the salvific work of Jesus. Abandoning satisfaction atonement is to challenge one way of talking about *how* Jesus saves. The challenge pointed out the multiple ways in which this particular explanation of the *how* of Jesus' saving work is linked to violence in some form. Proposing narrative Christus Victor as an alternative to satisfaction atonement is to propose a *how* explanation that focuses on Jesus' life as the reign of God rather than on Jesus' death as an act of God. Narrative Christus Victor is a biblical way of understanding the salvific work of Jesus without imaging God as one who abuses the perfect Son for the benefit of others. The God of narrative Christus Victor does suffer with Jesus in making the reign of God visible in the world. But this suffering was not the specific purpose of Jesus' mission, nor was it required by a divine equation.

Although the book has focused more on Anselm and satisfaction than on moral influence and classic Christus Victor atonement motifs, the discussion also pointed out problematic and violent dimensions of these latter images from a nonviolent perspective. And narrative Christus Victor is offered as an alternative to moral influence atonement and classic Christus Victor as well as to satisfaction atonement.

By this point, it should be evident that narrative Christus Victor is much more than an atonement motif. It poses a comprehensive way to see God working in the world, and thus suggests a reading of the Bible's story from beginning to end. In this story, God enters human history with the call of Abraham. The history of Israel shows their continuing effort to understand who they were as the people of God and how to understand their mission to make God's rule visible in the world. In Jesus, there is a new level of God's working in the world. Throughout this story it is the calling of God's people to be a visible witness to the reign of God made visible. Carrying out that mission then exposes the world as the world, which is the first step towards acknowledgment of the rule of God. One specific implication of this story is that it has no place for a relationship to God that is based on retributive justice or the idea that restoring justice means to punish. Approaching atonement from a nonviolent perspective in no way results in a narrow statement about ethics. On the contrary, it produces a wide-ranging discussion with implications for a wide array of doctrines in Christian theology. The sketch in this book has only begun to develop these implications.

As it has been sketched in these pages, narrative Christus Victor suggests a new reading of the history of the doctrines of atonement and Christology. It is reading shaped by an explicit claim that rejection of violence is intrinsic to the narrative of Jesus. These pages have revealed that the picture of the standard interpretation of both Christology and atonement changes considerably when studied through the lens of Jesus' nonviolence.

It should be evident that I have learned from the critique of satisfaction atonement in black and feminist and womanist theologies. It is equally evident that I do not follow their reconstructions, particularly those feminists who would do away with atonement or who attempt to restate Abelard. Narrative Christus Victor is the development of an atonement motif that encompasses the full story of the life, death, and resurrection of Jesus.

In narrative Christus Victor, individuals as well as the world are saved, although we still await the culmination of that salvation in the eschaton. In the intermediate time, Christians participate in that salvation when they accept God's call and are transformed from creatures aligned with evil to those who become co-laborers with Jesus in making God's rule present and visible on earth.

Narrative Christus Victor is not a reinterpretation or a reemphasis that attempts to rescue a problematic motif, as was the case for the authors cited in Chapter 7, who attempted to rescue satisfaction atonement from the charges made by feminists and womanists. Neither is narrative Christus Victor merely an effort to make a case for integrating a particular interest and favorite motif into a supposedly wider, more comprehensive mosaic of atonement doctrines.[1] This book has demonstrated why the sat-

---

1. Among recent advocates of Christus Victor atonement imagery are Thomas N. Finger and Darby Kathleen Ray. Finger calls Christus Victor the motif that best fits the "biblical material." However, his treatment deals neither with Revelation nor with correlation of atonement imagery with ecclesiological contexts, both of which figure prominently in the book in hand. Further, Finger's methodology is to adopt supposedly discrete elements from a variety of theologies over the centuries, and then to integrate these elements into a new theological mosaic or synthesis. This borrowing of motifs fails to recognize the intrinsically violent presuppositions and foundation of satisfaction atonement. And by the time these additional motifs from satisfaction and moral atonement theories are incorporated into Christus Victor with the aim of enriching it, the result is a conglomerate of images and emphases in which Christus Victor has all but disappeared from view into an atonement mosaic that is an ahistorical synthesis of all atonement views rather than a statement of Christus Victor. For an example of this methodology, see Thomas N. Finger, *Christian Theology: An Eschatological Approach, Volume 1* (Scottdale, Pa.: Herald Press [reprint, Thomas Nelson], 1985), pp. 325-48; Thomas N. Finger, *Christian Theology: An Eschatological Approach, Volume 2* (Scottdale, Pa.: Herald Press, 1989), pp. 174-91, 393-98. In contrast, in this book I have pointed out the violent components of satisfaction atonement, which indicates why it should be abandoned rather than grafted into narrative Christus Victor.

Darby Kathleen Ray's *Deceiving the Devil* is an interesting statement of Christus Victor,

isfaction motif that has dominated atonement thinking for nearly a millennium should be abandoned. And more importantly, it proposes narrative Christus Victor as a reading of the entire Bible story, making explicit an understanding that had fallen out of view. It is also a contemporary reading, one that speaks specifically to a variety of violence issues that are acknowledged by both detractors and defenders of satisfaction atonement.

I pose narrative Christus Victor as a conversation partner with black and feminist and womanist theologies. It addresses issues they raise. However, while it speaks with those contextual theologies, its message addresses all Christians, as do black, feminist, and womanist theology. In spite of their specific names, each of these theologies addresses every Christian from a particular perspective. But narrative Christus Victor is not a replacement for black, feminist, or womanist theology, and my proposal does not claim to speak for them. However, if it speaks truthfully to the issues they raise, which is their judgment to make, it can and should be restated in terms of the experiences that shape those theologies.

It is my hope that this book does show the way for narrative Christus Victor to replace Anselm as the Christian understanding of atonement. At the same time, it should be stated clearly that all theology is particular or specific to a context. It cannot be claimed that narrative Christus Victor is the ultimate atonement image and that our problem of how best to articulate the saving work of Christ has now been definitively solved for the remainder of life on earth. Since all theology is particular, that claim could never stand. At the same time, on the basis of what we know now, narrative Christus Victor is a viable expression of God's saving work in Christ that makes visible and real in our history the victory of the reign of God and invites our participation in it. It is an image of atonement that takes the Bible very seriously. I commend it as an expression of the gospel of Christ. Come Lord Jesus.

---

particularly in her recognition of it as a nonviolent atonement image. However, Ray's treatment lacks the foundation in Revelation and other biblical material, and depends primarily on early church theologians for its positive articulation. Ray also has a goal for Christus Victor similar to that of Finger, namely to fuse motifs of moral and satisfaction theories into Christus Victor for a comprehensive view of atonement (Darby Kathleen Ray, *Deceiving the Devil: Atonement, Abuse, and Ransom* [Cleveland: Pilgrim Press, 1998], pp. 142-45).

Works Cited

Anselm. "Why God Became Man." In *A Scholastic Miscellany: Anselm to Ockham*, edited and translated by Eugene R. Fairweather. The Library of Christian Classics, pp. 100-83. Philadelphia: Westminster, 1956.

Aulén, Gustaf. *Christus Victor: An Historical Study of the Three Main Types of the Idea of Atonement*. Translated by A. G. Herbert. New York: Macmillan Publishing, 1969.

Baker-Fletcher, Garth Kasimu. *Xodus: An African American Male Journey*. Minneapolis: Fortress Press, 1996.

Baker-Fletcher, Karen, and Garth Kasimu Baker-Fletcher. *My Sister, My Brother: Womanist and XODUS God-Talk*. Bishop Henry McNeal Turner/ Sojourner Truth Series in Black Religion, vol. 12. Maryknoll, N.Y.: Orbis Books, 1997.

Baldwin, Lewis V. *There Is a Balm in Gilead: The Cultural Roots of Martin Luther King, Jr.* Minneapolis: Augsburg Fortress, 1991.

Barrett, Anthony A. *Caligula: The Corruption of Power*. New Haven: Yale University Press, 1989.

Barrett, C. K. (Charles Kingsley). *The Gospel According to St. John: An Introduction with Commentary and Notes on the Greek Text*. New York: Macmillan, 1962.

Beker, J. Christiaan. *Paul the Apostle: The Triumph of God in Life and Thought*. Philadelphia: Fortress Press, 1980.

——. *Paul's Apocalyptic Gospel: The Coming Triumph of God*. Philadelphia: Fortress Press, 1982.

Bethune-Baker, J. F. *An Introduction to the Early History of Christian Doctrine: To the Time of the Council of Chalcedon.* London: Methuen & Co. Ltd., 1938.

Boring, M. Eugene. *Revelation.* Interpretation: A Bible Commentary for Teaching and Preaching. Louisville: John Knox Press, 1989.

Braaten, Carl E. "The Christian Doctrine of Salvation," *Interpretation* 35, no. 2 (April 1981): 117-31.

Brock, Rita Nakashima. "And a Little Child Will Lead Us: Christology and Child Abuse." In *Christianity, Patriarchy, and Abuse: A Feminist Critique,* edited by Joanne Carlson Brown and Carole R. Bohn, pp. 42-61. New York: Pilgrim Press, 1989.

Brock, Rita Nakashima. *Journeys by Heart: A Christology of Erotic Power.* New York: Crossroad, 1988.

Brown, Joanne Carlson, and Rebecca Parker. "For God So Loved the World?" In *Christianity, Patriarchy, and Abuse: A Feminist Critique,* edited by Joanne Carlson Brown and Carole R. Bohn, pp. 1-30. New York: Pilgrim Press, 1989.

Brown, Joanne Carlson. "Divine Child Abuse?" *Daughters of Sarah* 18, no. 3 (Summer 1992): 24-28.

Cannon, Katie Geneva. "Moral Wisdom in the Black Women's Literary Tradition." In *Katie's Canon: Womanism and the Black Soul of the Community,* pp. 57-68. New York: Continuum, 1995.

Cannon, Katie G. *Black Womanist Ethics.* Atlanta: Scholars Press, 1988.

―――. "'The Wounds of Jesus': Justification of Goodness in the Face of Manifold Evil." In *A Troubling in My Soul: Womanist Perspectives on Evil and Suffering,* edited by Emilie M. Townes. Bishop Henry McNeal Turner Series, vol. 8, pp. 219-31. Maryknoll, N.Y.: Orbis Books, 1993.

Collins, Adela Yarbro. *Crisis and Catharsis: The Power of the Apocalypse.* Philadelphia: Westminster, 1984.

Cone, James H. *A Black Theology of Liberation.* C. Eric Lincoln Series in Black Religion. Philadelphia: Lippincott, 1970.

―――. *A Black Theology of Liberation: Twentieth Anniversary Edition.* Maryknoll, N.Y.: Orbis Books, 1990.

―――. *Black Theology and Black Power.* Maryknoll, N.Y.: Orbis Books, 1997.

―――. "Black Spirituals: A Theological Interpretation," *Theology Today* 29, no. 1 (April 1972): 54-69.

―――. *For My People: Black Theology and the Black Church.* Maryknoll, N.Y.: Orbis Books, 1984.

―――. *God of the Oppressed.* Rev. ed. Maryknoll, N.Y.: Orbis Books, 1997.

————. *Martin and Malcolm and America: A Dream or a Nightmare.* Maryknoll, N.Y.: Orbis Books, 1991.

————. *My Soul Looks Back.* Maryknoll, N.Y.: Orbis Books, 1986.

————. *The Spirituals and the Blues: An Interpretation.* Maryknoll, N.Y.: Orbis Books, 1992.

Cone, James H., and Gayraud S. Wilmore, eds. *Black Theology: A Documentary History: Vol 1: 1966-1979.* Maryknoll, N.Y.: Orbis Books, 1993.

Conzelmann, Hans. *Acts of the Apostles: A Commentary on the Acts of the Apostles.* Edited by Eldon Jay Epp and Christopher R. Matthews, translated by James Limburg, A. Thomas Kraabel, and Donald H. Juel. Hermeneia. Philadelphia: Fortress Press, 1987.

Deats, Richard L., ed. *The Theory of Nonviolence.* Active Nonviolence: A Way of Life, a Strategy for Change, vol. 1. Nyack, N.Y.: The Fellowship of Reconciliation, 1991.

Douglas, Kelly Brown. *The Black Christ.* The Bishop Henry McNeal Turner Studies in North American Black Religion, no. 9. Maryknoll, N.Y.: Orbis Books, 1994.

————. "Teaching Womanist Theology." In *Living the Intersection: Womanism and Afrocentrism in Theology,* edited by Cheryl J. Sanders, pp. 147-55. Minneapolis: Fortress Press, 1995.

Douglass, Shelley, and Melinda Moore, eds. *The Practice of Nonviolence.* Active Nonviolence: A Way of Life, a Strategy for Change, vol. 2. Nyack, N.Y.: The Fellowship of Reconciliation, 1991.

Drake, H. A. *Constantine and the Bishops: The Politics of Intolerance.* Baltimore: Johns Hopkins University Press, 2000.

Driver, John. *Understanding the Atonement for the Mission of the Church.* Forward by C. René Padilla. Scottdale, Pa.: Herald Press, 1986.

Duff, Nancy J. "Atonement and the Christian Life: Reformed Doctrine from a Feminist Perspective," *Interpretation* 53, no. 1 (January 1999): 21-33.

Duff, Nancy J. *Humanization and the Politics of God: The Koinonia Ethics of Paul Lehmann.* Grand Rapids: Eerdmans, 1992.

Evans, James H., Jr. *We Have Been Believers: An African-American Systematic Theology.* Minneapolis: Fortress Press, 1992.

Finger, Thomas. "Christus Victor and the Creeds: Some Historical Considerations," *The Mennonite Quarterly Review* 72, no. 1 (January 1998): 31-51.

Finger, Thomas N. *Christian Theology: An Eschatological Approach, vol. 1.* Scottdale, Pa.: Herald Press (reprint, Thomas Nelson), 1985.

————. *Christian Theology: An Eschatological Approach, vol. 2.* Scottdale, Pa.: Herald Press, 1989.

Ford, J. Massyngberde. *Revelation: Introduction, Translation and Commentary.* The Anchor Bible. Garden City, N.Y.: Doubleday, 1975.

Friesen, Abraham. *Erasmus, the Anabaptists, and the Great Commission.* Grand Rapids: Eerdmans, 1998.

Friesen, Duane K. *Christian Peacemaking and International Conflict: A Realist Pacifist Perspective.* Scottdale, Pa.: Herald Press, 1986.

Girard, René. *The Girard Reader.* Edited by James G. Williams. New York: Crossroad, 1996.

―――. *Things Hidden Since the Foundation of the World.* Translated by Stephen Bann and Michael Metter. Stanford, Calif.: Stanford University Press, 1987.

Gorringe, Timothy. *God's Just Vengeance: Crime, Violence and the Rhetoric of Salvation.* Cambridge Studies in Ideology and Religion, no. 9. Cambridge University Press, 1996.

Grant, Jacquelyn. "The Sin of Servanthood: And the Deliverance of Discipleship." In *A Troubling in My Soul: Womanist Perspectives on Evil and Suffering,* edited by Emilie M. Townes. Bishop Henry McNeal Turner Series, vol. 8, pp. 199-218. Maryknoll, N.Y.: Orbis Books, 1993.

―――. *White Women's Christ and Black Women's Jesus: Feminist Christology and Womanist Response.* American Academy of Religion Series, no. 64. Atlanta: Scholars Press, 1989.

Haenchen, Ernst. *The Acts of the Apostles: A Commentary.* Philadelphia: Westminster, 1971.

Hardin, Michael. "Sacrificial Language in Hebrews: Reappraising René Girard." In *Violence Renounced: René Girard, Biblical Studies, and Peacemaking,* edited by Willard M. Swartley, pp. 103-12. Telford, Pa.: Pandora Press U.S.; co-publisher Herald Press, 2000.

Hays, Richard B. *The Moral Vision of the New Testament: Community, Cross, New Creation: A Contemporary Introduction to New Testament Ethics.* New York: HarperCollins, 1996.

Hengel, Martin. *Crucifixion: In the Ancient World and the Folly of the Message of the Cross.* Philadelphia: Fortress Press, 1977.

Heyward, Carter. *Saving Jesus From Those Who Are Right: Rethinking What It Means to Be Christian.* Minneapolis: Fortress Press, 1999.

Hopkins, Dwight N. *Introducing Black Theology of Liberation.* Maryknoll, N.Y.: Orbis Books, 1999.

Hopkins, Julie M. *Towards a Feminist Christology: Jesus of Nazareth, European Women, and the Christological Crisis.* Grand Rapids: Eerdmans, 1995.

House, H. Wayne, and John Howard Yoder. *The Death Penalty Debate: Two Opposing Views of Capital Punishment.* Dallas: Word Publishing, 1991.

Houts, Margo G. "Atonement and Abuse: An Alternative View," *Daughters of Sarah* 18, no. 3 (Summer 1992): 29-32.

Howard-Brook, Wes, and Anthony Gwyther. *Unveiling Empire: Reading Revelation Then and Now.* Maryknoll, N.Y.: Orbis Books, 1999.

Johns, Loren L. "'A Better Sacrifice' or 'Better Than Sacrifice'? Michael Hardin's 'Sacrificial Language in Hebrews.'" In *Violence Renounced: René Girard, Biblical Studies, and Peacemaking,* edited by Willard M. Swartley, pp. 120-31. Telford, Pa.: Pandora Press U.S.; co-publisher Herald Press, 2000.

Jones, A. H. M. *Constantine and the Conversion of Europe.* New York: Macmillan, 1948; reprint, Toronto: University of Toronto Press, 1978.

Josephus. "Jewish Antiquities 20." In *Jewish Antiquities, Book 20.* In *Josephus, Vol. 10,* translated by Louis H. Feldman. The Loeb Classical Library. Cambridge, Mass.: Harvard University Press, 1981.

————. "Jewish War 2." In *The Jewish War, Books 1-3.* In *Josephus, Vol. 2,* translated by H. St. J. Thackeray. The Loeb Classical Library. Cambridge, Mass.: Harvard University Press, 1976.

Juhnke, James C. *Vision, Doctrine, War: Mennonite Identity and Organization in America 1890-1930.* Mennonite Experience in America, vol. 3. Scottdale, Pa.: Herald Press, 1989.

Kaufman, Gordon D. *In Face of Mystery: A Constructive Theology.* Cambridge, Mass.: Harvard University Press, 1993.

————. *Systematic Theology: A Historicist Perspective.* 1968. New York: Scribner's, 1978.

Kelly, J. N. D. *Early Christian Doctrines.* Rev. ed. New York: Harper & Row, 1978.

Kirk-Duggan, Cheryl A. "African-American Spirituals: Confronting and Exorcising Evil Through Song." In *A Troubling in My Soul: Womanist Perspectives on Evil and Suffering,* edited by Emilie M. Townes. Bishop Henry McNeal Turner Series, vol. 8, pp. 150-71. Maryknoll, N.Y.: Orbis Books, 1993.

Kraus, C. Norman. *Jesus Christ Our Lord: Christology from a Disciple's Perspective.* Rev. ed. 1987. Scottdale, Pa.: Herald Press, 1990.

Kraybill, J. Nelson. *Imperial Cult and Commerce in John's Apocalypse.* Journal for the Study of the New Testament Supplement Series, vol. 132. Sheffield, U.K.: Sheffield Academic Press, 1996.

MacMullen, Ramsay. *Constantine.* London: Croom Helm, 1987.

Martin, Clarice J. "Biblical Theodicy and Black Women's Spiritual Autobiography: 'The Miry Bog, the Desolate Pit, a New Song in My Mouth.'" In *A Troubling in My Soul: Womanist Perspectives on Evil and Suffering*, edited by Emilie M. Townes. Bishop Henry McNeal Turner Series, vol. 8, pp. 13-36. Maryknoll, N.Y.: Orbis Books, 1993.

McClendon, James Wm., Jr. *Systematic Theology: Doctrine*. Systematic Theology, vol. 2. Nashville: Abingdon, 1994.

McDonald, H. D. *The Atonement of the Death of Christ in Faith, Revelation, and History*. Grand Rapids: Baker, 1985.

McIntyre, John. *St. Anselm and His Critics: A Re-Interpretation of the Cur Deus Homo*. Edinburgh: Oliver and Boyd, 1954.

Megill-Cobbler, Thelma. "A Feminist Rethinking of Punishment Imagery in Atonement," *Dialog* 35, no. 1 (Winter 1996): 14-20.

Pannenberg, Wolfhart. *Jesus — God and Man*. Translated by Lewis L. Wilkins and Duane A. Priebe. Philadelphia: Westminster, 1975.

Paul, Robert S. *The Atonement and the Sacraments: The Relation of the Atonement to the Sacraments of Baptism and the Lord's Supper*. New York: Abingdon, 1960.

Pelikan, Jaroslav. *The Growth of Medieval Theology (600-1300)*. The Christian Tradition: A History of the Development of Doctrine, vol. 3. Chicago: University of Chicago Press, 1978.

Philo. "The Embassy to Gaius." In *The Embassy to Gaius*. In *Philo, Vol. 10*, translated by F. H. Colson. The Loeb Classical Library. Cambridge, Mass.: Harvard University Press, 1971.

Pickstock, Catherine. *After Writing on the Liturgical Consummation of Philosophy*. Oxford: Blackwell, 1998.

Placher, William C. "Christ Takes Our Place: Rethinking Atonement," *Interpretation* 53, no. 1 (January 1999): 5-20.

Ray, Darby Kathleen. *Deceiving the Devil: Atonement, Abuse, and Ransom*. Cleveland: Pilgrim Press, 1998.

Reesor, Rachel. "Atonement: Mystery and Metaphorical Language," *Mennonite Quarterly Review* 68, no. 2 (April 1994): 209-18.

Rivkin, Ellis. *What Crucified Jesus? Messianism, Pharisaism, and the Development of Christianity*. With a foreword by Eugene J. Fisher. New York: UAHC Press, 1997.

Ruether, Rosemary Radford. *Sexism and God-Talk: Toward a Feminist Theology*. Boston: Beacon, 1983.

———. *Introducing Redemption in Christian Feminism*. Introductions in Feminist Theology, no. 1. Sheffield, U.K.: Sheffield Academic Press, 1998.

————. *Women and Redemption: A Theological History.* Minneapolis: Fortress Press, 1998.

Schlabach, Theron F. *Peace, Faith, Nation: Mennonites and Amish in Nineteenth-Century America.* The Mennonite Experience in America, vol. 2. Scottdale, Pa.: Herald Press, 1988.

Schürer, Emil. *The History of the Jewish People in the Age of Jesus Christ (175 B.C.–A.D. 135).* Vol. 1. Revised and edited by Geza Vermes and Fergus Millar. Edinburgh: T. & T. Clark, 1973.

Schwager, Raymund. *Jesus in the Drama of Salvation.* New York: Crossroad, 1999.

Seeberg, Reinhold. *Text-Book of the History of Doctrines.* Two volumes bound in one. Translated by Charles E. Hay. Grand Rapids: Baker, 1961.

Selby, Donald Joseph, and James King West. *Introduction to the Bible.* New York: Macmillan, 1971.

Southern, R. W. *Saint Anselm: A Portrait in a Landscape.* Cambridge: Cambridge University Press, 1990.

Stayer, James M. *Anabaptists and the Sword.* Lawrence, Kans.: Coronado Press, 1972.

Suetonius. "Claudius, Afterwards Deified." In *The Twelve Caesars: Gaius Suetonius Tranquillas.* Rev. ed., translated by Robert Graves, revised and introduced by Michael Grant. London: Penguin Books, 1989.

————. "Galba, Otho, and Vitellius." In *The Lives of the Caesars.* In *Suetonius, Vol. 2,* translated by J. C. Rolfe. The Loeb Classical Library, pp. 189-277. Cambridge, Mass.: Harvard University Press, 1979.

————. "Nero." In *The Twelve Caesars: Gaius Suetonius Tranquillas.* Rev. ed., translated by Robert Graves, revised and introduced by Michael Grant. London: Penguin Books, 1989.

Tacitus. "The Annals of Imperial Rome." In *The Annals of Imperial Rome.* Rev. ed., translated and introduced by Michael Grant. London: Penguin Books, 1988.

Terrell, JoAnne Marie. *Power in the Blood? The Cross in African American Experience.* The Bishop Henry McNeal Turner/Sojourner Truth Series in Black Religion, no. 15. Maryknoll, N.Y.: Orbis Books, 1998.

Thistlethwaite, Susan Brooks. *Sex, Race and God: Christian Feminism in Black and White.* New York: Crossroad, 1991.

Thompson, Leonard L. *The Book of Revelation: Apocalypse and Empire.* New York: Oxford University Press, 1990.

Townes, Emilie M., ed. *A Troubling in My Soul: Womanist Perspectives on Evil and Suffering.* Bishop Henry McNeal Turner Series, vol. 8. Maryknoll, N.Y.: Orbis Books, 1993.

Townes, Emilie M. "Living in the New Jerusalem." In *A Troubling in My Soul: Womanist Perspectives on Evil and Suffering,* edited by Emilie M. Townes. Bishop Henry McNeal Turner Series, vol. 8, pp. 78-91. Maryknoll, N.Y.: Orbis Books, 1993.

Ulrichsen, Jarl Henning. "Die Sieben Häupter und die Zehn Hörner Zur Datierung der Offenbarung Des Johannes," *Studia Theologica* 39 (1985): 1-20.

Van Braght, Thieleman J. *The Bloody Theater or Martyrs Mirror of the Defenseless Christians.* Translated by Joseph F. Sohm. Scottdale, Pa.: Mennonite Publishing House, 1950.

Van Dyk, Leanne. "Do Theories of Atonement Foster Abuse?" *Dialog* 35, no. 1 (Winter 1996): 21-25.

Volf, Miroslav. *Exclusion and Embrace: A Theological Exploration of Identity, Otherness, and Reconciliation.* Nashville: Abingdon, 1996.

Walker, Alice. *In Search of Our Mother's Garden.* San Diego: Harcourt Brace Jovanovich, 1983.

Weaver, J. Denny. *Anabaptist Theology in Face of Postmodernity: A Proposal for the Third Millennium.* With a foreword by Glen Stassen. The C. Henry Smith Series, vol. 2. Telford, Pa.: Pandora Press U.S.; co-publisher Herald Press, 2000.

————. "Atonement for the NonConstantinian Church," *Modern Theology* 6, no. 4 (July 1990): 307-23.

————. *Becoming Anabaptist: The Origin and Significance of Sixteenth-Century Anabaptism.* Scottdale, Pa.: Herald Press, 1987.

————. *Keeping Salvation Ethical: Mennonite and Amish Atonement Theology in the Late Nineteenth Century.* Foreword by C. Norman Kraus. Studies in Anabaptist and Mennonite History, no. 35. Scottdale, Pa.: Herald Press, 1997.

————. "Nicaea, Womanist Theology, and Anabaptist Particularity." In *Anabaptists and Postmodernity.* Edited by Susan Biesecker-Mast and Gerald Biesecker-Mast. The C. Henry Smith Series, vol. 1, pp. 251-80. Telford, Pa.: Pandora Press U.S.; co-published with Herald Press, 2000.

————. "Theology in the Mirror of the Martyred and Oppressed: Reflections on the Intersections of Yoder and Cone." In *The Wisdom of the Cross: Essays in Honor of John Howard Yoder,* edited by Stanley Hauerwas, Chris K. Hauerwas, Harry J. Huebner, and Mark Thiessen Nation, pp. 409-29. Grand Rapids: Eerdmans, 1999.

Whale, J. S. *Christian Doctrine: Eight Lectures Delivered in the University of Cambridge to Undergraduates of All Faculties.* Cambridge: Cambridge University Press, 1961.

Wheeler, David. "The Cross and the Blood: Dead or Living Images?" *Dialog* 35, no. 1 (Winter 1996): 7-13.

Williams, Daniel H. "Constantine, Nicaea and the 'Fall' of the Church." In *Christian Origins: Theology, Rhetoric and Community,* edited by Lewis Ayres and Gareth Jones, pp. 117-36. London and New York: Routledge, 1998.

Williams, Delores S. *Sisters in the Wilderness: The Challenge of Womanist God-Talk.* Maryknoll, N.Y.: Orbis Books, 1993.

———. "The Color of Feminism: Or Speaking the Black Woman's Tongue," *The Journal of Religious Thought* 43, no. 1 (Spring-Summer 1986): 42-58.

———. "A Crucifixion Double Cross?" *The Other Side* (September-October 1993): 25-27.

———. "A Womanist Perspective on Sin." In *A Troubling in My Soul: Womanist Perspectives on Evil and Suffering,* edited by Emilie M. Townes. Bishop Henry McNeal Turner Series, vol. 8, pp. 130-49. Maryknoll, N.Y.: Orbis Books, 1993.

Williams, George H. "The Sacramental Presuppositions of Anselm's *Cur Deus Homo,*" *Church History* 26, no. 3 (September 1957): 245-74.

Williams, George Huntston. *Anselm, Communion and Atonement.* Saint Louis, Mo.: Concordia Publishing House, 1960.

Wink, Walter. *Naming the Powers: The Language of Power in the New Testament.* The Powers, vol. 1. Philadelphia: Fortress Press, 1984.

———. *Unmasking the Powers: The Invisible Forces That Determine Human Existence.* The Powers, vol. 2. Philadelphia: Fortress Press, 1986.

———. *Engaging the Powers: Discernment and Resistance in a World of Domination.* The Powers, vol. 3. Minneapolis: Fortress Press, 1992.

Winter, Paul. *On the Trial of Jesus.* 2nd ed. Revised and edited by T. A. Burkill and Geza Vermes. New York: Walter de Gruyter, 1974.

Yoder, John Howard. "The Otherness of the Church." In *The Royal Priesthood: Essays Ecclesiological and Ecumenical,* edited and introduced by Michael G. Cartwright, foreword Richard J. Mouw, pp. 53-64. Grand Rapids: Eerdmans, 1994.

———. *Preface to Theology: Christology and Theological Method.* Elkhart, Ind.: Goshen Biblical Seminary; distributed by Co-op Bookstore, 1981.

———. "'See How They Go with Their Face to the Sun.'" In *For the Nations:*

Essays Public and Evangelical, pp. 51-78. Grand Rapids and Cambridge: Eerdmans, 1997.

―――. "That Household We Are." Unpublished paper, 1980.

―――. *What Would You Do?: A Serious Answer to a Standard Question.* Scottdale, Pa.: Herald Press, 1983.

―――. *The Case for Punishment.* John Howard Yoder's Home Page, 1995. Accessed 1 July 2000. Http://www.nd.edu/~theo/jhy/writings/home/welcome.htm.

―――. "The Constantinian Sources of Western Social Ethics." In *The Priestly Kingdom: Social Ethics as Gospel,* pp. 135-47. Notre Dame, Ind.: University of Notre Dame, 1984.

―――. *The Politics of Jesus: Vicit Agnus Noster.* 2nd ed. Grand Rapids: Eerdmans, 1993.

―――. *When War Is Unjust: Being Honest in Just-War Thinking.* 2nd ed. Maryknoll, N.Y.: Orbis Books, 1996.

Zehr, Howard. *Changing Lenses: A New Focus for Crime and Justice.* A Christian Peace Shelf Selection. Scottdale, Pa.: Herald Press, 1990.

Index

Abelard, Peter, 1, 2, 183; abusive imagery in, 129, 131; atonement motif, 18-19, 197; counterpart to Anselm, 81, 218; James Cone on, 105-6; feminist restatements of, 147, 227

Abraham, 66-67, 104, 161-62, 226

Abuse, 122, 131, 142, 148-49, 170, 177, 204; in atonement, 127-30, 131-32, 139, 142, 146, 151, 186, 191, 219; divine child, 5, 127-29, 131-32, 141, 146, 151, 154, 156, 167, 178, 184, 188, 191, 195, 203n.1, 223; women conditioned to accept, 5, 126-28, 134, 186, 191

Anabaptism, 110-11

Anselm of Canterbury, 1, 3, 5, 6, 8, 80; agent of Jesus' death, 200-203; atonement doctrine, 16, 18, 71-72, 187, 188-95, 197-202; atonement separated from ethics, 90-91; and black theology, 105-6; and Chalcedonian Christology, 92; *Cur Deus Homo*, 11, 16, 19, 80, 86-89, 92, 179, 188-89, 192-93, 198-99; defenses of, 180-88; distinguished from Luther/Calvin, 187, 198; dominant atonement view, 2, 6; and ecclesiology, 88-89, 97; and feminist theology, 128, 151, 191, 196, 198; feudal context, 88, 167, 192-95, 196, 201, 212, 213, 214; focus on death, 187; Jesus' particularity absent, 87-90; not Pauline, 54; rejected ransom theory, 81, 86, 87, 188-89; *Why the God-man*, 92

Anthony, Susan B., 164

Atonement: accomplishment of death, 71-72, 176, 197; agent of Jesus' death, 72-74, 176, 197; in black theology, 106-7, 118-20; Catholic view, 19; classic questions, 44-45; debated, 1, 18; ecclesiological implications, 13, 86-88, 90, 96-98, 213-14; in feminist theology, 124-25, 130-31, 135-36, 143-45, 152-53; history of doctrine, 13, 81-88, 97, 212-13; object of death, 18, 70, 138, 153, 197; Protestant views, 16-17, 19, 183, 192, 197, 202, 198; sinners' role in death of Jesus, 74-76, 215; subjective view, 18; in womanist theology, 164-68; in Xodus, 118-20; *See also* names of